GLEANINGS FROM ELISHA

GLEANINGS FROM ELISHA

HIS LIFE AND MIRACLES

by

ARTHUR W. PINK

MOODY PRESS
CHICAGO

© 1972 by
THE MOODY BIBLE INSTITUTE
OF CHICAGO

Library of Congress Catalog Card Number: 79-181591

Moody Paperback Edition, 1981

ISBN 0-8024-3000-7

16 17 18 19 20 Printing/VP/Year 93 92 91 90 89 88

CONTENTS

Chapter 1

ELISHA'S LIFE AND MIRACLES

THAT WHICH OCCUPIES the central and dominant place in what the Spirit has been pleased to record of the life of Elisha is the miracles performed by and connected with him. Far more miracles were wrought by him or were granted in answer to his prayers than any other of the Old Testament prophets. In fact the narrative of his history consists of little else than a record of supernatural acts and events. Nor need this at all surprise us, though it is strange that so few seem to grasp its implication and significance. The character of Elisha's mission and ministry was in thorough keeping with Israel's condition at that time. The very fact that these miracles were needed indicates the state into which Israel had fallen. Idolatry had held sway for so long that the true and living God was no longer known by the nation. Here and there were individuals who believed in the Lord, but the masses were worshipers of idols. Therefore by means of drastic interpositions, by awe-inspiring displays of His power, by supernatural manifestations of His justice and mercy alike, God forced even the skeptical to recognize His existence and subscribe to His supremacy.

Prophecy and Miracles

It is fitting here that we should make a few remarks upon the reason for and meaning of miracles. Prophecy and miracles partake of much the same nature. Prophecy is really an oral miracle, and miracles are virtually prophecies (forthtelling of God) in action. As God sends forth one of His prophets only in a time of marked declension and departure of His people from Himself, so miracles were quite unnecessary while the sufficiency of His Word was practically recognized. The one as much as the other lies entirely outside the ordinary line or course of things, neither occurring during what we

7

may term normal times. Which of the patriarchs, the priests, or the
kings performed any miracles? How many were wrought during
the lengthy reign of Saul, David, or Solomon? Why, then, were so
many wonders done during the ministry of Elijah and still more so
during that of Elisha?

The mission and ministry of Elisha was the same in character as
that which God did in Egypt by the hand of Moses. There Jehovah
was unknown: entirely so by the Egyptians, largely so by the Israelites. The favored descendants of Abraham had sunk as low as
the heathen in whose midst they dwelt, and God, by so many remarkable signs and unmistakable interventions, brought them back to
that knowledge of Himself which they had lost. Unless the Hebrews
in Egypt had been thoroughly convinced by these displays of divine
power that Moses was a prophet sent from God, they never would
have submitted to him as their leader. How reluctantly they owned
his authority on various occasions! So also in the conquest of Canaan, God wrought four miracles in favor of His people: one in the
water, in the crossing of Jordan; one in the earth, in throwing down
the walls of Jericho; one in the air, in destroying their enemies by
hail; and one in the heavens, by slowing the course of the sun and
the moon. Thereby the nations of Canaan were furnished with clear
proof of Jehovah's supremacy, that the God of Israel possessed universal dominion, that He was no local deity but the Most High reigning over all nature.

But, it may be asked, how do the miracles wrought by Christ
square with what has been said above? Surely they should present
no difficulty. Pause and ask the question, Why did He work miracles? Did not His teaching make clearly evident His divine mission?
The very officers sent to arrest Him had to acknowledge, "Never
man spake as this man." Did not the spotless holiness of His life
make manifest the heavenliness of His person? Even Pilate was
forced to testify, "I find no fault in Him." Did not His conduct on
the cross demonstrate that He was no imposter? The centurion and
his fellows owned, "Truly this was the Son of God" (Mt 27:54). Ah,
but men must be left without the shadow of an excuse for their unbelief. The whole world shall have it unmistakably shown before
their eyes that Jesus of Nazareth was none other than "God manifest in flesh." The Gentiles were sunk in idolatry; Judaism was reduced to a lifeless formality and had made void the Word of God by
traditions. Therefore did Christ reveal the wisdom and power of God

as none other before or since by a series of miracles which warranted His saying, "He that hath seen Me hath seen the Father."

Thus it will be seen that there is another characteristic which links closely together prophecy and miracles: the character of the times in which they occur supply the key both to their implication and their significance. Both of them may be termed abnormalities, for neither of them are given in the ordinary course of events. While conditions are relatively decent, God acts according to the ordinary working of the laws of creation and operations of His providence. But when the Enemy comes in like a flood, the Spirit of the Lord lifts up a more apparent and noticeable standard against him, coming out more into the open and obliging men to take cognizance of Him. But there is this difference: the one intimates there is a state of grievous departure from God on the part of His people; the other indicates that the knowledge of the true and living God has publicly disappeared, that He is no longer believed in by the masses. Drastic diseases call for drastic remedies.

Elijah and Elisha

The missions of Elijah and Elisha form two parts of one whole, the one supplementing the other, though there was a striking contrast between them. Therein we have an illustration of the spiritual significance of the number two. Whereas one denotes there is no other, two affirms there is another and therefore a difference. That difference may be for good or for evil, and therefore this number bears a twofold meaning according to its associations. The second that comes in may be for opposition or for support. The two, though different in character, may be one in testimony and friendship. "The testimony of two men is true" (Jn 8:17 and cf. Num 35:30). Thus two is also the number of witnesses, and the greater the contrast between the two witnesses the more valuable their testimony when they agree therein. Hence it is that all through the Scriptures we find two persons linked together to present a contrast: as in such cases as Cain and Abel, Abraham and Lot, Ishmael and Isaac, Jacob and Esau; or two bearing witness to the truth: as Enoch and Noah, Moses and Aaron, Caleb and Joshua, Naomi and Ruth, Ezra and Nehemiah, the sending forth of the apostles by twos (Mk 6:7 and cf. Rev 11:3).

This linking together of two men in their testimony for God con-

tains valuable instruction for us. It hints broadly at the twofoldness
of truth. There is perfect harmony and unity between the two great
divisions of Holy Writ, yet the differences between the Old and New
Testaments are apparent to every thoughtful reader of them. It
warns against the danger of lopsidedness, intimating the importance
of seeking to preserve the balance. The chief instruments employed
by God in the great Reformation of the sixteenth century were Luther and Calvin. They took part in a common task and movement,
yet how great was the difference between the two men and the respective parts they were called upon to play. Thus with Elijah and
Elisha: there are manifest parallels between them, as in the likeness
of their names, yet there are marked contrasts both in their missions
and their miracles. It is in the observing of their respective sim-
ilarities and dissimilarities that we are enabled to ascertain the special teaching which they are designed to convey to us.

At first glance it may appear that there is a much closer resemblance than antithesis between the two men. Both of them were
prophets, both of them dwelt in Samaria, and they were confronted
with much the same situation. The falling of Elijah's mantle upon
Elisha seems to indicate that the latter was the successor of the former, called upon to continue his mission. The first miracle performed by Elisha was identical with the last one wrought by his master: the smiting of the waters of the Jordan with the mantle, so that
they parted asunder for him (2 Ki 2:8, 14). At the beginning of
his ministry Elijah had said unto Ahab king of Israel, "As the Lord
God of Israel liveth, before whom I stand" (1 Ki 17:1). And when
Elisha came into the presence of Ahab's son he also declared, "As
the Lord of hosts liveth, before whom I stand" (2 Ki 3:14). As
Elijah was entertained by the widow of Zarepath and rewarded her
by restoring her son to life (1 Ki 17:22), so Elisha was entertained
by a woman at Shunem (2 Ki 4:8-10) and repaid her by restoring
her son to life (4:35-37).

Striking as the points of agreement are between the two prophets,
the contrasts in their careers and works are just as vivid and certainly more numerous. One appeared suddenly and dramatically
upon the stage of public action, without a word being told us of from
whence he sprang or how he had previously been engaged; but of
the other the name of his father is recorded, with an account of his
occupation at the time he received his call into God's service. The
first miracle of Elijah was that for the space of three and a half

years there should be neither dew nor rain according to his word, whereas the first public act of Elisha was to heal the springs of water (2 Ki 2:21, 22) and to produce an abundance of water (3:20). One of the most noticeable features of Elijah's life was his loneliness, dwelling apart from the apostate masses of the people; but Elisha seems to have spent most of his life in the company of the prophets, presiding over their schools. The different manner in which their earthly careers terminated is even more marked: the one was taken to heaven in a chariot of fire, and the other fell sick in old age and died a natural death.

The principal contrast between the two prophets appears in the character of the miracles wrought by and connected with them. The majority of those performed by Elijah were associated with death and destruction, whereas by far the greater of those attributed to Elisha were works of healing and restoration. If the former was the prophet of judgment, the latter was the prophet of grace; if the course of one was fittingly closed by a "whirlwind" removing him from this scene, a peaceful dove would be the more appropriate emblem of the other. Elisha's ministry consisted largely of divine interpositions in a way of mercy, interventions of sovereign goodness, rather than judicial dealings. He commenced his mission by a miracle of blessing, healing the death-dealing springs of water. What immediately followed was the establishing of his authority, the symbol of his extraordinary office. The work of Elijah was chiefly a protest against evil, while the work of Elisha was an almost continuous testimony to the readiness of God to relieve the distressed and respond to the call of need wherever that call came from a contrite and believing heart.

Unto many it may seem really astonishing that a ministry like that of Elisha should immediately follow after Elijah's, for in view of the desperate defiance he encountered we would naturally suppose the end had been reached, that the patience of God was at last exhausted. But if we take into account what has been before us above on the significance of miracles, we shall be less surprised. As we have pointed out, a state of general infidelity and idolatry forms the historical background, and thus is the reason for and purpose of His breaking through the darkness and making Himself manifest to a people who are God's, but know Him not. Now since God is "light" (1 Jn 1:5), that is, the ineffably holy one, it necessarily follows that when revealing Himself He will do so as the hater and punisher of sin. But it is equally true that God is "love" (1 Jn 4:8), that is, the infinitely benevolent one, and consequently when appearing more evidently before the eyes of His creatures, it is in wondrous works of kindness and benevolence. Thus we have the two sides of the divine character revealed in the respective ministries of Elijah and Elisha: deeds of vengeance and deeds of mercy.

While their two missions may certainly be considered separately, yet Elisha's ministry should be regarded primarily as the complement of Elijah's. The two, though dissimilar, make one complete whole — and only subordinately a thing apart. On the one hand Elijah's mission was mainly of a public character; on the other, Elisha's was more in private. The former had to do principally with the masses and those who had led them astray, and therefore his miracles consisted chiefly of judgments, expressive of God's wrath upon idolatry. The latter was engaged mostly with the Lord's prophets and people, and consequently his acts were mainly those of blessing, manifestations of the divine mercy. The comforting and assuring lesson in this for Christians today is, that even in a season of apostasy and universal wickedness, when His rod is laid heavily upon the nations, the Lord will neither forget nor forsake His own, but will appear unto them as "the God of all grace." Things may become yet worse than they are now. Even so the Lord will prove Himself to be "a very present help" to His people.

Coming now to the subordinate viewpoint and considering Elisha's career as the sequel to Elijah's, may we not find in it a message of hope in this dark, dark hour. Those with any measure of spiritual discernment cannot fail to perceive the tragic resemblance there is between the time in which Elijah's lot was cast and our own sad day. The awful apostasy of Christendom, the appalling multiplication of false prophets, the various forms of idolatry now so prevalent in our midst, and the solemn judgments from heaven which have been and are being visited upon us and the blatant refusal of the multitudes to pay any heed to them by mending their ways, all furnish an analogy which is too plain to be missed. There is therefore a real temptation to conclude that the end of all things is at hand — some say an end of the age, others the end of the world. Many thought the same when Napoleon was desolating Europe and again in 1914-18 but they were wrong, and it is quite likely that they who think the same today will have their conclusions falsified.

There is at least a warning for us here: Elijah was followed by Elisha! Who can tell what mercy God may yet show to the world?

We must be on our guard against missing the consolation which this portion of Scripture may contain for us. The darkest night is followed by the morning's light. Even if the present order of "civilization" is doomed to destruction, we know not what favors from God await this earth in generations to come. Of necessity there will be a time when this world and all its works will be burned up, and that event may be very near. On the other hand that event may be thousands of years away. If such be the case, then black as is the present outlook and blacker it may yet become, yet the clouds of divine judgment will again disperse and the sun of Righteousness arise once more with healing in His wings. More than once the times of Elijah have been substantially duplicated even during this Christian era, yet each time they were followed by an Elisha of mercy. Thus it may be again, yea will be unless God is now on the point of bringing down the curtain upon human history.

The Written Record

Very little indeed seems to have been written upon the life of Elisha, yet this is not difficult to account for. Though there is almost twice as much recorded about him than his predecessor, his history is not given in one connected piece or consecutive narrative. Rather it is disjointed, the current of his life being crossed again and again by references to others. The scattered allusions to the prophet's career do not lend themselves so readily to biographical treatment as do the lives of Abraham, Jacob, or David. Why is this? For there is nothing meaningless in Scripture; perfect wisdom directs the Holy Spirit in every detail. May it not be that we have a hint here of the method which will be followed by the Lord in that era which will possibly succeed the period of Christendom's history foreshadowed by Elijah's life? May not the broken and disconnected account of Elisha's deeds presage the form God's dealings will take in a future generation: that instead of being a regular stream they will be occasional showers of blessing at intervals?

Chapter 2

HIS CALL

IN THE INTRODUCTION we noted the close connection between the missions and ministries of Elijah and Elisha. Let us now consider the personal relation that existed between the two prophets themselves. This is something more than a point of interest. It throws light upon the character and career of the latter, and it enables us to discern the deeper spiritual meaning which is to be found in this portion of the Word. There was a twofold relation between them: one official, and the other more intimate. The former is seen in 1 Ki 19:16 where we learn that Elijah was commanded to "anoint Elisha to be prophet," and it is worthy of note that while it is generally believed all the prophets were officially "anointed" yet Elisha's case is the only one expressly recorded in Scripture. Next we learn that immediately following his call, Elisha "went after Elijah and ministered unto him" (19:21), so the relation between them was that of master and servant, confirmed by the statement that he "poured water on the hands of Elijah" (2 Ki 3:11).

But there was more than an official union between these two men; the ties of affection bound them together. There is reason to believe that Elisha accompanied Elijah during the last ten years of his earthly life, and during the closing scenes we are shown how closely they were knit together and how strong was the love of the younger man to his master. During their lengthy journey from Gilgal to the Jordan, Elijah said to his companion again and again, "Tarry ye here, I pray thee." But nothing could deter Elisha from spending the final hours in the immediate presence of the one who had won his heart or make him willing to break their communion. So they "still went on, and talked" (2 Ki 2:11). Observe how the Spirit has emphasized this. First "they went down to Bethel" (v. 2), but later "they two went on" (v. 6); "they two stood by Jordan" (v. 7); "they two went on dry ground" (v. 8). They refused to be separated. But when it was necessary, Elisha cried, "My father, my father" (a term of endearment), and in token of his deep grief "took hold of his own clothes and rent them in two pieces."

God's Command to Elijah

As the invariable rule of Scripture, it is the first mention which supplies the key to all that follows: "Elisha, the son of Shaphat, of Abel-melolah shalt thou anoint to be prophet in thy room" (1 Ki 19:16). Those words signify something more than that he was to be his successor. Elisha was to take Elijah's place and act as his accredited representative. This is confirmed by the fact that when he found Elisha, Elijah "cast his mantle upon him" (v. 19) which signified the closest possible identification. It is very remarkable to find that when Joash the king of Israel visited the dying Elisha he uttered the selfsame words over him as the prophet had used when Elijah was departing from this world. Elisha cried, "My father, my father, the chariot of Israel and the horsemen thereof" — the real defense of Israel (2:12), and Joash said, "O my father, my father, the chariot of Israel and the horsemen thereof" (2 Ki 13:14). That not only marked the identification of Elisha with Elijah, but the identification was actually acknowledged by the king himself.

Another detail which serves to manifest the relation between the two prophets is found in the striking reply made by Elisha to the question of his master: "Ask what I shall do for thee before I be taken from thee," namely, "I pray thee, let a double portion of thy spirit be upon me" (2 Ki 2:9). That his request was granted appears clear from the sequel. "If thou see me when I am taken from thee, it shall be so unto thee," and verse 12 assures us "and Elisha saw." Moreover, when the young prophets saw him smite the waters of the Jordan with his master's mantle so that they "parted hither and thither," they exclaimed, "The spirit of Elijah doth rest on Elisha" (v. 15). The "double portion" was that which pertained to the firstborn or oldest son and heir: "But he shall acknowledge the son of the hated for the firstborn, by giving him a double portion of all that he hath: for he is the beginning of his strength: the right of the firstborn is his" (Deu 21:17; and cf. 1 Ch 5:1).

Elisha, then, was far more than the historical successor of Elijah. He was appointed and anointed to be his representative — we might almost say, his "ambassador." He was the man who had been called by God to take Elijah's place before Israel. Though Elijah had left this scene and gone on high, yet he would be so in spirit. Elisha was to be in "his room" (1 Ki 19:16), for the starting point of his mission was the ascension of his master. Now what, we may ask, is the spiritual significance of this? What is the important instruction to be found in it for us today? Surely the answer is not far to seek. The relation between Elijah and Elisha was that of master and servant. Since the anointing of Elisha into the prophetic office is the only case of its kind expressly recorded in Scripture, are we not required to look upon it as a representative or pattern one? Since Elijah was a figure of Christ, is it not evident that Elisha is a type of those servants specially called to represent Him here upon earth?

The conclusion drawn above is manifestly confirmed by all the preliminary details recorded of Elisha before he entered upon his life's work. Those details may all be summed up under the following heads: his call, the testings to which he was submitted and from which he successfully emerged, the oath he was required to follow, and the special endowment which he received equipping him for his service. The closer these details are examined and the more they are prayerfully pondered, the more evidently will it appear to anointed eyes that the experiences through which Elisha passed are those which, substantially, each genuine servant of Christ is required to encounter. Let us consider them in the order named. First, the call of which he was the recipient. This was his induction into the sacred ministry. It was a clear and definite call by God, the absence of which makes it the height of presumption for any one to invade the holy office.

Elijah Summons to Elisha

The summons which Elisha received to quit his temporal avocation and to henceforth devote the whole of his time and energies to God and His people is noted in, "So he departed thence, and found Elisha the son of Shaphat, who was ploughing with twelve yoke of oxen before him, and he was with the twelfth: and Elijah passed by him and cast his mantle upon him" (1 Ki 19:19). Observe how that here, as everywhere, God took the initiative. Elisha was not seeking Him, but the Lord through Elijah sought him out. Elisha was not found in his study but in the field, not with a book in his hand, but at the plow. As one of the Puritans said when commenting thereon,

"God seeth not as man seeth, neither does He choose men because they are fit, but He fits them because He hath chosen them." Sovereignty is stamped plainly upon the divine choice, as appears also in the calling of the sons of Zebedee while "mending their nets" (Mt 4:21), of Levi while he was "sitting at the receipt of custom" (Mt 9:9), and Saul of Tarsus when persecuting the early Christians.

Though Elisha does not appear to have been seeking or expecting a call from the Lord to engage in His service, yet it is to be noted that he was actively engaged when the call came to him, as was each of the others alluded to above. The ministry of Christ is no place for idlers and drones, who wish to spend much of their time driving around in fancy cars or being entertained in the homes of their members and friends. No, it is a vocation which calls for constant self-sacrifice, and which demands tireless devotion to the performance of duty. Those then are most likely to be sincere and energetic in the ministry who are industrious and businesslike in their temporal avocation. Alas, how many who wish to shirk their natural responsibilities and shelve hard work have entered the ministry to enjoy a life of comparative ease.

Elisha means "God is Saviour" and his father's name *Shaphat* signifies "judge." *Abel-meholah* is literally "meadow of the dance" and was a place in the inheritance of Issachar, at the north of the Jordan valley. Elisha's father was evidently a man of some means for he had "twelve yoke of oxen" engaged in plowing, yet he did not allow his son to grow up in idleness as is so often the case with the wealthy. It was while Elisha was usefully engaged, in the performance of duty, undertaking the strenuous work of plowing, that he was made the recipient of a divine call into special service. This was indicated by the approach of the prophet Elijah and his casting his mantle — the insignia of his office — upon him. It was a clear intimation of his own investiture of the prophetic office. This call was accompanied by divine power, the Holy Spirit moving Elisha to accept the same, as may be seen from the promptness and decidedness of his response.

Before we look at his response, let us consider the very real and stern test to which Elisha was subjected. The issue was clearly drawn. To enter upon the prophetic office, to identify himself with Elijah, meant a drastic change in his manner of life. It meant the giving up of a lucrative worldly position, the leaving of the farm, for the servant and soldier of Jesus Christ must not "entangle himself with the affairs of this life" (2 Ti 2:4). (Paul's laboring at "tent-making" was quite the exception to the rule and a sad reflection upon the parsimoniousness of those to whom he ministered.) It meant the breaking away from home and natural ties. Said the Lord Jesus, "He that loveth father or mother more than me is not worthy of me: and he that loveth son or daughter more than me is not worthy of me" (Mt 10:37). If such immoderate affection was an effectual bar to Christian discipleship (Lk 14:26), how much more so from the Christian ministry. The test often comes at this very point. It did so with the present writer, who was called to labor in a part of the Lord's vineyard thousands of miles from his native land, so that he did not see his parents for thirteen years.

Elisha's Response to the Call

There was first, then, the testing of Elisha's affections, but he shrank not from the sacrifice he was now called upon to make. "And he left the oxen and ran after Elijah." Note the alacrity, the absence of any reluctance. And he said, "Let me, I pray thee, kiss my father and my mother and I will follow thee." Observe his humble spirit. He had already taken the servant's place, and would not even perform a filial duty without first receiving permission from his master. Let any who may be exercised in mind as to whether they have received a call to the ministry search and examine themselves at this point, to see if such a spirit has been wrought in them. The nature of Elisha's request shows clearly that he was not a man devoid of natural feelings, but an affectionate son, warmly attached to his parents. Far from being an excuse for delaying his obedience to the call, it was a proof of his promptness in accepting it and of his readiness to make a deliberate break from all natural ties.

"And he [Elijah] said unto him, Go back again: for what have I done to thee?" (1 Ki 19:20). It was as though the prophet said, "Do not act impulsively, but sit down and count the cost before you definitely commit yourself." Elijah did not seek to influence or persuade him. "It is not to me but to God you are accountable — it is His call which you are to weigh." He knew quite well that if the Holy Spirit were operating, He would complete the work and Elisha would return to him.

Oh that the rank and file of God's people would heed this lesson. How many a young man, never called of God, has been pressed into the ministry by well-meaning friends who had more zeal than knowledge. None may rightly count upon the divine blessing in the service of Christ unless he has been expressly set apart thereto by the Holy Spirit (Ac 13:2). One of the most fearful catastrophies which has come upon the churches (and those terming their's "assemblies") during the past century has been the repetition of what God complained of of old: "I have not sent these prophets, yet they ran" (Jer 23:21). To intrude into the sacred office calls down heaven's curse (2 Sa 6:6-7).

But Elisha's acceptance of this call from God not only meant the giving up of a comfortable worldly position and the breaking away from home and natural ties; it also involved his following or casting his lot with one who was very far from being a popular hero. Elijah had powerful enemies who more than once had made determined attempts on his life. Those were dangerous times, when persecution was not only a possibility but a probability. It was well then for Elisha to sit down and count the cost; by consorting with Elijah, he would be exposed to the malice of Jezebel and all her priests. The same is true in principle of the Christian minister. Christ is despised and rejected of men, and to be faithfully engaged in His service is to court the hostility not only of the secular but of the religious world as well. It was on religious grounds that Jezebel persecuted Elijah, and it is by the false prophets of Christendom and their devotees that the genuine ministers of God will be most hated and hounded. Nothing but love for Christ and His people will enable Elisha to triumph over his enemies.

"And he returned back from him and took a yoke of oxen and slew them and boiled their flesh with the instruments of the oxen, and gave unto the people and they did eat." This farewell feast was a token of joy at his new calling, an expression of gratitude to God for His distinguishing favor, and the burning of the oxen's tackle a sign that he was bidding a final adieu to his old employment. Those oxen and tools of industry, wherein his former labors had been bestowed, were now gladly devoted to the celebration of the high honor of being called to engage in the service of God Himself. Those who rightly esteem the sacred ministry will freely renounce every other interest and pleasure, though called upon to labor amid poverty and persecution; yea, they who enter into the work of our heavenly Master without holy cheerfulness are not at all likely to prosper therein. Levi the publican made Christ "a great feast in his own house" to celebrate his call to the ministry, inviting a great company thereto (Lk 5:27-29).

"Then he arose and went after Elijah." See here the power of the Holy Spirit! The evidence of God's effectual call is a heart made willing to respond. Divine grace is able to subdue every lust, conquer every prejudice, surmount every difficulty. Elisha left his worldly employment, the riches to which he was heir, his parents and friends, and threw in his lot with one who was an outcast. Thus it was with Moses, who "refused to be called the son of Pharaoh's daughter; Choosing rather to suffer affliction with the people of God, than to enjoy the pleasures of sin for a season; Esteeming the reproach of Christ greater riches than the treasures in Egypt: for he had respect unto the recompence of the reward" (Heb 11:24-26). Love for Christ and His saints, faith in His ultimate "Well done," were the motive-springs of his actions. And such must prompt one entering the ministry today.

"Then he arose and went after Elijah and ministered unto him" (1 Ki 19:21). That was the final element in this initial test. Was he prepared to take a subordinate and lowly place, to become a servant, subjecting himself to the will of another? That is what a servant is: one who places himself at the disposal of another, ready to take orders from him, desirous of promoting his interests. He who would be given important commissions must prove himself. Thus did God approve of Stephen's service to the poor (Ac 7:1, 2). Because Philip disdained not to serve tables (Ac 6:2, 5) he was advanced to the rank of missionary to the Gentiles (Ac 8:5, 26). On the other hand, Mark was discontented to be merely a servant of an apostle (Ac 13:5, 13) and so lost his opportunity of being trained for personal participation in the most momentous missionary journey ever undertaken. Elisha became the servant of God's servant, and we shall see how he was rewarded.

Chapter 3

HIS TESTINGS

IN OUR LAST CHAPTER we pointed out that the peculiar relation which existed between Elijah and Elisha foreshadowed that which pertains to Christ and His servants, and that the early experiences through which Elisha passed are those which almost every genuine minister of the gospel is called upon to encounter. All the preliminary details recorded of the prophet before his mission commenced must have their counterpart in the early history of any who are used of God in the work of His kingdom. Those experiences in the case of Elisha began with a definite call from the Lord, and that is still His order of procedure. That call was followed by a series of very real testings, which may well be designated as a preliminary course of discipline. Those testings were many and varied. There were seven in number, which at once indicates the thoroughness and completeness of the ordeals through which Elisha went and by which he was schooled for the future. If we are not to ignore here the initial one, there will of necessity be a slight overlapping between this section and what was before us in our last chapter.

First, the Testing of His Affections

This occurred at the time he received his call to devote the whole of his time and energies to the service of God and His people. A stern test it was. Elisha was not one who had failed in temporal matters and now desired to "better his position," nor was he deprived of those who cherished him and were therefore anxious to enter a more congenial circle. Far from it. He was the son of a well-to-do farmer, living with parents to whom he was devotedly attached. Response to Elijah's casting of the prophetic mantle upon him meant not only the giving up of favorable worldly prospects, but the severing of happy home ties. The issue was plainly drawn:

which should dominate — zeal for Jehovah or love for his parents? That Elisha was very far from being one of a cold and unfeeling disposition is clear from a number of things. When Elijah bade him remain at Bethel, he replied, "I will not leave thee" (2 Ki 2:2); and when his master was caught away from him, he evidenced his deep grief by crying out, "My father! My father," and by rending his garments asunder (v. 12).

No, Elisha was no stoic, and it cost him something to break away from his loved ones. But he shrank not from the sacrifice demanded of him. He "left the oxen" with which he had been ploughing and "ran after Elijah" asking only, "Let me, I pray thee, kiss my father and my mother, and I will follow thee" (1 Ki 19:20). When permission was granted, a hasty farewell speech was made and he took his departure; and the sacred narrative contains no mention that he ever returned home even for a brief visit. Dutiful respect, yea, tender regard, was shown for his parents, but he did not prefer them before God. The Lord does not require His servants to callously ignore their filial duty, but He does claim the first place in their hearts. Unless one who is contemplating an entrance into the ministry is definitely prepared to accord Him that, he should at once abandon his quest. No man is eligible for the ministry unless he is ready to resolutely subordinate natural ties to spiritual bonds. Blessedly did the spirit prevail over the flesh in Elisha's response to this initial trial.

Second, the Testing of His Sincerity

This occurred at the outset of the final journey of the two prophets. "And it came to pass when the Lord would take up Elijah into heaven by a whirlwind that Elijah went with Elisha from Gilgal. And Elijah said unto Elisha, Tarry here, I pray thee" (2 Ki 2:1-2). Various reasons have been advanced by the commentators as to why the Tishbite should have made such a request. Some think it was because he wished to be alone, that modesty and humility would not suffer that his companion should witness the very great honor which was about to be bestowed upon him. Others suppose it was because he desired to spare Elisha the grief of a final leave-taking. But in view of all that follows, and taking this detail in connection with the whole incident, we believe these words of the prophet bear quite a different interpretation, namely, that Elijah was now making proof of Elisha's determination and attachment to him. At the time of his call

Elisha had said, "I will follow thee," and now he was given the opportunity to go back if he were so disposed.

There was one who accompanied the apostle Paul for a while, but later he had to lament, "Demas hath forsaken me, having loved this present world, and is departed unto Thessalonica" (2 Ti 4:10). Many have done likewise. Daunted by the difficulties of the way, discouraged by the unfavorable response to their efforts, and their ardor cooled, they concluded they had mistaken their calling; or, because only small and unattractive fields opened to them, they decided to better themselves by returning to worldly employment. To what numbers do those solemn words of Christ apply: "No man, having put his hand to the plough, and looking back, is fit for the kingdom of God" (Lk 9:62). Far otherwise was it with Elisha. No fleeting impression had actuated him when he declared to Elijah, "I will follow thee." And when he was put to the test as to whether or not he was prepared to follow him to the end of the course, he successfully gave evidence of his unwavering fidelity. "As the Lord liveth, and as thy soul liveth, I will not leave thee" was his unflinching response. Oh for like stability.

Third, the Testing of His Will or Resolution

From Gilgal, Elijah and his companion had gone on to Bethel, and there he encountered a subtle temptation, one which had prevailed over any whose heart was not thoroughly established. "And the sons of the prophets that were at Beth-el came forth to Elisha and said unto him, Knowest thou that the Lord will take away thy master from thy head to day?" (2 Ki 2:3). Which was as much as saying, Why think of going on any further, what is the use of it, when the Lord is on the point of taking him from you? And mark it well, they who here sought to make him waver from his course were not the agents of Jezebel but those who were on the side of the Lord. Nor was it just one who would deter Elisha, but apparently the whole body of the prophets endeavored to persuade him that he should relinquish his purpose. It is in this very way God tries the mettle of His servants: to make evident to themselves and others whether they are vacillating or steadfast, whether they are regulated wholly by His call and will or whether their course is directed by the counsels of men.

A holy independence should mark the servant of God. Thus it

was with the chief of the apostles: "I conferred not with flesh and blood" (Gal 1:16). Had he done so, what trouble would he have made for himself; had he listened to the varied advice the other apostles would offer, what a state of confusion his own mind would have been in! If Christ is my Master, then it is from Him, and from Him alone, I must take my orders. Until I am sure of His will I must continue to wait upon Him; once it is clear to me, I must set out on the performance of it, and nothing must move me to turn aside. So it was here. Elisha had been Divinely called to follow Elijah, and he was determined to cleave to him unto the end, even though it meant going against well-meant advice and offending the whole of his fellows. "Hold ye your peace" was his reply. This was one of the trials which this writer encountered over thirty years ago, when his pastor and Christian friends urged him to enter a theological seminary, though they knew that deadly error was taught there. It was not easy to take his stand against them, but he is deeply thankful he did so.

Fourth, the Testing of His Faith

"And Elijah said unto him, Elisha, tarry here, I pray thee; for the LORD hath sent me to Jericho" (2 Ki 2:4). "Tarry here." They were at Bethel, and this was a place of sacred memories. It was here that Jacob had spent his first night as he fled from the wrath of his brother. Here he had been favored with that vision of the ladder whose top reached unto heaven and beheld the angels of God ascending and descending on it. Here it was Jehovah had revealed Himself and given him precious promises. When he awakened, Jacob said, "Surely the Lord is in this place . . . this is none other but the house of God and this is the gate of heaven" (Gen 28). Delectable spot was this: the place of divine communion. Ah, one which is supremely attractive to those who are spiritually minded, and therefore one which such are entirely loath to leave. What can be more desirable than to abide where such privileges and favors are enjoyed! So felt Peter on the holy mount. As he beheld Christ transfigured and Moses and Elijah talking with Him, he said, "Lord, it is good for us to be here: if thou wilt let us make here three tabernacles; one for thee, and one for Moses, and one for Elijah." Let us remain and enjoy such blessing. But that could not be.

God still tests His servants at this very point. They are in some place where the smile of heaven manifestly rests upon their labors. The Lord's presence is real, His secrets are revealed to them, and intimate communion is enjoyed with Him. If he followed his own inclinations he would remain there, but he is not free to please himself: he is the servant of another and must do His bidding. Elijah had announced, "the LORD hath sent me to Jericho" and if Elisha were to "follow" him to the end then to Jericho he too must go. True, Jericho was far less attractive than Bethel, but the will of God pointed clearly to it. It is not the consideration of his own tastes and comforts which is to actuate the minister of Christ but the performance of duty, no matter where it leads to. The mount of transfiguration made a powerful appeal unto Peter, but at the base thereof there was a demon-possessed youth in dire need of deliverance! (Mt 17:14-18). Elisha resisted the tempting prospect, saying again, "I will not leave thee." Oh for such fidelity.

Fifth, the Testing of His Patience

This was a twofold test. When the two prophets arrived at Jericho, the younger one suffered a repetition of what he had experienced at Bethel. Once again "the sons of the prophet" from the local school accosted him, saying, "Knowest thou that the Lord will take away thy master from thy head today?" Elijah himself they left alone, but his companion was set upon by them. It is the connection in which this occurs that supplies the key to its meaning. The whole passage brings before us Elisha being tested first in one way and at one point and then at another. That he should meet with a repetition at Jericho of what he had encountered at Bethel is an intimation that the servant of God needs to be especially on his guard at this point. He must not put his trust even in "princes," temporal or spiritual, but cease entirely from man, trusting in the Lord and leaning not on his own understanding. Though it was annoying to be pestered thus by these men, Elisha made them a courteous reply, yet one which showed them he was not to be turned away from his purpose: "Yea, I know it, hold ye your peace."

"And Elijah said unto him, Tarry, I pray thee, here; for the LORD hath sent me to Jordan." This he said to prove him, as the Saviour tested the two disciples on the way to Emmaeus when He "made as though he would have gone further" (Lk 24:28). Much ground had been traversed since they had set out together from Gilgal. Was

Elisha growing tired of the journey, or was he prepared to persevere to the end? How many grow weary of well doing and fail to reap because they faint. How many fail at this point of testing and drop out when Providence appears to afford them a favorable opportunity of so doing. Elisha might have pleaded, "I may be of some service here to the young prophets, but of what use can I be to Elijah at the Jordan?" Philip was being greatly used of God in Samaria (Ac 8: 12) when the angel of the Lord bade him arise and go south "unto Gaza, which is desert" (v. 26). And he arose and went, and God honored his obedience. And Elisha said to his master, "I will not leave thee," no, not at the eleventh hour; and great was his reward.

Sixth, the Testing of His Character

"And it came to pass, when they were gone over [the Jordan], that Elijah said unto Elisha, Ask what I shall do for thee, before I be taken away from thee" (2 Ki 2:9). Here is clear proof that Elijah had been making trial of his companion when he had at the different stopping places, bade him "Tarry here" or remain behind, for certainly he would have extended no such offer as this had Elisha been disobedient and acting in self-will. Clearly the Tishbite was so well pleased with Elisha's devotion and attendance that he determined to reward him with some parting blessing: "Ask what I shall do for thee." If this was not the most searching of all the tests, certainly it was the most revealing. What was his heart really set upon? What did he desire above all else? At first glance it seemed surprising that Elijah should fling open so wide a door and offer to supply anything his successor should ask. But not only had they spent several years together; Elisha's reaction to the other testings convinced him that this faithful soul would ask nothing which was incongruous or which God could not give.

"And Elisha said, I pray thee, let a double portion of thy spirit be upon me." He rose above all fleshly and worldly desires, all that the natural heart would crave, and asked for that which would be most for the glory of God and the good of His people. Elisha sought neither wealth nor honors, worldly power nor prestige. What he asked for was that he might receive that which marked him out as Elijah's firstborn, the heir of his official patrimony (Deu 21:17). It was a noble request. The work to which he was called involved heavy responsibilities and the facing of grave dangers, and for the discharge of his duties he needed to be equipped with spiritual power. That is what every servant of God needs above everything else: to be "endued with power from on high." The most splendid faculties, the ablest intellect, the richest acquirements, count for nothing unless they be energized by the holy One.

The work of the ministry is such that no man is naturally qualified for it; only God can make any meet for the same. For that endowment the apostles waited upon God for ten days. To obtain it Elisha had to successfully endure the previous testings, pass through Jordan, and keep his eye fixed steadily upon his master.

Seventh, the Testing of His Endowment

When we ask God for something it is often His way to test our earnestness and importunity by keeping us waiting for it, and then when He grants our request, He puts our fidelity to the proof in the use we make of it. If it is faith that is bestowed, circumstances arise which are apt to call into exercise all our doubts and fears. If it is wisdom which is given, situations soon confront us where we are sorely tempted to give way to folly. If it is courage which is imparted, then perils will have to be faced which are calculated to make the stoutest quake. When we receive some spiritual gift, God so orders things that opportunity is afforded for the exercise of it. It was thus with Elisha. A double portion of Elijah's spirit was granted him, and the prophetic mantle of his master fell at his feet. What use would he make of it? As this comes up in our next chapter, suffice it now to say that he was confronted by the Jordan — he was on the wrong side of it and no longer was there any Elijah to divide asunder its waters!

We turn now from the testings to which Elisha was subjected unto the course which he had to take. The spiritual significance of his journey has also to receive its counterpart in the experiences of the servant of Christ. That journey began at Gilgal (2 Ki 2:1), and none can work acceptably in the kingdom of God until his soul is acquainted with what that place stands for. It was the first stopping-place of Israel after they entered Canaan, and where they were required to tarry before they set out on the conquest of their inheritance (Jos 5:9). It was there that all the males who had been born in the wilderness were circumcised. Now "circumcision" speaks of separation from the world, consecration to God, and the knife's application to the flesh. Figuratively it stood for the cutting off of the old life, the rolling away of "the reproach of Egypt." There is a circumcision "of the heart" (Ro 2:29), and it is that which is the distinguishing mark of God's spiritual children, as circumcision of the flesh had identified His earthly people. Gilgal, then, is where the path of God's servant must necessarily begin. Not until he unsparingly mortifies the flesh, separates from the world, and consecrates himself unreservedly to God is he prepared to journey further.

From Gilgal Elisha passed on to "Bethel," which means "the house of God." As we have seen, it was originally the place of hallowed memories, but in the course of time it had been grievously defiled. Bethel had been horribly polluted; for it was there that Jeroboam set up one of his golden calves, appointed an idolatrous priesthood, and led the people into terrible sin (1 Ki 12:28, 33). Elisha must visit this place so that he might be suitably affected with the dishonor done unto the Lord.

History has repeated itself. The house of God, the professing church, is defiled, and the servant of Christ must take to heart the apostate condition of Christendom today if his ministry is to be effective. From Bethel they proceeded to Jericho, a place that was under God's curse (Jos 6:26). The servant of God needs to enter deeply into the solemn fact that this world is under the curse of a holy God. And what is that "curse"? Death (Ro 6:23), and it is of that the Jordan (the final stopping-place) speaks. That too must be passed through in the experience of his soul if the minister is to be effective.

Chapter 4

FIRST MIRACLE
PASSAGE THROUGH JORDAN

THE RELATION BETWEEN Elijah and Elisha was that of master (2 Ki 2:16) and servant (2 Ki 3:11), and thus it set forth that which exists between Christ and His ministers. For some time Elijah himself occupied the state of action; but upon the completion of his mission and after a miraculous passage through Jordan, he was supernaturally removed to heaven. Thus it was with the One whom he foreshadowed: when the Saviour had finished the work given Him to do and had risen in triumph from the grave, He ascended on High. But men were appointed by Him to serve as ambassadors in the world from which He departed, to act in His name and perpetuate His mission. So it was with His type. Elisha was to succeed Elijah and carry forward what he had inaugurated. In order to do this he had been called by him. Then we saw in our last chapter how Elisha was subjected to a series of testings, which shadowed forth the disciplinary experiences by which the servant of Christ approves himself and through which he is schooled for his life's work. Then we viewed the path which Elisha was required to tread and pointed out briefly its spiritual significance in connection with the preparatory history of the minister of the gospel. One other preliminary feature remains for our consideration, namely, the endowment Elisha received.

It will be remembered that when Elijah had put to his companion that searching question, "Ask what I shall do for thee, before I be taken away from thee," Elisha had replied, "I pray thee, let a double portion of thy spirit be upon me." This we believe showed three things.

First, it revealed his modesty and humility, being an acknowledg-

29

ment of his weakness and insufficiency. He was conscious of his unfitness for his mission and felt that nothing but a plentiful supply of the Spirit which had rested upon the Tishbite would be enough for the tasks confronting him. Happy is the young servant of Christ who is aware of his own impotence, for in felt weakness lies his strength. Happy is the one who has experimentally learned the force of that word, "Not by might, nor by power, but by my spirit, saith the LORD" (Zec 4:6).

Second, if Elisha were to take Elijah's place at the head of the schools of the prophets, then he needed a superior endowment to theirs — a double supply of the Spirit of wisdom and power.

Third, as the accredited servant of God, he needed more than the rank and file of His people: not only the Spirit's indwelling, but also the Spirit's resting upon him.

We have only to turn to the final discourse of our Lord to His apostles, recorded in John 14-16, to discover the part which the Holy Spirit must play if His servants are to be duly equipped for their work. First, He declared He would pray the Father that another Paraclete or Comforter should be given them, who would abide with them forever (14:16). Then He promised that this blessed Comforter, sent in His name, would teach them all things (16:13). It was by means of the Spirit of truth given unto them that they would be enabled to bear testimony unto their Master (15:26-27). He would guide them into all truth, show them things to come, and glorify Christ by a fuller revelation to them of the mystery of His person, office, and work (16:13-15). In the book of Acts we see how those promises were made good. These servants were already indwelt by the Spirit of life (Jn 20:22) but the "power of the Holy Ghost" was to come upon them (Ac 1:8). This took place on the day of Pentecost, when "there appeared unto them cloven tongues like as of fire, and it sat upon each of them. And they [the apostles, 1:26] were all filled with the Holy Ghost" (2:3-4).

This, then, is the deep need of the servant of Christ: that he be endowed by the Spirit, for without such an anointing his labors can only prove ineffective. It was thus that Christ Himself was furnished (Mt 3:16; Ac 10:38), and the disciple is not greater than his Lord. Much has been said and written on this subject of the minister being endowed and empowered by the Holy Spirit, and varied indeed are the directions given as to what must be done in order to enter into this blessing. Personally, we have long been convinced that the position occupied by the apostles was unique, and therefore we are certainly not warranted in praying and looking for any supernatural endowment such as they received. On the other hand we must be careful not to go to an opposite extreme and conclude there is no special and distinct anointing by the Spirit which the servants of God need today. Elisha shows otherwise, for this case we believe is a typical and representative one.

Taking it for granted then that most of our readers will concur in the last remarks, we proceed to the important question. What is required of the minister if he is to enjoy a double portion of the Spirit? In answering this inquiry we will restrict ourselves to what is recorded of Elisha. In his case there were two things. First, the passage through Jordan, for it is to be duly noted that Elijah did not ask him "what shall I do for thee" until they had gone through its divided waters. Now, the Jordan stands for death, and death must be experimentally passed through before we can know the power of resurrection. The minister has to die to self, to all self-pleasing and self-seeking, before the Spirit of God will use him. Second, the prophet had to keep his eye fixed steadily upon his master if his desire was to be realized (2 Ki 2:10). It is all summed up in those words of Paul, "Not I, but Christ" (Gal 2:20). Just in proportion as self is set aside and the magnifying of Christ is the goal of my ministry, is an ungrieved Spirit likely to use me.

"And it came to pass, as they still went on, and talked, that, behold, there appeared a chariot of fire, and horses of fire, and parted them both asunder; and Elijah went up by a whirlwind to heaven. And Elisha saw it" (2 Ki 2:11-12). Of course he did. God never disappoints those who renounce self and are occupied solely with Christ. Elijah had made the granting of Elisha's request turn upon this very thing: "If thou seest me when I am taken from thee, it shall be so unto thee." Additional incentive then had the young prophet to keep his gaze steadfastly on his master. Those who follow on to know the Lord, who press forward in the race set before them, who allow nothing to turn them aside from fully following Christ, are permitted to behold things which are hidden not only from the world but also from their halfhearted brethren. A vision of the unseen is ever the reward which God grants to faith and fidelity. It was so with Abraham (Gen 22:11-12), with Moses (Ex 19:3-4), with Stephen (Ac 7:55), with John (Rev 1:1).

But something more than spiritual vision was granted unto Elisha, namely spiritual perception. He not only saw, but understood the significance of what he beheld. "And Elisha saw it, and he cried, My father, my father, the chariot of Israel, and the horsemen thereof." (2 Ki 2:12). Only as we ponder carefully the words of that sentence will the force of it be apparent. He did not say "the chariot of fire," nor even "the chariot of God," but "the chariot of Israel." What did he mean? And why preface that explanation with the cry "My father, my father"? He was interpreting for us the wondrous vision before him, the supernatural phenomenon described in the preceding verse. There was a divine suitability in Elijah's being removed from this scene in a chariot of fire driven by horses of fire. No other conveyance could have been more suitable and suggestive, though we have met no writer who appears to have grasped the significance of it. Why did God send a fiery chariot to conduct His servant to heaven? Let us endeavor to find the answer to that question.

Scripture interprets Scripture, and if we turn to other passages where "chariots" and "horses" are mentioned we shall obtain the key which opens to us the meaning of the one here before us. "Some trust in chariots and some in horses: but we will remember the name of the Lord our God" (Ps 20:7). Israel had good reason for saying that. Go back to the beginning of their national history. Behold them in their helplessness before the Red Sea as "Pharaoh's horses, his chariots, and his horsemen" (Ex 14:23) menaced their rear. Ah, but behold the sequel! They are all safe on the other side, singing "The Lord is a man of war: the Lord is his name. Pharoah's chariots and his host hath he cast into the sea: . . . The depths have covered them: . . . Thy right hand, O Lord, is become glorious in power: thy right hand, O Lord, hath dashed in pieces the enemy" (Ex 15:3-6). The ungodly may look to such things as horses and chariots for protection and prowess, but the saints will find their sufficiency in the name of the Lord their God.

It is sad indeed to see how woefully the favored nation of Israel failed at this very point. "They soon forgat his works;" yea, they "forgat God their saviour" (Ps 106:13, 21) and relied upon the arm of flesh. They even sought alliances with the heathen until one of their prophets had to cry, "Woe to them that go down to Egypt for help; and stay on horses, and chariots, because they are many; and in horsemen, because they are very strong; but they look not unto the Holy One of Israel, neither seek the Lord!" (Is 31:1). Now set over against this our present passage and is not its meaning clear? As Elisha beheld that awe-inspiring sight, his soul perceived its significance: "My father, my father, the chariot of Israel and the horsemen thereof." His master, had been in the band of the Lord of Israel's real chariot and horses, their true defense against Jezebel and Baal's prophet which are bent on their destruction. The nation was too carnal, too much given to idolatry to recognize what they were losing in the departure of Elijah; but Elisha realized it was "the chariot of Israel," which was being taken from them.

First, the Time of the Miracle

This brings us then to the time when Elisha performed his first miracle. It was what men generally would deem a most unpropitious one, when the prophet's spirits were at their lowest ebb. His beloved master had just been taken from him and deeply did he feel the loss. "He took hold of his own clothes, and rent them in two pieces" (2 Ki 2:12). That action was emblematic of his grief, as a comparison of Genesis 37:34 and Joshua 7:6, shows; yet it was a temperate sorrow, a controlled sorrow, and not an inordinate one. He only rent his garments in two pieces; had he done more they would have been wastefully ruined. His action may also have betokened Israel's rejection of Elijah (cf. 1 Sa 15:26-28). But severe as his loss was and heavy as his heart must have been, Elisha did not sit down in despair and wring his hands with inconsolable dejection. Pining over the loss of eminent ministers accomplishes no good to those left behind, but rather enfeebles them. Man's extremity is God's opportunity. The darkest hour of all is the best time to prove His sufficiency. This is what Elisha did now.

Second, the Object of the Miracle

Consider now the object on which it is wrought. A formidable one it was, none less than the river Jordan. He had friends, the prophets at Jericho, on the other side; the problem was how to come to them. Probably he was unable to swim, or surely he would have done so, since miracles are not wrought where there is no urgent need for them. There was no boat to take him over; how then was he to cross? A very real difficulty confronted him.

Let us note that he looked the difficulty squarely in the face. He "went back, and stood by the bank of the Jordan" (2 Ki 2:13), instead of foolishly playing the part of an ostrich, which buries its head in the sand when menaced by danger. To close our eyes to difficulties gets us nowhere, nor is anything gained by underestimating or belittling them. The Jordan was a challenge to Elisha's faith; so he regarded it and so he dealt with it. That is why God lets His servants and saints be confronted with difficulties: to try them and see of what metal they are made.

Third, the Instrument and Means for the Miracle

"He took up also the mantle of Elijah that fell from him, and went back, and stood by the bank of Jordan" (2 Ki 2:13). When his master's mantle fluttered to his feet, Elisha knew beyond doubt that heaven had granted his request. Not only had he seen Elijah at the moment of his departure, but the gift of his prophetical garment was an additional token of receiving a double portion of his spirit. And now came the test: what use would he make of his master's mantle! Testing always follows the bestowment of a divine gift. After Solomon had asked the Lord for "an understanding heart" that he might judge His people wisely and well and "discern between good and bad," he was quickly confronted by the two women each claiming the living child as hers (1 Ki 3:9, 16-27). No sooner did the Spirit of God descend upon Christ than He led Him into the wilderness to be tempted of the devil. Scarcely had the apostles been endowed with power from on High and begun to speak with other tongues, than they were charged with being "full of new wine." So here: Elijah's mantle fell at his feet, but before Elisha smote the Jordan!

Fourth, the Mode of the Miracle

This is of deep interest and importance, for it inculcated a truth of the greatest possible moment. "And he took the mantle of Elijah that fell from him, and smote the waters" (2 Ki 2:14). That was what the mantle had been given to him for — not to be idolized as a venerable memento, but to be made practical use of. "For whosoever, hath to him shall be given" (Lk 8:18), which means that he that has in reality, evidences it by improving the same, by investing it for interest. By cleaving so steadfastly to his master, Elisha had already given proof that he was indwelt by the Spirit, and now the double portion became his. This too he used, and used in the right way. He followed strictly the example his master had left him. In the context we are told, "Elijah took his mantle, and wrapped it together, and smote the waters" (2 Ki 2:8). Now his disciple did precisely the same thing. Is not the lesson for us clear? If the servant of Christ would work miracles, his ministry must be patterned closely after his Master's example.

Fifth, the Meaning of the Miracle

In view of all that has been before us, this should now be apparent. As we have sought to show, Elisha is to be regarded all through the piece as the representative servant, as a figure of the ministers of Christ: in their call, their testings, the path they must tread, their spiritual endowment; and the miracles he performed are not to be taken as exceptions to the rule. What then is the meaning and message of this first miracle, the smiting of and dividing asunder the waters of the Jordan? Clearly it is victory over death, ministerial victory. The servant of Christ is sent forth to address those who are dead in trespasses and sins. What an undertaking! How is he to prevail over the slaves and subjects of Satan? As Elisha did over the Jordan! He must be divinely equipped: he must obtain a double portion of the Spirit. By acting as Elijah did: using what has been given him from above. As he smote the waters in the exercise of faith, he said "Where is the LORD God of Elijah?" or, "Give proof that Thou art with me too."

Sixth, the Value of the Miracle

"And when he also had smitten the waters, they parted hither and thither: and Elisha went over" (2 Ki 2:14). There was the proof that though Elijah was not present, the God of Elijah was! There was the proof that he had received a double portion of his master's spirit. There was the proof that by using the same means as his master had employed, God was pleased to honor his faith and grant the same result. Three times in Scripture do we read of a miraculous crossing of the Jordan. See Joshua 3:17 for the first example. Typifying, I believe, the victory of Christ over the grave, the deliverance of the church from spiritual death, and the resurrection of our bodies in the day to come.

Seventh, the Recognition of the Miracle

"And when the sons of the prophets which were to view at Jericho saw him, they said, The spirit of Elijah doth rest on Elisha. And they came to meet him, and bowed themselves to the ground before him" (2 Ki 2:15). The miracle they had witnessed convinced them, and they accepted him as the successor or representative of Elijah. The parted waters of the Jordan demonstrated the presence of the Holy Spirit. So the regeneration of souls makes manifest that the servant of God has been endowed with power from on high, and those with spiritual perception will accept and honor him as such, for faithful ministers are to be esteemed "very highly in love for their work's sake" (1 Th 5:13). If Romanists have gone to one extreme in exalting the priesthood and making it a barrier to prevent the individual Christian from having direct dealings with God Himself, the democratic spirit of our day has swung so far to the other side as to level all distinctions. Those who have received a double portion of the Spirit are to "be counted worthy of double honor" if they "rule well" (1 Ti 5:17).

Chapter 5

SECOND MIRACLE
SALT-HEALED WATERS

"AND THEY SAID UNTO HIM, Behold now, there be with thy servants fifty strong men; let them go, we pray thee, and seek thy master: lest peradventure the Spirit of the Lord hath taken him up, and cast him upon some mountain, or into some valley" (2 Ki 2: 16). Two things must be borne in mind in connection with this request, lest we be too severe in our criticism of those who made it.

First, these young prophets had known that Elijah was to be removed from Elisha that day, as is clear from their words to him on a former occasion: "Knowest thou that the LORD will take away thy master from thy head to day?" (2 Ki 2:5). As to how they had learned of this, we cannot be sure; nor do we know how full was their information. Yet it seems clear they knew nothing more than the general fact that this was the day which would terminate the earthly career of the renowned Tishbite.

Second, we are told, "And fifty men of the sons of the prophets went, and stood to view afar off: and they two [Elijah and Elisha] stood by Jordan" (v. 7). Here again we cannot be certain what it was or how much they actually saw. Perhaps, some are ready to exclaim, if they were definitely on the lookout, they must have seen the remarkable translation of Elijah, for the "chariot of fire and the horses of fire" in midair would surely have been visible to them. Not necessarily. Probably that "fire" was very different from any that we are acquainted with. Moreover we must bear in mind that on a later occasion "the mountain was full of horses and chariots of fire round about Elisha," yet his own personal attendant saw them not until the prophet asked, "LORD, I pray thee, open his eyes, that he may see" (2 Ki 6:17)! We are therefore inclined to believe that as these young prophets watched, Elijah suddenly and mysteriously disappeared from their view, without their actually seeing his miraculous translation to heaven. Consequently they felt that something unprecedented and supernatural had taken place, and they ascribed it to a divine intervention, as their reference to "the Spirit of the LORD" intimates.

Though they must have realized that an event quite extraordinary had occurred, yet they were uneasy, fearful that something unpleasant had befallen their teacher. They were deeply concerned, and veneration and love for Elijah prompted their petition. Let us seek to put ourselves in their place and then ask, Would we have acted more intelligently? At any rate, was their request any more foolish than Peter's on the mount of transfiguration when he said to Christ, "If thou wilt, let us make here three tabernacles; one for thee, and one for Moses, and one for Elijah" (Mt 17:4)! Moreover it should be observed that they did not rashly take matters into their own hands, but respectfully submitted their request to Elisha. Before criticizing them too harshly let us make sure that our hearts are as warmly attached to God's servants as theirs, and that we are as troubled over their departure as they were.

Elisha tersely refused their request. "Ye shall not send." But why did he not explain to them the uselessness of such a quest, by informing them exactly what had happened to Elijah? Probably because he concluded that if the Lord had intended them to know of His servant's miraculous exit from this scene, He would have opened their eyes to behold what he himself had been permitted to see. Not all of the twelve witnessed Christ's transfiguration either. Moreover, is there not a hint here as to why this privilege had been withheld from them, in the statement that "they stood to view afar off"? Not so Elisha, who followed his master fully. It is only those who "draw near" that enjoy the highest privileges of grace. Finally we may learn from Elisha's reticence that there are some experiences which are too sacred to describe to others. Oh for more of such holy reserve and modesty in this day of curiosity and vulgar intruding into one another's spiritual privacy.

"And when they urged him till he was ashamed, he said, Send. They sent therefore fifty men; and they sought three days, but found him not" (2 Ki 2:17). Let it not be forgotten that up to this time only one individual from all mankind had gone to heaven without passing through the portals of death, and it is very doubtful if the contemporaries of Enoch (or those who lived later) knew of his translation, for the words, "He was not found" (Heb 11:5) intimate that search was also made for him. Elisha's being "ashamed" means that he felt if he were to continue refusing them they would likely think he was being influenced by an undue desire to occupy Elijah's place of honor. "And when they came again to him, (for he tarried at Jericho,) he said unto them, Did I not say unto you, Go not?" (2 Ki 2:18). Now *they* must have felt ashamed. "This would make them the more willing to acquiesce in his judgment another time" (Matthew Henry).

First, the Order of the Miracle

This brings us to Elisha's next miracle. First, let us consider the order of it. It was Elisha's second one, and the scriptural significance of that numeral casts light upon this point. One expresses unity and sovereignty. One stands all alone; but where there are two, another element has come in. So in the first miracle Elisha acted alone. But here in this one Elisha is not alone. A second human element is seen in connection with it — the "men of Jericho." They were required to furnish a "new cruse" with "salt therein" before the wonder was performed. Probably this very fact will prove a serious difficulty to the thoughtful reader. Those who have followed closely the preceding chapters will remember how we pointed out again and again that Elisha is to be regarded as a representative character, as a figure of the servants of Christ. Some may conclude the type fails us at this point, for it will be said, Surely you do not believe that ministers of the gospel demand something at the hands of sinners in order to be saved! Our answer will be given under the meaning of this miracle.

Second, the Place of the Miracle

Let us take note of the place where this occurred: it was at Jericho. This too is very illuminating. Jericho had been the first city of the Canaanites to defy the children of Israel, for it was closed and barred against them (Jos 6:1). Whereupon it was pronounced "accursed," and orders were given that Israel should not appropriate anything in it unto themselves: "And ye, in any wise keep yourselves from the accursed thing, lest ye make yourselves accursed, when ye take of the accursed thing" (Jos 6:18). By the power of Jehovah,

Jericho was overthrown, following which His people "burnt the city with fire, and all that was therein" (v. 24). Afterward the fearful denunciation went forth, "Cursed be the man before the LORD, that riseth up and buildeth this city Jericho" (v. 26). But both of those divine prohibitions were flouted. The first was by Achan, who "saw among the spoils a goodly Babylonish garment, and two hundred shekels of silver, and a wedge of gold" (Jos 7:21), which he coveted and stole, for which he and his family were stoned to death and their bodies destroyed by fire.

The second prohibition was broken centuries later, in the reign of the apostate Ahab: "In his days did Hiel the Bethelite build Jericho" (1 Ki 16:34). Thus Jericho was the city of the curse. It was the first place in Canaan where defiance of the Lord and His people was displayed. It was there that Israel, in the person of Achan, committed their first sin in the land of promise. A fearful curse was pronounced against the man who should have the effrontery to rebuild the city. That there is an unmistakable parallel between these things and what occurred in Eden scarcely needs pointing out. But we must not anticipate. That which is now before us is the fact that, in defiance of the divine threat, Jericho had recently been rebuilt — probably the attractiveness of its locality was the temptation to which Hiel yielded (as the pleasantness of the fruit in Eve's eyes induced her to partake: Gen 3:6), for we are told "And the men of the city said unto Elisha, Behold, I pray thee, the situation of this city is pleasant" (2 Ki 2:19).

Third, the Object of the Miracle

"And the men of the city said unto Elisha, Behold, I pray thee, the situation of this city is pleasant, as my Lord seeth: but the water is naught, and the ground barren" (v. 19). Herein God had evidenced His displeasure on that accursed rebuilding of Jericho by making its water unwholesome and the ground barren, or as the margin notes, "causing to miscarry." The Jewish commentators understood this to mean that these waters caused the cattle to cast their young, the trees to shed their fruit before it was mature, and even the women to be incapable of bearing children. The Hebrew word which is rendered "the water is naught" ("ra") is a much stronger one than the English denotes. In the great majority of cases it is translated "evil" (as in Gen 6:5; Pr 8:13), and "wicked" no less than thirty-one times. Its first occurrence is in "the tree of knowledge of good and evil" (Gen 2:9)! But it signifies not only evil but that which is harmful or injurious to others, being translated "the hurtful sword" (Ps 144:10).

Jericho then was a pleasant location, but there was no good water for its inhabitants or their flocks and herds. This was a serious matter, a vital consideration, for the Israelites were an essentially pastoral people. (Observe how often we find mention of the "wells" in their early history: Gen 16:14; 21:25; 26:15, 22; 29:2; Num 21: 16-18, etc.) Jericho in spite of all its ideal qualities then lacked the one thing essential.

How this reminds us of another and later incident in the career of Elisha: "Now Naaman, captain of the host of the king of Syria, was a great man with his master, and honourable, because by him the LORD had given deliverance unto Syria: he was also a mighty man in valour, but he was a leper" (2 Ki 5:1). In spite of his exalted position, his wealth, his exploits, he lacked the one thing needful — health. He was a leper and that nullified everything else. And thus it is with every man in his natural sinful condition; however favored by creation and by providence, the springs of his life are defiled.

Fourth, the Means Used for the Miracle

"And he said, Bring me a new cruse, and put salt therein. And they brought it to him. And he went forth unto the spring of the waters, and cast the salt in there" (vv. 20-21). The appropriateness of this particular means for counteracting the effects of the curse is at once apparent. Salt is the grand purifier and preserver. It is by means of the salty vapors which the rays of the sun distill from the ocean that the atmosphere of our earth is kept healthy for its inhabitants. That is why the sea breezes act as such a tonic to the invalid and the convalescent. Salt prevents putrefaction. Hence, after the backs of prisoners were scourged, salt was rubbed into the wounds; though extremely painful, it prevented blood poisoning. Salt is the best seasoning; how insipid and unsavory are many foods without a sprinkling of it. Salt is the emblem of divine holiness and grace, and so we read of the "covenant of salt" (Num 18:19; 2 Ch 13:5). Hence also the exhortation, "Let your speech be alway with grace, seasoned with salt" (Col 4:6), the savor of true piety. The

ministers of Christ are therefore denominated "the salt of the earth"
(Mt 5:13).

Fifth, the Instrument of the Miracle

Obviously the salt itself could not heal those unwholesome waters,
any more than the "rods" or twigs of the trees with their "white
streaks" that Jacob set before the flocks, were able to cause the
cattle to bring forth young ones that were "ringstreaked, speckled
and spotted" (Gen 30:37-39). Though the men of Jericho were
required to furnish the salt, and though the prophet now cast the
same into the springs, yet he made it clear this would avail nothing
unless the blessing of Jehovah accompanied the same. His power
must operate if anything good was to be accomplished. Therefore
we find that as Elisha cast in the salt he declared "Thus saith the
LORD, I have healed the waters; there shall not be from thence any
more death or miscarrying" (2 Ki 2:21, ASV). Thereby the prophet
disclaimed any inherent power of his own. Yet he was instrumentally employed of God, for the very next verse says, "So the waters
were healed unto this day, according to the saying of Elisha which
he spake"! How very similar to Paul's experience, which he expressed,
"I have planted, Apollos watered [they were the instruments]; but
God gave the increase" (1 Co 3:6).

Sixth, the Meaning or Typical Significance of the Miracle

The first key to the meaning is found in the order of it. Under that
point we intimated that probably some readers would find a difficulty in the men of Jericho being required to furnish the salt and be
inclined to object that surely the minister of the gospel (for as a
figure of such Elisha is to be viewed here) does not demand anything at the hand of sinners in order for them to be saved. But such
a difficulty is self-created through entertaining vague and general
concepts instead of distinguishing sharply between things that differ.
When we speak of "salvation" we refer to something that is many-
sided. If on the one hand we must guard most carefully against the
error of man's contributing to his regeneration, on the other we must
watch against swinging to the opposite extreme and denying that
man is required to concur with God in connection with his reconciliation, preservation, etc. The typical picture which is here set be-

fore us is divinely perfect; yet we need to view it closely if we are to see its details in their proper perspective.

The first miracle, the smiting of the Jordan, suggests the ministerial power of the evangelist over spiritual death, in connection with salvation. But this second miracle foreshadows a later, second experience in the history of those truly converted. This miracle at Jericho speaks of neutralizing the effects of the curse, overcoming the power of innate depravity. And here the minister of the gospel acts not alone, for in this matter there is the conjunction of both the divine and the human elements. Thus the second key to its meaning lies in the place where it occurred. It is true that the conjunction of the divine and human elements in conversion cannot be so closely defined as to express the same in any theological formula; nevertheless the reality of those two elements can be demonstrated both from Scripture and experience. We do not like the expression "man's cooperating with God" for that savors too much of a dividing of the honors, but man's "concurring with God" seems to be both permissible and necessary.

The third key is contained in the fact that these men of Jericho are represented as taking the initiative, coming unto Elisha, acquainting him with their need, supplicating his assistance! Apparently they knew from his dress that Elisha was a prophet; and as he no doubt still carried Elijah's mantle, they hoped he would use his power on their behalf. The servant of God ought to be readily identified by his (emblematic) "garments" or spiritual graces, easily accessible and approachable, one to whom members of a community will gladly turn in their troubles. Elisha did not repulse them by saying this lay outside his line of things, that his concern lay only with the young prophets. Instead he at once intimated his willingness to help. Yet something was required of them (compare 4:41 and 5:10 for other illustrations of the same principle). They were told to provide a "new cruse" with salt therein. That was a test as to whether they were willing to follow the prophet's instructions. They promptly heeded. How different from many who disregard the directions of God's servants!

This miracle then does not give us a history of the servant of God going to those who are utterly unconcerned, dead in trespasses and sins, but rather that of awakened souls, seeking help, acquainting the minister with their need. In the first miracle it is God acting in sovereign power, enabling His servant to ministerially triumph over death; here it is His servant addressing human responsibility. In bidding awakened and inquiring sinners to provide a "new cruse and put salt therein," he is saying to them, "Cast away from you all your transgressions, whereby ye have transgressed; and make you a new heart and a new spirit" (Eze 18:31 and cf. Ja 4:8). These men of Jericho could not have procured the new cruse and the salt unless God had first placed it at their hands, and the sinner cannot bring a responsive and obedient heart to the minister until God has previously quickened him. That this miracle is, instrumentally, attributed to the "saying of Elisha" (the Hebrew term *dabar* is rendered "word" in 1 Ki 17:2, 8) denotes that awakened sinners are delivered from the effects of the curse as they obey the instructions of God's faithful servants.

Seventh, the Permanency of the Miracle

"Thus saith the LORD, I have healed these waters; there shall not be from thence any more death or miscarrying: so the waters were healed unto this day, according to the word of Elisha which he spake" (2 Ki 2:21-22, ASV). It was no superficial and temporary change that was wrought, but an effectual and permanent one. "I know that, whatsoever God doeth, it shall be for ever: nothing can be put to it, nor any thing taken from it" (Ec 3:14). Herein we see again the appropriateness of the salt, the emblem of incorruption, used in the covenant to express its perpetuity. Placing in a "new cruse" and then casting into "the springs of water" give figures of the new and honest heart, out of which are "the issues of life" (Pr 4:23).

The nature of fallen men, even the most attractive specimens, is like unwholesome water and barren soil; it must be renewed by God before any good works can be produced. Make the tree good and its fruit will be good. The miracle is attributed, instrumentally, not to the faith or the prayer of Elisha (though there was both), but to his word. By His response God avouched His prophet and sustained his testimony in Israel.

Chapter 6

THIRD MIRACLE
TWO AVENGING BEARS

"AND HE WENT UP FROM THENCE unto Beth-el: and as he was going up by the way, there came forth little children out of the city, and mocked him, and said unto him, Go up, thou bald head; go up, thou bald head. And he turned back, and looked on them, and cursed them in the name of the LORD. And there came forth two she bears out of the wood, and tare forty and two children of them" (2 Ki 2:23-24).

First, the Connection of the Miracle

In seeking to give an exposition of this miracle let us observe its connection. It will be noted that our passage opens with the word "And." Since there is nothing meaningless in Scripture, it should be duly pondered. It evidently suggests that we should observe the relation between what we find here and that which immediately precedes. The context records the wonders which God wrought through Elisha at the Jordan and at Jericho. Thus the truth which is here pointed to by the conjunction is plain: when the servant has been used by his Master he must expect to encounter the opposition of the enemy.

There is an important if unpalatable truth illustrated here, one which the minister of Christ does well to take to heart if he would be in some measure prepared for and fortified against bitter disappointment. After a period of blessing and success, he must expect sore trials. After he has witnessed the power of God attending his efforts he may count upon experiencing something of the rage and

power of Satan; for nothing infuriates the devil so much as beholding his victims delivered from spiritual death and set free. Elisha
has been favored both at the Jordan and at Jericho, but here at
Bethel he hears the hiss of the serpent and the roaring of the lion
against him. Yes, the minister of the gospel is fully aware of this
principle and even often reminds his hearers of it. He knows it was
the case with his Master; for after the Spirit of God had descended
upon Him and the Father had testified to His pleasure in Him, He
was at once led into the wilderness to be tempted of the devil. Yet
how quickly is this forgotten when he himself is called to pass
through this contrasting experience.

It is one thing to know this truth theoretically, and it is quite another to have a personal acquaintance with it. The servant of
Christ is informed that the smile of heaven upon his labors will
arouse the enmity of his great adversary, yet how often is he taken
quite unaware when the storm of opposition bursts upon him! It
ought not to be so, but so often it is. "Think it not strange concerning the fiery trial which is to try you" (1 Pe 4:12). Various indeed
are the ups and downs which are encountered by those who labor in
the Christian vineyard. What a striking contrast is here presented to
our view! At Jericho Elisha is received with respect, the young
prophets render obeisance to him, and the men of the city seek his
help. Here at Bethel he is contemptuously ridiculed by the children.
At Jericho, the city of the curse, he is an instrument of blessing; at
Bethel, which signifies "the house of God" and where blessing might
therefore be expected, he solemnly pronounces a curse upon those
who mock him.

Second, the Occasion of the Miracle

The insulting of God's servant occasioned this miracle. As Elisha
was approaching Bethel, "there came forth little children out of the
city and mocked him." Upon reading this incident it is probable
that some will be inclined to say that it seems that children then
were much like what they are now — wild, rude, lawless, totally
lacking in respect for their seniors. From this analogy the conclusion will be drawn: therefore we should not be surprised nor unduly
shocked at the present-day delinquency of some of our youth. But
such a conclusion is entirely unwarranted. It is true there is "nothing new under the sun" and that fallen human nature has been the

same in every age. But it is not true that the tide of evil has always flowed uniformly and that each generation has witnessed more or less the same appalling conduct which now stigmatizes the young in every part of the world. No, very far from it.

When there was an ungrieved Spirit in the churches, the restraining hand of God was held upon the baser passions of mankind. That restraint operated largely through parental control — moral training in the home, wholesome instruction and discipline in the school, and adequate punishment of young offenders by the state. But when the Spirit of God is "grieved" and "quenched" by the churches, the restraining hand of the Lord is removed, and there is a fearful moral aftermath in all sections of the community. When the divine law is thrown out by the pulpit, there inevitably follows a breakdown of law and order in the social realm, which is what we are now witnessing all over the so-called civilized world. That was the case to a considerable extent twenty-five years ago; and as the further an object rolls down hill the swifter becomes its momentum, so the moral deterioration of our generation has proceeded apace. As the majority of parents were godless and lawless, it is not to be wondered at that we now behold such reprehensible conduct in their offspring.

Older readers can recall the time when juveniles who were guilty of theft, wanton destruction of property, and cruelty to animals were sternly rebuked and punished for their wrong doing. But a few years later such conduct began to be condoned, and "boys will be boys" was used to gloss over a multitude of sins. So, far from being shocked, many parents were pleased and regarded their erring offspring as smart, precocious, and cute. Educational authorities and psychologists insisted that children must not be suppressed and repressed but "directed." These professionals prated about the evils inflicted on the child's character by "inhibitions," and corporal punishment was banished from the schools. Today the parent who acts according to Proverbs 13:24, 19:18, 22:15, and 23:14 will not only be called a brute by his neighbors, but is likely to be summoned before the courts for cruelty; and instead of supporting him the magistrate will probably censure him. The present permissive treatment of children is not normal but abnormal. What is recorded in our passage occurred in the days of Israel's degeneracy! Child delinquency is one of the plain marks of a time of apostasy. It was so then; it is so now.

Third, the Location of the Miracle

As with the former miracles, the place where this one happened also throws much light upon that which occasioned it. Originally Bethel was called "the house of God" (Gen 28:16-19), but now it had become a habitation of the devil, one of the principal seats of Israel's idolatry. It was here that Jeroboam had set up one of the calves. Afraid that he might not be able to retain his hold upon those who had revolted from Rehoboam, especially if they should go up to Jerusalem and offer sacrifices in the temple, he "made two calves of gold, and said unto them. It is too much for you to go up to Jerusalem: behold thy gods, O Israel, which brought thee up out of the land of Egypt. And he set the one in Bethel, and the other put he in Dan. . . . And he made an house of high places and made priests of the lowest of the people which were not of the sons of Levi. And Jeroboam ordained a feast for the eighth month, on the fifteenth day of the month, like unto the feast that is in Judah, and he offered upon the altar. So did he in Bethel, sacrificing unto the calves that he had made: and he placed in Bethel the priests of the high places which he had made" (1 Ki 12:28-29, 31-33).

Thus it will be seen that, far from Bethel being a place which basked in the sunshine of Jehovah's favor, it was one upon which His frown now rested. Its inhabitants were no ordinary people, but high rebels against the Lord, openly defying Him to His face, guilty of the most fearful abominations. This it was which constituted the dark background of the scene that is here before us. This accounts for the severity of the judgment which fell upon the youngest of its inhabitants; this explains why these children conducted themselves as they did. What occurred here was far more than the silly prank of innocent children; it was the manifestation of an inveterate hatred of the true God and His faithful servant. Israel's worship of Baal was far more heinous than the idolatry of the Canaanites, for it had the additional and awful guilt of apostasy. And apostates are always the fiercest persecutors of those who cleave to the truth, for the very fidelity of the latter is a witness against and a condemnation of those who have forsaken it.

Fourth, the Awfulness of the Miracle

The fearful doom which overtook those children must be considered in the light of the enormity of their offense. Our degenerate generation has witnessed so much condoning of the greatest enormities that it may find it difficult to perceive how this punishment fitted the crime. The character of God has been so misrepresented by the pulpit, His claims so little pressed, the position occupied by His servants so imperfectly apprehended, that there must be a returning to the solemn teaching of Holy Writ if this incident is to be viewed in its proper perspective. God had said, "Touch not mine annointed, and do my prophets no harm" (Ps 105:15). They are His messengers, His accredited representatives, His appointed ambassadors, and an insult done to them is regarded by God as an insult against Himself. Said Christ to His ministers, "He that receiveth you receiveth me, and he that receiveth me receiveth him that sent me" (Mt 10:40); conversely, he that despises and rejects the one sent forth by Christ, despises and rejects Him. How little is this realized today! The curse of God now rests on many a place where His ministers were mocked.

"And we went up from thence unto Bethel; and as he was going up by the way, there came forth little children out of the city and mocked him, and said unto him, Go up, thou bald head." After the vain search which had been made for Elijah (2 Ki 2:17), it is likely that some inkling of his supernatural rapture was conveyed to the prophets at Jericho, and from them to their brethren at Bethel (v. 3). Hence we may conclude that his remarkable translation had been noised abroad — received with skepticism and ridicule by the inhabitants of Bethel. In their unbelief they would mock at it. Today apostate leaders of Christendom do not believe that the Lord Jesus actually rose again from the dead and that He ascended to heaven in a real physical body, and they make fun of the Christian's hope of his Lord's return and of being caught up to meet Him in the air (1 Th 4:16-17). Thus in saying, "Go up, thou bald head," the children were, in all probability, scoffing at the tidings of Elijah's translation — scoffs put into their mouths by their elders.

Thomas Scott says,

> They had heard that Elijah was "gone up to heaven" and they insultingly bade Elisha follow him, that they might be rid of him also, and they reviled him for the baldness of his head. Thus they united the crimes of abusing him for a supposed bodily infirmity, contemptuous behaviour towards a venerable person, and enmity against him as the prophet of God. The sin therefore of these children was

very heinous: yet the greater guilt was chargeable on their parents, and their fate was a severe rebuke and awful warning to them.

How true it is that "the curse causeless shall not come" (Pr 26:2). "And he turned back and looked on them," which indicates he acted calmly, and not on the spur of the moment. "And he cursed them in the name of the LORD," not out of personal spite, but to vindicate his insulted Master. Had Elisha sinned in cursing these children, divine providence would have prevented it. This was a fair warning from God of the awful judgment about to come upon Israel for their sins.

Fifth, the Ethics of the Miracle

The passage before us is one which infidels have been quick to seize upon, and lamentable indeed have been many of the answers returned to them. But the Word has survived every opposition of its enemies and all the puerile apologies of its weak-kneed friends. Nor are the Scriptures in any danger whatever in this skeptical and blatant age. Being the Word of God, they contain nothing which His servants have any need to be ashamed of, nothing which requires any explaining away. It is not our province to sit in judgment upon Holy Writ: our part is to tremble before it (Is 66:2) knowing that one day we shall be judged by it (Jn 12:48). As Jehovah was able to look after the sacred ark without the help of any of His creatures (2 Sa 6:6-7), so His truth is in need of no carnal assistance from us. It is to be received without question and believed in with all our hearts. It is to be preached and proclaimed in its entirety without hesitation or reservation.

Certain so-called Christian apologists have replied to the taunts of infidels by a process of what is termed "toning down" the passage, arguing that it was not little children but young men who were cursed by the prophet and torn to pieces by the bears: but such an effeminate explanation is as senseless as it is needless. We quite agree with Thomas Scott when he says,

> Some learned men have endeavored to prove that these offenders were not young children but grown-up persons, and no doubt the word rendered "children" is often used in that sense. The addition, however of the word "little" seems to clearly evince they were not men, but young boys who had been brought up in idolatry and taught to despise the prophets of the Lord.

Others roundly condemn Elisha, saying he should have meekly endured their taunts in silence and that he sinned grievously in cursing them. It is sufficient to point out that his Master deemed otherwise. Instead of rebuking His servant, He sent the bears to fulfill his curse, and there is no appeal against His decision.

Some Bible teachers have asserted mistakenly that this drastic punishment was necessary because the Old Testament period was governed by the law, but that under New Testament grace, this would not warrant immediate judgment. Let such teachers remember that Ananias and Sapphira fell dead as soon as they sinned against the Holy Spirit (Acts 5).

God is even now giving the most awe-inspiring and wide-reaching proof of His wrath against those who flout His Law, visiting the earth with sorer judgments than any He has sent since the days of Noah! The New Testament equally with the Old teaches "it is a righteous thing with God to recompense tribulation to them that trouble you" (2 Th 1:6). In the incident before us, God was righteously visiting the sins of the fathers upon the children, as He was by the death of their children also smiting the parents in their tenderest parts. At almost the end of the Old Testament era we read that Israel "mocked the messengers of God, and despised his words, and misused his prophets, until the wrath of the LORD arose against his people, till there was no remedy" (2 Ch 36:16). Here at Bethel God was giving a warning, a sample of His coming wrath, unless they reformed their ways and treated His servants better.

Sixth, the Meaning of the Miracle

At first glance it certainly appears that there can be no parallel between the above action of Elisha and that which should characterize the servants of Christ, and many are likely to conclude that it can only be by a wide stretch of imagination or a flagrant wresting of this incident that it can be made to yield anything pertinent for this age. But it must be remembered that we are not looking for a literal counterpart but rather a spiritual application. Viewing it thus, our type is solemnly accurate. Ministers of the gospel are "unto God a sweet savour of Christ, in them that are saved, and in them that perish: To the one we are the savour of death unto death; and to the other the savour of life unto life" (2 Co 2:14-15). Certainly the evangelist has no warrant to anathamatize any who oppose him, but he can point out that they are accursed of God who love not Christ and who obey not His law (1 Co 16:22; Gal 3:10).

Seventh, the Sequel of the Miracle

This is recorded in the closing verse of 2 Kings 2. "And he went from thence to mount Carmel, and from thence he returned to Samaria." In the violent death of those children as the outcome of Elisha's malediction, we behold the estating of the prophet's divine authority, the sign of his extraordinary office, and the fulfillment of the prediction that he should "slay" (1 Ki 19:17)! After his unpleasant experience at Bethel, the prophet went to Carmel, which had been the scene of Elijah's grand testimony to a prayer-answering God (1 Ki 18). By heading for the mount this servant of God intimated his need for the renewing of his strength by communion with the Most High and by meditation upon His holiness and power. Samaria was the country where the apostate portion of Israel dwelt, and by going there, Elisha manifested his readiness to be used of his Master as He saw fit in that dark and difficult field of labor.

There is only space left for us to barely mention some of the more outstanding lessons to be drawn from this solemn incident. First, "Behold therefore the goodness and severity of God" (Ro 11:22): if the previous miracle exemplified His "goodness," certainly this one demonstrated His "severity," and the one is as truly a divine perfection as the other!

Second, the words as well as actions of children, even "little children," are noticed by God! (Pr 20:11). They should be informed of this and warned against showing disrespect to God's servants.

Third, what must have been the grief of those parents when they beheld the mangled bodies of their little ones! But how much greater the anguish of parents in the day of judgment when they witness the everlasting condemnation of their offspring if it has been occasioned by their own negligence and evil example.

Chapter 7

FOURTH MIRACLE
VALLEY OF DITCHES

First, the Background of the Miracle

IT HAS PLEASED the Holy Spirit in this instance to provide a somewhat lengthy and complicated miracle, so it will be wise for us to patiently ponder the account He has given of what led up to and occasioned this exercise of God's wonder-working power. Just as a diamond appears to best advantage when placed in a suitable setting, so we are the more enabled to appreciate the works of God when we take note of their connections. This applies equally to His works in creation, in providence, and in grace. We are always the losers if we ignore the circumstances which occasion the varied actings of our God. The longer and darker the night, the more welcome the morning's light, and the more acute our need and urgent our situation, the more manifest is the hand of Him that relieves and His goodness in ministering to us. The same principle holds good in connection with the Lord's undertaking for our fellows, and if we were not so self-centered we should appreciate and render praise for the one as much as for the other.

In 2 Kings 3 we read, "Now Jehoram the son of Ahab began to reign over Israel in Samaria the eighteenth year of Jehoshaphat king of Judah, and reigned twelve years. And he wrought evil in the sight of the LORD; but not like his father, and like his mother: for he put away the image of Baal, that his father had made. Nevertheless he cleaved unto the sins of Jeroboam the son of Nebat, which made Israel to sin; he departed not therefrom" (vv. 1-3). Five things are taught us in these verses about that "abominable thing" which God "hates" and which is the cause of all the suffering and sorrow that is in the world, namely, sin.

1. *God Himself personally observes our wrongdoing.* It was "in

53

the sight of the LORD" that the guilty deeds of Jehoram were performed. How much evil doing is perpetrated secretly and under
cover of darkness, supposing none are witness. But though evildoing
may be concealed from human gaze, it cannot be hidden from the
omnipresent One, for, "The eyes of the LORD are in every place (by
night as well as by day), beholding the evil and the good" (Pr 15:
3). What curb this ought to place on us.

2. *God records our evil deeds.* Here is a clear case in point. The
evil which Jehoram wrought in the sight of the Lord is set down
against him, likewise that of his parents before him, and further back
still "the sin of Jeroboam." Unspeakably solemn is this: God not
only observes but registers against men every infraction of His Law.
They commit iniquity and think little or nothing of it, but the very
One who shall yet judge them has noted the same against them. It
may all be forgotten by them, but nothing shall fade from what God
has written. And when the dead, both small and great, stand before
Him, the "books" will be opened, and they will be "judged out of
those things which were written in the books, according to their
works" (Rev 20:12). And my reader, there is only one possible way
of escape from receiving the awful wages of your sins, and that is
to throw down the weapons of your warfare against God, cast yourself at the feet of Christ as a guilty sinner, put your trust in His re-
deeming and cleansing blood. Then God will say, "I have blotted
out, as a thick cloud, thy transgressions" (Is 44:22).

3. *God recognizes degrees in evildoing.* Jehoram displeased the
Lord; yet it is said, "but not like his father, and like his mother."
Christ declared to Pilate, "he [Judas] that delivered me unto thee
hath the greater sin" (Jn 19:11). Again we are told, "He that despised Moses' law died without mercy under two or three witnesses:
Of how much sorer punishment, suppose ye, shall he be thought
worthy, who hath trodden under foot the Son of God" (Heb 10:
28-29). There are many who ignore this principle and suppose that
since they are sinners it makes no difference how much wickedness
they commit. They madly argue, "I might as well be hung for a
sheep as a lamb," but are only treasuring up unto themselves wrath
against the day of wrath (Ro 2:5), for "every transgression and
disobedience" will yet receive "a just recompence of reward" (Heb
2:2).

4. *God observes whether our reformation is partial or complete.*
This comes out in the fact that we are told Jehoram "put away the

image [or 'statue'] that his father had made," but he did not destroy it, and a few years later Baal worship was restored. God's Word touching this matter was plain: "thou shalt utterly overthrow them, and quite break down their images" (Ex 23:24). Sin must be dealt with by no unsparing hand, and when we resolve to break away, we must burn our bridges behind us or they are likely to prove an irresistible temptation to return to our former ways.

5. *God duly notes our continuance in sin.* Here it is recorded that Jehoram not only "cleaved unto the sins of Jeroboam" but also that "he departed not therefrom" which greatly aggravated his guilt. To enter upon a course of wrongdoing is horrible wickedness, but to deliberately persevere in it is much worse. How few heed that word "break off thy sins by righteousness" (Dan 4:27).

"And Mesha king of Moab was a sheepmaster, and rendered unto the king of Israel an hundred thousand lambs, and an hundred thousand rams, with the wool. But it came to pass, when Ahab was dead, that the king of Moab rebelled against the king of Israel" (2 Ki 3:4-5). In fulfillment of Balaam's prophecy (Num 24:17) David had conquered the Moabites. They became his "servants" (2 Sa 8:2), and they continued in subjection to the kingdom of Israel until the time of its division, when their vassalage and tribute was transferred to the kings of Israel, as those of Edom remained to the kings of Judah. But upon the death of Ahab they revolted. Here we see the divine Providence crossing His sons in their affairs. This rebellion on the part of Moab should be regarded in the light of "When a man's ways please the LORD, he maketh even his enemies to be at peace with him" (Pr 16:7); but when our ways displease Him, evil from every quarter menaces us. Temporal as well as spiritual prosperity depends entirely on God's blessing. To make His hand more plainly apparent, God frequently punishes the wicked after the manner of their sins. He did so to Ahab's sons: they had turned from the Lord, and Moab was moved to rebel against them.

As we ponder this incident we are made to realize that there is no new thing under the sun. Discontent, strife, jealousies, and bloodshedding have characterized the relations of one nation to another all through history. Instead of mutual respect and peace, "living in malice and envy, hateful, and hating one another" (Titus 3:3) have marked them all through the years. How aptly were the great empires of antiquity symbolized by "four great beasts" (Dan 7:3) — wild, ferocious, and cruel ones, at that! Human depravity is a solemn reality, and neither education nor legislation can eradicate or sublimate it. What, then, are the ruling powers to do? Deal with it with a firm hand: "For rulers are not a terror to good works, but to the evil. . . . He beareth not the sword in vain: for he [the governmental and civil ruler] is the minister of God [to maintain law and order], a revenger [to enforce law and order] . . . upon him that doeth evil" (Ro 13:4).

"But it came to pass, when Ahab was dead, that the king of Moab rebelled against the king of Israel." The Moabites were the descendants of the son which Lot had by his elder daughter. They occupied a territory to the southeast of Judah and east of the Red Sea. They were a strong and fierce people — "the mighty men of Moab" (Ex 15:15). Balak, who sent for Balaam to curse Israel, was one of their kings. Even as proselytes they were barred from entering the congregation of the Lord unto the tenth generation. They were idolators (1 Ki 11:33). For at least a hundred and fifty years they had apparently paid a heavy annual tribute, but upon the death of Ahab they had decided to throw off the yoke and be fined no further.

"And king Jehoram went out of Samaria the same time, and numbered all Israel" (2 Ki 3:6). There was no turning to the Lord for counsel and help. He was the One who had given David success and brought the Moabites into subjection, and Jehoram should have turned to Him now that they rebelled. But he was a stranger to Jehovah; nor did he consult the priests of the calves, so apparently he had no confidence in them either. How sad is the case of the unregenerate in the hour of need; no divine comforter in sorrow, no unerring counsellor in perplexity, no sure refuge when danger menaces them. How much men lose even in this life by turning their backs upon the One who gave them being. Nothing less than spiritual madness can account for the folly of those who "observe lying vanities" and "forsake their own mercies" (Jon 2:8). Jonah had to learn that lesson in a hard school. Alas, the vast majority of our fellows never learn it, as they ultimately discover to their eternal undoing. Will that be the case with you, my reader?

"And he went and sent to Jehoshaphat the king of Judah, saying, The king of Moab hath rebelled against me: wilt thou go with me against Moab to battle?" (2 Ki 3:7). Both Thomas Scott and Matthew Henry suppose that it was merely a political move on the part of Jehoram when he "put away the image of Baal that his father had made." They think this external reformation was designed to pave the way for obtaining the help of Jehoshaphat, who was a God-fearing, though somewhat vacillating, man. The words of Elisha to him in verses 13-14 certainly seem to confirm this view, for the servant of God made it clear that he was not deceived by such a device and addressed him as one who acted the part of a hypocrite. Any student of history is well aware that many religious improvements have been granted by governments simply from what is termed "state policy" rather than from spiritual convictions or a genuine desire to promote the glory of God. Only the One who looks on the heart knows the real motives behind much that appears fair on the surface.

"And he said, I will go up: I am as thou art, my people as thy people, and my horses as thy horses" (v. 7). It seems strange that Jehoshaphat was willing to unite with Jehoram in this expedition, for he had been severely rebuked on an earlier occasion for having "joined affinity with Ahab" (2 Ch 18:1-3). Jehu the prophet said to him, "Shouldest thou help the ungodly, and love them that hate the LORD? therefore is wrath upon thee from before the LORD" (2 Ch 19:2). How, then, is his conduct to be explained on this occasion? No doubt his zeal to heal the breach between the two kingdoms had much to do with it, for 2 Chronicles 18:1-3 intimates he was anxious to promote a better spirit between Judah and Israel. Moreover, the Moabites were a common enemy, for we learn from 2 Chronicles 20:1 that at a later date the Moabites, accompanied by others, came against Jehoshaphat to battle. But it is most charitable to conclude that Jehoshaphat was deceived by Jehoram's reformation. Yet we should mark the absence of his seeking directions from the Lord on this occasion.

Second, the Urgency of the Miracle

"And he said, Which way shall we go up? And he answered, The way through the wilderness of Edom. So the king of Israel went, and the king of Judah, and the king of Edom: and they fetched a compass of seven days' journey: and there was no water for the host, and for the cattle that followed them. And the king of Israel said, Alas! that the LORD hath called these three kings together to deliver them into the hand of Moab" (2 Ki 3:8-10). Note that Jehoram was quite willing for the king of Judah to take the lead, and that he made his plans without seeking counsel of God. The

course he took was obviously meant to secure the aid of the Edomites, but by going so far into the wilderness they met with a desert
where there was no water. Thus the three kings and their forces
were in imminent danger of perishing. This struck terror into the
heart of Jehoram and at once his guilty conscience smote him —
unbelievers know sufficient truth to condemn them! "The foolishness of man perverteth his way: and his heart fretteth against the
LORD" (Pr 19:3). What an illustration of that is furnished by the
words of Jehoram on this occasion.

"But Jehoshaphat said, Is there not here a prophet of the LORD,
that we may enquire of the LORD by him? And one of the king of
Israel's servants answered and said, Here is Elisha the son of Shaphat,
which poured water on the hands of Elijah. And Jehoshaphat said,
The Word of the LORD is with him. So the king of Israel and
Jehoshaphat and the king of Edom went down to him" (2 Ki 3:
11-12). Here we see the difference between the unrighteous and the
righteous in a time of dire calamity. The one is tormented with a
guilty conscience and thinks only of the Lord's wrath; the other has
hope in His mercy. In those days the prophet was the divine mouth-
piece, so the king of Judah made inquiry for one, and not in vain.
It is blessed to observe that as the Lord takes note of and registers
the sins of the reprobate, so He observes the deeds of His elect,
placing on record here the humble service which Elisha had rendered to Elijah. Appropriately was Elisha termed "the chariot of
Israel and the horsemen thereof" (2 Ki 13:14). He was their true
defense in the hour of danger, and to him did the three kings turn
in their urgent need.

Third, the Discrimination of the Miracle

"And Elisha said unto the king of Israel, What have I to do with
thee? get thee to the prophets of thy father, and to the prophets of
thy mother" (2 Ki 3:13). Mark both the dignity and fidelity of
God's servant. Far from feeling flattered because the king of Israel
consulted him, he deemed himself insulted and let him know he
discerned his true character. It reminds us of the Lord's words
through Ezekiel, "These men have set up their idols in their hearts,
and put the stumblingblock of their iniquity before their face: should
I be enquired of at all by them?" (Eze 14:3).

"And the king of Israel said unto him, Nay: for the LORD hath called these three kings together, to deliver them into the hand of Moab," as much as to say, "Do not disdain me; our case is desperate."

"And Elisha said, "As the LORD of hosts liveth, before whom I stand, surely, were it not that I regard the presence of Jehoshaphat the king of Judah, I would not look toward thee, nor see thee" (2 Ki 3:14). Little do the unrighteous realize how much they owe, under God, to the presence of the righteous in their midst.

Fourth, the Requirement of the Miracle

"But now bring me a minstrel" (2 Ki 3:15). In view of 1 Samuel 16:23, Scott and Henry conclude that his interview with Jehoram had perturbed Elisha's mind and that soothing music was a means to compose his spirit, that he might be prepared to receive the Lord's mind. Possibly they are correct, yet we believe there is another and more important reason. In the light of such passages as "Sing unto the LORD with the harp; . . . and the voice of a psalm" (Ps 98:5), and "Jeduthun, who prophesied with a harp, to give thanks and to praise the LORD" (1 Ch 25:3 and cf. v. 1), we consider that Elisha was here showing regard for and rendering submission to the order established by God. The Hebrew word for "minstrel" signifies "one who plays on a stringed instrument," as an accompaniment to the psalm he sang. Thus it was to honor God and instruct these kings that Elisha sent for the minstrel. "And it came to pass when the minstrel played, that the hand of the Lord (cf. Eze 1:3, 3:22) came upon him." The Lord ever honors those who honor Him.

Fifth, the Testing of the Miracle

"And he said, Thus saith the LORD, Make this valley full of ditches. For thus saith the LORD, Ye shall not see wind, neither shall ye see rain; yet that valley shall be filled with water, that ye may drink, both ye, and your cattle, and your beasts" (2 Ki 3:16-17). A pretty severe test was this, when all outward sign of fulfillment was withheld. It was a trial of their faith and obedience, and entailed a considerable amount of hard work. Had they treated the prophet's prediction with derision, they would have scorned to go to so much trouble. It was somewhat like the order Christ gave to His disciples as He bade them make the multitudes "sit down" when there was nothing in sight to feed so vast a company, only a few loaves and

fishes. The sequel shows they heeded Elisha and made due prepara-
tion for the promised supply of water. As Henry says, "They that
expect God's blessings must prepare room for them."

Sixth, the Meaning of the Miracle

The very number of this miracle helps us to apprehend its significance. It was the fourth of the series, and in the language of scripture numerics it stands for the earth — for instance, the four seasons
and the four points of the compass. What we have in this miracle
is one of the Old Testament foreshadowments that the gospel was not
to be confined to Palestine but would yet be sent forth throughout
the earth.

Prior to His death Christ bade His disciples, "Go not into the way
of the Gentiles, and into any city of the Samaritans enter ye not: but
Go rather to the lost sheep of the house of Israel" (Mt 10:5-6 and
cf. Jn 4:9); but after His resurrection He said, "Go ye therefore, and
teach all nations" (Mt 28:19). But there is more here. "Salvation
is of the Jews" (Jn 4:22), and we Gentiles are "their debtors" (Ro
15:26-27).

Strikingly is this typified here, for it was solely for the sake of the
presence of Jehoshaphat this miracle was wrought and that the water
of life was made available for the Israelites and the Edomites! Thus
it is a picture of the minister of the gospel engaged in missionary
activities that is here set forth.

Seventh, the Timing of the Miracle

"And it came to pass in the morning, when the meat-offering was
offered, that, behold, there came water by the way of Edom, and
the country was filled with water" (2 Ki 3:20). This hour was chosen
by the Lord for the performing of this miracle to intimate to the
whole company that their deliverance was vouchsafed on the ground
of the sacrifices offered and the worship rendered in the temple in
Jerusalem. It was at the same significant hour that Elijah had made
his effectual prayer on Mount Carmel, (1 Ki 18:36), when another
notable miracle was wrought. So too it was at the hour "of the
evening oblation" that a signal blessing was granted unto Daniel
(Dan 9:21). Typically, it teaches us that it is through the merits of the
sacrifice of Christ that the life-sustaining gospel of God now flows
unto the Gentiles.

Chapter 8

FIFTH MIRACLE
A POT OF OIL

IN CREATION we are surrounded with both that which is useful and that which is ornamental. The earth produces a wealth of lovely flowers as well as grain and vegetables for our diet. The Creator has graciously provided things which charm our eyes and ears as well as supply our bodies with food and raiment. The same feature marks God's Word. The Scriptures contain something more than doctrine and precept: there are wonderful types which display the wisdom of their Author and delight those who are able to trace the merging of the shadow into the substance, and there are mysterious prophecies which demonstrate the foreknowledge of their giver, and minister pleasure to those granted the privilege of beholding their fulfillment. These types and prophecies form part of the internal evidence which the Bible furnishes of its divine inspiration, for they give proof of a wisdom which immeasurably transcends that of the wisest of mortals. Nevertheless one has to turn unto the doctrinal and preceptive portions of Holy Writ in order to learn the way of salvation and the nature of that walk which is pleasing to God.

In our earlier writings we devoted considerable attention to the types and prophecies, but for the last decade, we have concentrated chiefly upon the practical side of the truth. Observation taught us that many of those who were keenly interested in a Bible reading on some part of the tabernacle or an attempt to explain some of the predictions of Daniel, appeared quite bored when we preached upon Christian duty or deportment; yet they certainly needed the latter for they were quite deficient therein. A glorious sunset is an exquisite sight, but it would supply no nourishment to one that was starving. The perfumes of a garden may delight the senses, but they would be a poor substitute for a good breakfast to a growing child. Only after the soul has fed upon the doctrine of Scripture and put into practice its precepts is it ready to enjoy the beauties of the types and explanations of the mysteries of prophecy.

This change of emphasis in our writings has lost us hundreds of readers. Yet if we could relive the past fifteen years, we would follow the same course. The solemn days through which we are passing demand, as never before, that first things be put first. There are plenty of writers who cater to those who read for intellectual entertainment; our longing is to minister to those who yearn for a closer walk with God. What would be thought of a farmer who in the spring wasted his time in the woods listening to the music of the feathered songsters, while his fields were allowed to remain unplowed and unsown? Would it not be equally wrong if we dwelt almost entirely on the typical significance of the miracles of Elisha, while ignoring the simpler and practical lessons they contain for our hearts and lives? Balance is needed here as everywhere, and if we devote more space than usual on this occasion to the spiritual meaning of the miracle before us (and similarly in the "Dagon" articles), it will not be because we have made or shall make a practice of so doing.

First, the Connection of the Miracle

> Great service had Elisha done in the foregoing chapter for the three kings: to his prayers and prophecies they owed their lives and triumphs. One would have expected that the next chapter should have told us what honours and what dignities were conferred on Elisha for this: that he should have been immediately preferred at court, and made prime-minister of state; that Jehoshaphat should have taken him home with him and advanced him in the kingdom. No, the wise man delivered the army, but no man remembered the wise man (Eccl 9:15). Or, if he had preferment offered him, he declined it: he preferred the honor of doing good in the schools of the prophets, before that of being great in the courts of kings. God magnified him and that sufficed him: magnified him indeed, for we have him here employed in working no less than five miracles (Henry).

He who has, by grace, the heart of a true servant of Christ, would not, if he could, exchange places with the monarch on his throne or the millionaire with all his luxuries.

Second, the Beneficiary of the Miracle

"Now there cried a certain woman of the wives of the sons of the
prophets unto Elisha, saying, Thy servant my husband is dead; and
thou knowest that thy servant did fear the LORD: and the creditor is
come to take unto him my two sons to be bondmen" (2 Ki 4:1).
The one for whom this miracle was wrought was a woman, "the
weaker vessel" (1 Pe 3:7). She was a widow, a figure of desola-
tion: "how doth the city sit solitary, that was full of people! how is
she become as a widow!" (Lam 1:1). Contrast the proud boast of
corrupt Babylon: "I sit a queen, and am no widow, and shall see
no sorrow" (Rev 18:7). Not only was she bereft of her husband
but she was left destitute, in debt and without the means of paying
it. A more pitiable and woeful object could scarcely be conceived.
In her sad plight she went to the servant of Jehovah and told him
her dire situation. Her husband may have died while Elisha was absent with the kings in their expedition against the Moabites, and
thus he was unacquainted with her troubles.

Third, the Urgency of the Miracle

The situation confronting this poor widow was indeed a drastic
one. Her human provider and protector had been removed by the
hand of death. She had been left in debt and had not the where-
withal to pay it, a burden that would weigh heavily on a conscientious soul. And now she was in immediate danger of having her
two sons seized and taken from her by the creditor to serve as bondmen to him. Observe that in the opening words of 2 Kings 4 it is
not said, "Now there came a certain woman of the wives of the
sons of the prophets unto Elisha" but "there cried a certain woman,"
which indicates the pressure of her grief and the earnestness of her
appeal to the prophet. Sometimes God permits His people to be
brought very low in their circumstances; nor is this always by way
of chastisement or because of their folly. We do not think that
such was her case. The Lord is pleased to bring some to the end
of their own resources that His delivering hand may be more plainly
seen acting on their behalf.

One of the outstanding characteristics of the regenerate is that
they are given honest hearts (Lk 8:15). Therefore is it their careful
endeavor to "provide things honest in the sight of all men" and to
"owe no man anything" (Ro 12:17, 13:8). They are careful to

live within their income and not to order an article unless they can pay for it. It is because so many hypocrites under the cloak of a Christian profession have been so dishonest in financial matters and so unscrupulous in trade, that reproach has so often been brought upon the churches. Yet, in certain exceptional cases, even the most thrifty and upright may run into debt. It was so with her. The deceased husband of this widow was a man who "did fear the LORD" (2 Ki 4:1); nevertheless he left his widow in such destitution that she was unable to meet the claims of her creditor. There has been considerable speculation by the commentators as to the cause of this unhappy situation, most of which this writer finds himself quite unable to approve. What then is his own explanation?

In seeking the answer to the above question three things need to be borne in mind. First, as we pointed out in our introduction to this study, a prophet was an abnormality; that is, there was no place for him, no need of him in the religious life of Israel during ordinary times. It was only in seasons of serious declension or apostasy that he appeared on the scene. Thus, no stated maintenance was provided for him, as it was for the priests and Levites under the law. Consequently the prophet was dependent upon the gifts of the pious or the productions of his own manual labors. Judging from the brief records of Scripture, one gathers the impression that most of them enjoyed little more than the barest necessities of life.

Second, for many years past Ahab and Jezebel had been in power, and not only were the pious persecuted but the prophets went in danger of their lives (1 Ki 18:4).

Third, it seems likely to us that this particular prophet obtained his subsistence from the oil obtained from an olive grove, and that probably there had been a failure of the crop during the past year or two — note how readily the widow obtained from her "neighbors" not a few "empty vessels."

"And Elisha said unto her, what shall I do for thee?" Possibly the prophet was himself momentarily nonplussed, conscious of his own helplessness. Possibly his question was designed to emphasize the gravity of the situation. "It is beyond my power to extricate you." More likely it was to make her look above him. "I too am only human." Or again, it may have been to test her. "Are you willing to follow my instructions?" Instead of waiting for her reply, the prophet at once asked a second question, "Tell me, what hast thou in the house?" (2 Ki 4:2). Perhaps this was intended to press upon the widow the seriousness of her problem, for the prophet must have known that she possessed little or nothing, or why should she have sought him? Or, in the light of her answer, its force may have been an admonition not to despise small mercies. Her "not anything, save a pot of oil" reminds of Andrew's "but what are they among so many" (Jn 6:9). Ah, do not we often reason similarly!

Fourth, the Test of the Miracle

"Then he said, Go, borrow thee vessels abroad of all thy neighbours, even empty vessels; borrow not a few" (2 Ki 4:3). It was a test both of her faith and her obedience. To carnal reason it would appear that the prophet was only mocking her, for of what possible service could a lot of empty vessels be to her? But if her trust was in the Lord, then she would be willing to submit herself to and comply with His word through His servant.

Are not His thoughts and ways ever the opposite of ours? Was it not so when He overthrew the Midianites? What a word was that to Gideon: "The people that are with thee are too many for me to give the Midianites into their hands, lest Israel vaunt themselves against me, saying, Mine own hand hath saved me" (Judg 7:2). And in consequence, his army was reduced from over twenty-two thousand to a mere three hundred (vv. 3-7); and when that little company went forth, it was with trumpets and "empty pitchers" and lamps inside the pitchers in their hands (v. 16)! Ah, my reader, we have to come before the Lord as "empty vessels" — emptied of our self-sufficiency — if we are to experience His wonder-working power.

Fifth, the Requirement of the Miracle

"And when thou art come in, thou shalt shut the door upon thee and upon thy sons, and shalt pour out into all those vessels, and thou shalt set aside that which is full" (2 Ki 4:4). This was to avoid ostentation. Her neighbors were not in on the secret, nor should they be permitted to witness the Lord's gracious dealings with her. It reminds us of Christ's raising of the daughter of Jairus: when He arrived at the house it was filled with a skeptical and scoffing company, and the Saviour "put them all out" (Mk 5:40) before He went in and performed the miracle. The same principle stands today in connection with the operations of divine grace. The world is totally ignorant of this mystery — God's filling of empty vessels: "the Spirit of truth; whom the world cannot receive, because it seeth him not, neither knoweth him" (Jn 14:17). Yes, she must shut the door, so "that in retirement she and her sons might the more leisurely ponder and adore the goodness of the Lord" (Scott).

Sixth, the Means of the Miracle

This was the "pot of oil" which appeared to be so utterly inadequate to meet the demands of the widow's creditor. It was so in itself, but under the blessing of God it proved amply sufficient. The five barley loaves and the two small fishes (Jn 6:9) seemed quite useless for feeding a vast multitude, but in the hands of the Lord they furnished "as much as they would," and even "when they were filled" there remained a surplus of twelve baskets full. Ah, it is the little things which God is pleased to use. A pebble from the brook when slung by faith is sufficient to overthrow the Philistine giant. A "little cloud" was enough to produce "a great rain" (1 Ki 18:44-45). A "little child" was employed by Christ to teach His disciples humility (Mt 18:2). A "little strength" supplied by the Spirit enables us to keep Christ's Word and not deny his name (Rev 3:8). Oh, to be "little" in our own sight (1 Sa 15:17). It is blessed to see that this widow did not despise the means, but promptly obeyed the prophet's instructions, her faith laying hold of the clearly-implied promise in "all those vessels" (2 Ki 4:4).

Seventh, the Significance of the Miracle

In this miracle we have a most blessed, striking, and remarkable, typical picture of the grand truth of redemption, a subject which is, we fear, rather hazy in the minds even of many Christians. The gospel is preached so superficially today, its varied glories are so lost in generalizations, that few have more than the vaguest idea of its component parts. Redemption is now commonly confused with atonement; the two are quite distinct, one being an effect of the other. The sacrifice which Christ offered unto divine holiness and justice was "that he might bring us to God" (1 Pe 3:18) — a comprehensive expression covering the whole of our salvation, both in the removal of all hindrances and in the bestowal of all requisites. In order to bring us to God it was necessary that all enmity between us and God should be removed — that is reconciliation; that the guilt of our transgressions should be cancelled — that is remission of sins;

that we should be delivered from all bondage — that is redemption; that we should be made, both experimentally and legally, righteous — that is regeneration and justification.

Redemption, then is one of the grand effects or results of the atonement, the satisfaction which Christ rendered unto the law. God's elect are debtors to the law, for they have broken it; and they are prisoners to His justice, for they are "by nature the children of wrath, even as others" (Eph 2:3). And our deliverance (or "salvation") is not a mere emancipation when adequate compensation has been made. No, while it is true our redemption is of grace and affected by sovereign power, yet it is so because a ransom is offered, a price paid, in every way equivalent to the discharge secured. In the words, "I will ransom them from the power of the grave; I will redeem them from death" (Ho 13:14) we are taught that the latter is the consequence of the former. Ransom is the paying of the price required. Redemption is the setting free of those ransomed, and this deliverance is by the exercise of divine power. "Not accepting deliverance" (Heb 11:35); the Greek word "deliverance" here is commonly rendered "redemption"; they refused to accept it from their afflictions on the dishonorable terms (apostasy) demanded by their persecutors.

Redemption necessarily presupposes previous possession. It denotes the restoration of something which has been lost, and returned by the paying of a price. Hence we find Christ saying by the Spirit of prophecy, "I restored that which I took not away" (Ps 69:4)! This was strikingly illustrated in the history of Israel, who on the farther shores of the Red Sea sang, "Thou in thy mercy hast led forth the people which thou hast redeemed" (Ex 15:13). First, in the book of Genesis, we see the descendants of Abraham sojourning in the land of Canaan. Later, we see the chosen race in cruel servitude, in bondage to the Egyptians, groaning amid the brick kilns, under the whip of their taskmasters. Then a ransom was provided in the blood of the pascal lamb, following which, the Lord by His mighty hand brought them out of serfdom and brought them into the promised inheritance. That is a complete picture of redemption.

There are many who perceive that Christians were a people in bondage, lost to God, but recovered and restored to Him; yet some fail to perceive they belonged to the Lord before Christ freed them. The elect belonged to Christ long before He shed His blood to ransom them, for they were chosen in Him before the foundation of the world (Eph 1:4) and made over to Him as the Father's love-gift (Jn 17:9). But they too fell and died in Adam, and therefore did He come to seek and to save that which was lost. Christ purchased the church of God with His own blood (Ac 20:28) and therefore does the Father say to Him, "By the blood of thy covenant I have sent forth thy prisoners out of the pit wherein is no water" (Zec 9:11). He has a legal right to them. There is no unavailing redemption: all whom Christ purchased or ransomed shall be redeemed; that is, delivered from captivity, set free from sin. Judicially they are so now, experientially too in part (Jn 8:36), but perfectly so only when glorified — hence the future aspect in Luke 21:28 and Romans 8:23.

Now observe how all the leading features of redemption are typically brought out in 2 Kings 4.

1. *The object of it is a widow.* She had not always been thus. Formerly she had been married to one who "feared the Lord," but death had severed that happy bond and left her desolate and destitute — apt figure of God's elect, originally in union with Him, and then through the fall alienated from Him (Eph 4:18).

2. *Her creditor was enforcing his demands.* He had actually come to seize her sons "to be bondmen." The Hebrew word rendered "creditor" in 2 Kings 4:1 signifies "one who exacts" what is justly due to him, and is so translated in Job 11:6. It looks back to, "And if thy brother that dwelleth by thee be waxen poor, and be sold unto thee; thou shalt not compel him to serve as a bondservant: But as an hired servant, and as a sojourner, he shall be with thee, and shall serve thee unto the year of jubile" (Lev 25:39-40). Our Lord had reference to this practice in His parable of Matthew 18:23-25. Thus the "creditor" of 2 Kings 4:1 who showed no mercy to the poor widow is a figure of the stern and unrelenting law.

3. *The widow was quite unable to pay her creditor.* So we are utterly incompetent to satisfy the demands of the law or effect our own redemption.

4. *She, like us, could rely only on the mere favor of God.* "Being justified freely by his grace through the redemption that is in Christ Jesus" (Ro 3:24). That is exactly what we should expect to find in this miracle, for five is the number of grace (see Gen 43:34, 45:22; 1 Co 14:19). Note also the means used, the "oil" mul-

tiplied. Oil is a figure of the superabounding grace of God (Ps 23: 5; Is 61:3).

5. *Yet it was a grace that was wrought "through righteousness"* (Ro 5:21). It obtained the freedom of the widow's sons by meeting the full due of her creditor.

6. *Both aspects of redemption are seen here.* First, the price: "Sell the oil, and pay thy debt" (v. 7); Second, the power: the miraculous supply of oil.

7. *It was not a general and promiscuous redemption.* It was a definite and particular one. For a "widow" was the special object of God's notice (Deu 24:19; Ps 68:5; Ja 1:27), and not a mere abstraction of "freewillism."

Chapter 9

SIXTH MIRACLE
A GREAT WOMAN

First, the Connection of the Miracle

OUR PRESENT NARRATIVE opens with the word "And" which intimates that the incident described here is closely related to the preceding miracle, though we must not conclude that this by any means exhausts its force. Sometimes the Spirit of God has placed two things in juxtaposition for the purpose of comparison that we may observe the resemblances between them; at other times, it is with the object of pointing a contrast, that we may consider the points of dissimilarity.

Here it is the latter: note the following antitheses. In the former case the woman's place of residence is not given (2 Ki 4:1), but here it is (v. 8). The first was a widow (v. 1); this woman's husband was alive (v. 9). The former was financially destitute; this one was a woman of means. The one sought out Elisha; the prophet approached the other. Elisha provided for the former; this one ministered unto him. The widow had "two sons," but the married woman was childless. The one was put to a severe test (vv. 3-4); the other was not.

Second, a Word on the Location of the Miracle

The place where this miracle was wrought cannot be without significance, for there is nothing meaningless in Holy Writ, though in this instance we confess to having little or no light. The one who was the beneficiary of this miracle resided at Shunem, which appears to mean "uneven." This place is mentioned only twice elsewhere in the Old Testament. First, in Joshua 19:18, from which we learn that it was situated in the territory allotted to the tribe of Issachar. Second, in 1 Samuel 28:4, where we are told it was the place that the Philistines gathered themselves together and pitched in battle array against Israel, on which occasion Saul was so terrified that, after inquiring in vain of the Lord, he sought out the witch of Endor. Matthew Henry tells us that "Shunem lay in the road between Samaria and Carmel, a road which Elisha was accustomed to travel, as we gather from 2:25." It seems to have been a farming district, and in this pastoral setting a lovely domestic scene is laid.

Third, the Beneficiary of the Miracle

"And it fell on a day, that Elisha passed to Shunem, where was a great woman" (2 Ki 4:8). The Hebrew word (*gadol*) is used in varied connections. In Genesis 1:16, 21 and many other passages it refers to material or physical greatness. In Exodus 32:21, "great sin," it has a moral force. In 2 Kings 5:1, Job 1:3, and Proverbs 25:6 it is associated with social eminence. In Psalm 48:1 and numerous other places, it is predicated of the Lord Himself.

This woman was one of substance or wealth, as is intimated by the servants her husband had and their building and furnishing a room for the prophet. God has His own among the rich and noble. This woman was also "great" spiritually. She was great in hospitality; in discernment, perceiving that Elisha was "a holy man of God"; in meekness, by owning her husband's headship; in thoughtfulness for others, the care she took in providing for the prophet's comfort; in contentedness, 2 Kings 4:13; in wisdom, realizing Elisha would desire retirement and quietness; and in faith, confidently counting upon God to show Himself strong on her behalf and work a further miracle as we shall see.

"And it fell on a day, that Elisha passed to Shunem, where was a great woman; and she constrained him to eat bread." Elisha seems to have resided at or near Mount Carmel (2:25, 4:25); but went his circuit through the land to visit the seminaries of the prophets and to instruct the people, which probably was his employment when he was not sent on some special service. "At Shunem there lived a woman of wealth and piety, who invited him to come to her house, and with some difficulty prevailed" (Scott). Several practical points are suggested by this. The minister of the gospel should not be forward in pressing himself upon people, but should wait un-

til he is invited to partake of their hospitality. Nor should he deliberately court the intimacy of the "great," except with the object
of doing them good. "Mind not high things, but condescend to men
of low estate" (Ro 12:16) is one of the rules God has given His people to walk by, and His servants should set them an example in this
matter.

The Lord's servants, like those to whom they minister, have their
ups and downs, not only in their inward experience but also in external circumstances. Yes, they have their ups as well as their downs.
They are not required to spend all their days in caves or sojourning
by brooks. If there are those who oppose, God also raises up others
to befriend them. Was it not thus with our blessed Lord when He
tabernacled here? Though for the most part He "had not where to
lay his head," yet there were many women who "ministered unto him
of their substance" (Lk 8:2-3), and the home at Bethany welcomed
Him. So with the apostle Paul; though he was made as the off-
scouring of all things to the Jewish nation, yet the saints loved and
esteemed him highly for his work's sake. If he was cast into prison,
yet he also makes mention of "Gaius mine host" (Ro 16:23). It
has ever been thus. The experience of Elisha was no exception, as
the present writer can testify, for in his extensive journeyings the
Lord opened the hearts and homes of many of His people unto him.

Hospitality (Ro 12:13) is required of the saints, and of God's servants too (1 Ti 3:2; Titus 1:8), and that "without grudging" (1 Pe
4:9), and this held good equally during the Old Testament era. It is
to be noted that this woman took the initiative, for she did not wait
until asked by Elisha or one of his friends. From the words "as often as he passed by" we gather that she was on the lookout for him.
She sought occasion to do good. Nor was her hospitality any formal
thing, but earnest and warmhearted. Hence it may strike us as all
the more strange that the prophet demurred and that she had to constrain him to enter her home. This intimates that the servant of God
should not readily respond to every invitation received, especially
from the wealthy. "Seekest thou great things for thyself? seek them
not" (Jer 45:5) is to regulate his conduct. Elisha responded to
her importunity, and after becoming better acquainted with her,
never failed to partake of her kindness whenever he passed that way.

"And she said unto her husband, Behold now, I perceive that this
is an holy man of God, which passeth by us continually. Let us
make a little chamber, I pray thee, on the wall; and let us set for

him there a bed, and a table, and a stool, and a candlestick: and it shall be, when he cometh to us, that he shall turn in thither" (2 Ki 4:9-10). Herein we have manifest several other features of her moral greatness. Apparently she was the owner of this property, for her husband is not termed a "great man." Yet we find her conferring with him and seeking his permission. Thereby she took her proper place and left her sisters an admirable example. The husband is "the head of the wife, even as Christ is the head of the church," and therefore explains the command, "Wives, submit yourselves unto your own husbands, as unto the Lord" (Eph 5:22-23). Instead of taking matters into her own hands and acting independently, this "great woman" sought her husband's consent and cooperation. How much domestic strife would be avoided if there was more of this mutual conferring.

This lady of Shunem was endowed with spiritual discernment, for she perceived that Elisha was a holy man of God. The two things are not to be separated; it is those who walk in subjection to the revealed will of God who are granted spiritual perception: "He that is spiritual judgeth [discerneth] all things" (1 Co 2:15), and the spiritual person is the one who is regulated by the precepts of Holy Writ, who is humble and meek and takes the place which the Lord has appointed. "If therefore thine eye be single, thy whole body shall be full of light" (Mt 6:22); it is acting in self-will which beclouds the vision. "I understand more than the ancients" said David. And why so? "Because I keep thy precepts" (Ps 119:100). It is when we forsake the path of obedience that our judgment is clouded and our perception dimmed.

While admiring the virtues and graces of this woman, we must not overlook the tribute she paid to Elisha. Observe how she refers to him. Not as a "charming" or "nice man"; how incongruous such an appellation for a servant of God! No, it was not any such carnal or sentimental term she employed. Nor did she allude to him as a "learned man," for scholarship and spirituality by no means always go together. Rather as "an holy man of God" did she designate the prophet. What a description! What a searching word for every minister of the gospel to take to heart. It is "holy men of God" who are used by the Spirit (2 Pe 1:21). And how did she perceive the prophet's holiness? Perhaps by finding him at prayer, or reading the Scriptures. Certainly from the heavenliness of his conversation and general demeanor. Ah, my reader, the servant of God should need no distinctive manner of dress in order for people to identify him. His walk, his speech, his deportment ought to be sufficient.

Returning to the "great woman," let us next take note of her constancy. The inviting of Elisha into her home was actuated by no fleeting mood of kindness, which came suddenly upon her and as suddenly disappeared; it rather was a steady and permanent thing. Some people are mere creatures of impulse. But the conduct of those who act on principle is stable.

How often a church is elated when a minister is installed, and its members cannot do too much to express their appreciation for him; but how soon such enthusiasm often cools off. The best of us are spasmodic if not fickle, and need to bear in mind the injunction "let us not be weary in well doing" (Gal 6:9). It is blessed to see that this woman did not tire of ministering to God's servant but continued to provide for his need and comfort, and at considerable trouble and expense.

Fourth, the Occasion of the Miracle

"And it fell on a day, that he came thither, and he turned into the chamber, and lay there. And he said to Gehazi his servant, Call this Shunammite. And when he had called her, she stood before him" (2 Ki 4:11-12). Elisha did not complacently accept as a matter of course the loving hospitality which had been shown him, as though it were something due him by virtue of his office. No, he was truly grateful and anxious to show his appreciation. In this he differed from some ministers we have met, who appeared to think they were fully entitled to such kindness and deference. While resting from his journey, instead of congratulating himself on his good fortune, he thought upon his benefactress and wondered how he could best make some return. She was in no financial need; apparently she lacked none of the good things of this life. What then should be done for her? He was at a loss to know; but instead of dismissing the thought, he decided to interrogate her directly.

Fifth, the Peculiarity of the Miracle

"And he said unto him, Say now unto her, Behold, thou hast been careful for us with all this care; what is to be done for thee? wouldest thou be spoken for to the king, or to the captain of the host? And she answered, I dwell among mine own people" (2 Ki 4:13).

This miracle differed from most of those we have previously considered in that it was unsought, proposed by the prophet himself. He suggested that royal honors might be bestowed on herself or husband if she so desired. Thomas Scott says,

> Elisha had no doubt acquired considerable influence with Jehoram and his captains by the signal deliverance and victory obtained for him (3:4-27), and though he would ask nothing for himself, he was willing to show his gratitude on behalf of his kind hostess by interposing on her behalf, if she had any petition to present.

Yet we feel that the prophet knew her too well to imagine her heart was set upon such trifles as earthly dignities, and that he gave her this opportunity to declare herself more plainly.

"And she answered, I dwell among mine own people" (v. 13). It looks as though the prophet's offer to speak to the king for her intimated that positions of honor could be procured for her and her husband in the royal household. Her reply seems to show this, for it signified, "I am quite satisfied with the portion God has given me. I desire no change or improvement in it." How very rare is such contentment! She was indeed a "great woman." Also, today there are so few like her. As Henry points out, "It would be well with many, if they did but know when they are well off." But they do not. A roving spirit takes possession of them, and they suppose they can improve their lot by moving from one place to another, only to find as the old adage says, "A rolling stone gathers no moss." "The wicked are like the troubled sea, when it cannot rest" (Is 57:20), but it should be far otherwise with the people of God. It is much to be thankful for when we can contentedly say, "I dwell among mine own people."

Sixth, the Nature of the Miracle

"And he said, What then is to be done for her? And Gehazi answered, Verily she hath no child, and her husband is old. And he said, Call her. And when he had called her, she stood in the door. And he said, About this season, according to the time of life, thou shalt embrace a son. And she said, Nay, my lord, thou man of God, do not lie unto thine handmaid. And the woman conceived, and bare a son at that season that Elisha had said unto her" (2 Ki 4:14-17). Observe the prophet's humility: in his perplexity, he did not disdain to confer with his servant. He was now pleased to use his interests in the court of heaven, which was far better than seeking a favor from Jehoram. It should be remembered that in Old Testament times the giving of a son to those who had long been childless was a special mark of God's favor and power, as in the cases of Abraham, Isaac, Manoah, and Elkanah. We are not sure whether her language was that of unbelief or of overwhelming astonishment; but having received a prophet in the name of a prophet, she received "a prophet's reward" (Mt 10:41).

Seventh, the Meaning of the Miracle

This may be gathered from the miracle preceding. There we had before us a typical picture of redemption, a setting free from the exactions of the law, a deliverance from bondage. What then is the sequel of this? Surely it is that which we find in the lives of the redeemed, namely, their bringing forth fruit unto God. This order of cause and effect is taught us in "being made free from sin . . . ye have your fruit unto holiness" (Ro 6:22 and cf. 1 Co 6:20). But it is not the products of the old nature transformed bringing forth after its own evil kind, for the "flesh" remains the same unto the end. No, it is altogether supernatural, the "fruit of the spirit," the manifestation of the graces of the new nature communicated by God at the new birth. Accordingly we have here the fruit of the womb, yet not by the ordinary workings of nature, but, as in the case of John the Baptist (Lk 1:7, 57), that which transcends nature, which issues only from the wonder-working power of God.

It is to be carefully noted in this connection that the beneficiary of our miracle is designated a "great woman." As we have pointed out in a previous paragraph, this appellation denotes that she was one upon whom divine providence had smiled, furnishing her liberally with the things of this life. But she was also morally and spiritually "great." In both respects she was an appropriate figure of that aspect of salvation which is here before us. Redemption finds its object, like the widow of the foregoing miracle, in distress — poor, sued by the law, unable to meet its demands. But redemption does not leave its beneficiaries thus. No, God deals with them according to "the riches of his grace" and they can now say, "He 'hath made us kings and priests unto God and his Father' " (Rev 1:6). The righteousness of Christ is imputed to them, and they are "great" indeed in the eyes of God. They are "the excellent, in whom is all my delight" (Ps 16:3) is how He speaks of them. Such are the ones in whom and by whom the fruits of redemption are brought forth.

Everything recorded of this woman indicates that she was one of the Lord's redeemed. She honored and ministered unto one of His servants, in a day when prophets were far from being popular. Moreover, Elisha accepted her hospitality, which he surely would not have done unless he discerned in her the marks of grace. The very fact that at first she had to "constrain" him to partake of her kindness indicates he would not readily receive favors from anybody and everybody. But having satisfied himself of her spirituality, "as oft as he passed by, he turned in thither to eat bread." Let it be remarked that that expression to "eat bread" means far more to an Oriental than to us. It signifies an act of communion, denoting a bond of fellowship between those who eat a meal together. Thus by such intimacy of communion with the prophet, this woman gave further evidence of being one of God's redeemed.

As the procuring of our redemption required miracles (the divine incarnation, the death of the God-man, His resurrection), so the application of it unto its beneficiaries cannot be without supernatural operations, both before and after. Redemption is received by faith; but before saving faith can be exercised, the soul must be quickened, for one who is dead to God cannot move toward Him. The same is true of our conversion, which is a right about-face, the soul turning from the world unto God. This is morally impossible until a miracle of grace has been wrought upon us: "Turn thou me, and I shall be turned" (Jer 31:18). Such a miracle as regeneration and conversion, whereby the soul enters into the redemption purchased by Christ, is necessarily followed by one which shows the miraculous fruits of redemption. Such is the case here, as we see in the child bestowed upon the great woman. Remarkably enough, that gift came to her unsought and unexpected. And is it not thus in the experience of the Christian? When he came to Christ as a sin-burdened soul, redemption was all that he thought about; there was no asking for or anticipation of subsequent fruit.

Chapter 10

SEVENTH MIRACLE
A CHILD RESTORED

"AND THE WOMAN CONCEIVED, and bare a son at that season that Elisha had said unto her, according to the time of life" (2 Ki 4:17). As Matthew Henry pointed out,

> We may well suppose, after the birth of this son, that the prophet was doubly welcome to the good Shunammite: he had thought himself indebted to her, but from henceforth, as long as she lives, she will think herself in his debt, and that she can never do too much for him. We may also suppose that, the child was very dear to the prophet, as the son of his prayers, and very dear to the parents as the son of their old age.

What is more attractive than a properly trained and well-behaved child! And what is more objectionable than a spoiled and naughty one? From all that is revealed of this great woman, we cannot doubt that she brought up her boy wisely and well, that she added to the delightfulness of her home, that he was a pleasure and not a trial to visitors. Alas that there are so few of her type now left. Godly and well-conducted homes are the choicest asset which any nation possesses.

First, the Occasion of the Miracle

"And when the child was grown, it fell on a day, that he went out to his father to the reapers" (v. 18). The opening clause does not signify that he was now a fully-developed youth, but that he had passed out of infancy into childhood. This is quite obvious from a number of things in the sequel. When he was taken ill, a "lad" carried him back home (v. 19); for some time he "sat on her knees"

78

(v. 20), and later she — apparently unaided — carried him upstairs and laid him on the prophet's bed (v. 21). Yet the child had grown sufficiently so as to be able to run about and be allowed to visit his father in the harvest field. While there, he was suddenly stricken with an ailment, for "he said unto his father, My head, my head" (v. 19). It is hardly likely that this was caused by a sunstroke, for it occurred in the morning, a while before noon. Seemingly the father did not suspect anything serious, for instead of carrying him home in his own arms, he sent him back with one of his younger workers. How incapable we are of foreseeing what even the next hour may bring forth!

"And when he had taken him, and brought him to his mother, he sat on her knees till noon" (v. 20). What a lovely picture of maternal devotion! How thankful should each one be who cherishes the tender memories of a mother's love, for there are tens of thousands in this country who were born of parents devoid of natural affection, who cared more for cocktail lounges and the parties than for their offspring. But powerful as true mother love is, it is impotent when the grim reaper draws near, for our verse adds "and then died." Death strikes down the young as well as the old, as the tombstones in our cemeteries bear ample witness. Sometimes it gives more or less advance notice of its gruesome approach; at others, as here, it smites with scarcely any warning. How this fact ought to influence each of us! To put it on its lowest ground, how foolish to make an idol of one who may be snatched away at any moment. With what a light hand should we grasp all earthly objects. So, then, the occasion of this miracle is the death of the child.

Second, the Mystery of the Miracle

How often the Lord's dealings seem strange to us. Hopes are suddenly blighted, prospects swiftly changed, and loved ones snatched away. "All flesh is grass" (Is 40:6), "which to day is and to morrow is cast into the oven" (Mt 6:30). Thus it was here. The babe had survived the dangers of infancy, only to be cut down in childhood. That morning, apparently full of life and health, he trotted merrily off to the harvest field; at noon he lay a corpse on his mother's knee. But in her case such a visitation was additionally inexplicable. The boy had been given to her by the divine bounty because of the kindness she had shown to one of God's servants; and now, to carnal reason, it looked as though He was dealing most unkindly with her. A miracle had been wrought in bestowing the child, and now that miracle is neutralized. Yes, God's ways are frequently "a great deep" unto human intelligence. Yet let the Christian never forget that those ways are ever ordered by infinite love and wisdom.

It is indeed most blessed to observe how this stricken mother conducted herself under her unexpected and severe trial. Here, as throughout the whole of this chapter, her moral and spiritual greatness shines forth. There was no wringing her hands in despair, no giving way to inordinate grief. Nor was there any murmuring at Providence, any complaint that God had ceased to be gracious unto her. It is in such crises and by their demeanor under them that the children of God and the children of the devil are manifest. We do not say that the former always conduct themselves as the great woman, yet they sorrow not as do others who have no hope. They may be staggered and stunned by a crushing affliction, but they do not give way to an evil heart of unbelief and become avowed infidels. There may be stirrings of rebellion within, and Satan will seek to foster hard thoughts against God, but he cannot induce the true child to curse Him and commit suicide. Divine grace is a glorious reality, and in his measure every Christian is given to prove the sufficiency of it in times of stress and trial.

Third, the Expectation of the Miracle

"And she went up, and laid him on the bed of the man of God, and shut the door upon him, and went out" (2 Ki 4:21). This must be pondered in the light of her subsequent actions if we are to perceive the meaning of her conduct here. There was definite purpose on her part; and in view of what immediately follows, it seems clear that these were the actions of faith. She cherished the hope that the prophet would restore her son to her. She made no preparations for the burial of the child, but anticipated his resurrection by laying him upon Elisha's bed. Her faith clung to the original blessing: God, by the prophet's promise and prayers, had given him unto her, and now she takes the dead child to God (as it were) and goes to seek the prophet. Her faith might be tried even to the straining point, but in that extremity she interpreted the inexplicable dealings of God by those dealings she was sure of, reasoning from the past to the future, from the known to the unknown. The child had been given unto her unasked, and she refused to believe he had now been irrecoverably taken away from her.

Her faith was indeed put to a severe test, for not only was her child dead, but at the very time she seemed to need him the most, Elisha was many miles away! Ah, that was no accident but was wisely and graciously ordered by God. How so? That there might be fuller opportunity for bringing forth the evidences and fruits of faith. A faith which does not triumph over discouragements and difficulties is not worth much. The Lord often causes our circumstances to be most unfavorable in order that faith may have the freer play and rise above them. Such was the case here. Elisha might be absent, but she could go to him. Most probably she had heard of the raising of the widow's son at Zarephath (1 Ki 17:23) by Elijah, and she knew that the spirit of Elijah now rested on Elisha (2 Ki 2:15). And therefore with steadfast confidence, she determined to seek him. That she did act in faith is clear from Hebrews 11:35, for that chapter which chronicles the achievements of faith of the Old Testament saints says that through faith "women received their dead raised to life again." There were but two who did so, and the great woman of Shunem was one of them.

"And she called unto her husband, and said, Send me, I pray thee, one of the young men, and one of the asses, that I may run to the man of God, and come again" (2 Ki 4:22). While faith triumphs over difficulties, it does not act unbecomingly by forcing a way through them and setting aside the requirements of propriety. Urgent as the situation was, she did not rush away without informing her husband of her intention. The wife should have no secrets from her partner, but take him fully into her confidence; failure at this point leads to suspicions, and where they exist love is soon chilled. Nor did this stricken mother content herself with scribbling a hurried note, telling her husband to expect her return within a day or so. No, once again she took her proper place and owned her subjection to him. Though she made known to him her desire, she demanded nothing, but respectfully sought his permission, as her "I pray thee" plainly shows. Faith is bold and venturesome, but it does not act unseemly and insubordinately.

Thomas Scott says,

> It is happy and comely when harmony prevails in domestic life: when the husband's authority is tempered with affection, and un-

suspecting confidence; when the wife answers that confidence with deference and submission, as well as fidelity, and when each party consults the other's inclinations, and both unite in attending on the ordinances of God and supporting His cause.

But such happiness and harmony is attainable only as both husband and wife seek grace from God to walk in obedience to His precepts, and as family worship is duly maintained. If the wife suffers herself to be influenced by the spirit which is now so common in the world and refuses to own the lordship of her husband (1 Pe 3:6), or if the husband acts as a tyrant and bully by failing to love, nourish, and cherish his wife (Eph 5:25, 29) and "giving honour unto the wife, as unto the weaker vessel" (1 Pe 3:7), then the smile of God will be forfeited, their prayers will be "hindered," and strife and misery will prevail in the home.

"And he said, Wherefore wilt thou go to him to day? it is neither new moon nor sabbath. And she said, It shall be well" (2 Ki 4:23). While we admire her virtues, her husband appears in a much less favorable light. His question might suggest that he was still ignorant of the death of his son, yet that scarcely seems likely. If he had made no inquiry about the child he must have been strangely lacking in tender regard for him, and his wife's desire to undertake an arduous journey at such a time ought to have informed him that some serious emergency had arisen. It is difficult to escape the conclusion that his language was more an expression of irritability, that he resented being left alone in his grief. At any rate, his words served to throw light upon another praiseworthy trait in his wife: that it was her custom to attend the prophet's services on the feast days and the sabbath. Though a great woman, she did not disdain those unpretentious meetings on Mount Carmel. No genuine Christian, however wealthy or high his station, will consider it beneath him to meet with his poorer brethren and sisters.

Those words of her husband may be considered from another angle, namely, as a further testing of her faith. Even where the deepest affection exists between husband and wife, there is not always spiritual equality, not even where they are one in the Lord. One may steadily grow in grace while the other makes little or no progress. One may enter more deeply into an experimental acquaintance with the truth, which the other is incapable of understanding and discussing. One may be given a much increased measure of faith without the other being similarly blessed. None can walk by the faith of another, and it is well for those of strong faith to remember that. Certainly there was no cooperation of faith in this instance; the husband of our great woman seemed to discourage rather than to encourage her. She might have reasoned with herself, *Perhaps this is an intimation from God that I should not seek unto Elisha.* But faith would argue, *This is but a further testing of me, and since my reliance is in the Lord, I will neither be daunted nor deterred.* It is by our reactions to such testings that the reality and strength of our faith is made evident. Faith must not expect a smooth and easy path.

"And she said, It shall be well." That was the language of firm and unshaken confidence. "Then she saddled an ass, and said to her servant, Drive and go forward, slack not thy riding for me, except I bid thee" (2 Ki 4:24). Her husband certainly does not shine here. Had he discharged the duties of love, he would have undertaken this tiring journey instead of his wife, or at the very least offered to accompany her. But he would not exert himself enough to saddle the ass for her, but left her to do that. How selfish many husbands are! How slack in bearing or at least sharing their wives' burdens! Marriage is a partnership or it is nothing except in name; and the man who allows his wife to become a drudge and does little or nothing to make her lot lighter and brighter in the home, is not worthy to be called "husband." Nor is it sufficient reply to say, It is only lack of thought on his part. Inconsiderateness and selfishness are synonymous terms, for unselfishness consists largely in thoughtfulness of others. The best that can be said for this man is that he did not actually forbid his wife to start out for Carmel.

We know not how far distant Shunem was from Carmel, but it appears that the journey was long and hard, in a mountainous country. But love is not quenched by hardships, and faith is not rendered inoperative by difficulties. And in the case of this mother, both of these graces were operative within her. Love can brook no delay and thinks not of personal discomfort, as her language to the servant shows. It is also the nature of faith to be speedy and to look for quick results; patience is a distinct virtue which is only developed by much hard schooling. An intense earnestness possessed the soul of this woman, and where such earnestness is joined with faith, it refuses all denial. While our faith remains a merely mental and mechanical thing it achieves nothing, but when it is intense and fervent it will produce results. True, it requires a deep sense of need, often the pressure of an urgent situation, to evoke this earnestness. That is why faith flourishes most in times of stress and trial, for it then has its most suitable opportunity to declare itself.

"So she went and came unto the man of God to mount Carmel. And it came to pass, when the man of God saw her afar off, that he said to Gehazi his servant, Behold, yonder is that Shunammite" (2 Ki 4:25). There are several things of importance to be noticed here. First, like his predecessor, Elisha was the man of the mount (2 Ki 2:25), symbolical of his spiritual elevation, his affections set upon things above. Second, mark how he conducts himself: not in haughty pride of fancied self-superiority. He did not wait for the woman to reach him, but dispatched his servant to meet her, thereby evidencing his solicitude. Third, was it not a gracious token from the Lord to cheer her heart near the close of a trying journey? How tender are God's mercies! Fourth, "that Shunammite" denotes either that she was the only pious person in that place or that she so towered above her brethren and sisters in spirituality that such an appellation was quite sufficient for the purpose of identification.

"Run now, I pray thee, to meet her, and say unto her, Is it well with thee? is it well with thy husband? is it well with the child? And she answered, It is well" (2 Ki 4:26). Incidentally, this shows that younger men engaged in the Lord's service and occupying lowlier positions are required to execute commissions from their seniors (cf. 2 Ti 4:11-13). We do not regard the woman's "it is well" as expressing her resignation to the sovereign will of God, but rather as the language of trustful expectation. She seems to have had no doubt whatever about the outcome of her errand. It appears to us that throughout the whole of this incident, the great woman regarded the death of her child as a trial of faith. Her "it is well" looked beyond the clouds and anticipated the happy outcome. Surely we must exclaim, Oh woman, great is thy faith. Yes, and great too was its reward, for God never puts to confusion those who really count upon Him showing Himself strong on their behalf. Let us not forget that this incident is recorded for our learning and encouragement.

"And when she came to the man of God to the hill, she caught him by the feet: but Gehazi came near to thrust her away. And the man of God said, Let her alone; for her soul is vexed within her: and the LORD hath hid it from me, and hath not told me" (2 Ki 4:

27). We are reminded of the two women who visited the Lord's sepulchre and that He eventually met them saying, "All hail. And they came and held him by the feet, and worshipped him" (Mt 28: 9). In the case before us, the great woman appears to have rightly viewed Elisha as the ambassador of God, and to have humbly signified that she had a favor to ask of him. In the rebuffing from Gehazi, we see how her faith met with yet another trial. And then the Lord tenderly interposed through His servant and rebuked the officious attendant. The Lord was accustomed to reveal His secrets unto the prophets (Amos 3:7), but until He did so they were as ignorant and as dependent upon Him as others, as this incident plainly shows.

Here was still a further test of faith; the prophet himself was in the dark, unprepared for her startling request. But the Lord has just as good a reason for concealing as for revealing. In the case before us, it is not difficult to perceive why He has withheld from Elisha all knowledge of the child's death; He would have him learn from the mother herself, and that, that she might avow her faith. "Then she said, Did I desire a son of my lord? did I not say, Do not deceive me?" (2 Ki 4:28). Those were powerful arguments to move Elisha to act on her behalf. "As she did not impatiently desire children, she could not think that her son had been given her, without solicitation, merely to become the occasion of her far deeper distress" (Scott). The second question evidenced that her dependence was entirely upon the word of God through His servant. "However the providence of God may disappoint us, we may be sure the promise of God never did, nor ever will deceive us: hope in that will not make us ashamed" (Henry).

Chapter 11

SEVENTH MIRACLE
HIS MOTHER'S FAITH

IN THE LAST CHAPTER we dwelt, first, upon the occasion of this miracle, namely, the death of the "great woman's" son. Second, we considered the mystery of it. To all appearances, the child had been quite well and full of life in the morning, yet by noon he was a ·corpse. In this case such a disaster was doubly inexplicable, for the son had been given to her by the divine bounty because of the kindness she had shown to one of God's servants; and now, to carnal reason, it looked as though He was dealing most unkindly with her. Furthermore, the wonder-working power of God had been engaged in bestowing a son upon her, and now this miracle was neutralized by his suddenly being snatched away. Third, we expanded upon its expectation. It is inexpressibly blessed to behold how this stricken mother reacted to the seeming catastrophe; throughout the whole narrative it is made evident that she regarded this affliction as a trial of her faith, and grandly did her confidence in God triumph over it.

Fourth, the Means of the Miracle

"Then he said to Gehazi, Gird up thy loins, and take my staff in thine hand, and go thy way: if thou meet any man, salute him not; and if any salute thee, answer him not again: and lay my staff upon the face of the child" (2 Ki 4:29). Some think the prophet believed that the child was only in a swoon. Yet we can hardly conceive of the mother leaving the boy under such circumstances; rather she would have sent a message by one of her servants. Nor is it likely that Elisha's instructions to the servant would be so peremptorily expressed if such had been the case. Matthew Henry says "I know not what to make of this." Another of the Puritans suggests that, "It was done out of pure conceit, and not by Divine instinct, and therefore it failed of the effect." Thomas Scott acknowledged, "It is difficult to determine what the prophet meant by thus sending Gehazi." He had divided Jordan by using Elijah's mantle, and perhaps he thought that the prophet's design was to teach Gehazi a much needed lesson. However, this much seems clear from the incident: no servant of God should delegate to another that which it is his own duty to do.

"And the mother of the child said, As the LORD liveth, and as thy soul liveth, I will not leave thee. And he arose, and followed her" (2 Ki 4:30). It is clear from her words that, whatever was or was not the prophet's design in ordering his servant to hurry to where the child lay, she regarded his action as another testing of her faith. She evidently had no confidence in Gehazi, or in Elisha's staff as such. She was not to be put off in this way. Her language was both impressive and emphatic, signifying, "I swear that I will not return home unless you come with me. The situation is desperate; my expectation is in you, Elisha, as the Lord's ambassador, and I refuse to take any no." Here we behold the boldness and perseverance of her faith. Whether there was any unwillingness on Elisha's part to set out on this journey, or whether he was only putting her to the test, we cannot be sure; but such earnestness and importunity won the day and now stirred the prophet to action.

"And Gehazi passed on before them, and laid the staff upon the face of the child; but there was neither voice, nor hearing. Wherefore he went again to meet him, and told him, saying, The child is not awaked" (v. 31). Young's concordance gives "denier" as the meaning of the name Gehazi. If the various references made to him are carefully compared it will be seen that his character and conduct were all alike and in keeping with his name.

Why Elisha should have had such a man for his personal attendant we know not; yet in view of there being a Judas in the disciples, we need not be unduly surprised. First, we see him seeking to officiously thrust away the poor mother when she cast herself at his master's feet (v. 27). Here we note the absence of prayer unto the Lord, and the nonsuccess of his efforts. Later, we find him giving expression to selfish unbelief, a complete lack of confidence in the power of Elisha (v. 43). Finally, his avarice masters him and he lies to Naaman, and is stricken with leprosy for his deception (5:

20-27). Thus in the verse before us, we have a picture of the unavailing efforts of an unregenerate minister, and his failure made manifest to others.

"And when Elisha was come into the house, behold, the child was dead, laid upon his bed" (2 Ki 4:32). In previous paragraphs we have dwelt much upon the remarkable faith of the child's mother. Yet we must not allow it to so occupy our attention as to obscure the faith of the prophet, for his was equally great. It was no ordinary demand which was now made upon him, and only one who was intimately acquainted with God would have met it as he did. The death of this child was not only quite unexpected by him, but must have seemed bewilderingly strange. Yet though he was in the dark as to the reason of this calamity, he refused to accept it as final. The mother had taken her stand upon the divine bounty and kindness, expecting an outcome in keeping with God's grace toward her, and no doubt the prophet now reasoned in the same way. Though he had never before been faced with such a desperate situation, he knew that with God all things are possible. The very fact that the dead child had been placed upon his bed was a direct challenge to his faith, and nobly did he meet it.

"He went in therefore, and shut the door upon them twain, and prayed unto the LORD" (v. 33). We are not quite clear whether "them twain" refers to himself and the child or to the mother, and Gehazi, who had most probably accompanied him; but whichever it was, his action in closing the door denoted his desire for privacy. The prophet practiced what he preached to others. In the miracle recorded at the beginning of chapter four, Elisha had bidden the widow "shut the door upon" herself and her sons (v. 4) so as to avoid ostentation, and here Elisha follows the same course. Moreover, he was about to engage the Lord in most urgent and special prayer, and that is certainly something which calls for aloneness with God. The minister of the gospel needs to be much on his guard on this point, precluding everything which savors of advertizing his piety like the Pharisees did (see Mt 6:5-6). Here, then, was the means of this miracle: the unfaltering faith of the mother and now the faith of the prophet, expressed in prayer unto his Master — acknowledging his own helplessness, humbly but trustfully presenting the need to Him, counting upon His almighty power and goodness.

Fifth, the Procedure of the Miracle

"And he went up, and lay upon the child, and put his mouth upon his mouth, and his eyes upon his eyes, . . . and the flesh of the child waxed warm" (v. 34). The means used by the prophet and the policy he followed are so closely linked together that they merge into one another without any break, the faith of Elisha finding expression in prayer. Considering the extraordinary situation here, how that act of the prophet's serves to demonstrate that he was accustomed to count upon God in times of emergency, to look for wondrous blessings from Him in response to his supplications. He was fully persuaded nothing was too hard for Jehovah and therefore no petition too large to present unto him. The more faith looks to the infinite power and all-sufficiency of the One with whom it has to do, the more is He honored. Next, the prophet stretched himself on the body of the little one, which was expressive of his deep affection for him and his intense longing for the lad's restoration, as though he would communicate his own life and thereby revive him.

Those who are familiar with the life and miracles of Elijah will at once be struck with the likeness between Elisha's actions here and the conduct of his predecessor on a similar occasion. In fact so close is the resemblance between them, it is evident the one was patterned after that of the other — showing how closely the man of God must keep to the scripture model if he would be successful in the divine service. First, Elijah had taken the lifeless child of the Zarephath widow, carried him upstairs, and laid him on his own bed, thereby preventing any human eyes from observing what transpired. Next, he "cried unto the Lord" and then "he stretched himself upon the child" (1 Ki 17:19-21). In addition to what had been pointed out in the previous paragraph, we believe this stretching of the prophet on the one for whom he prayed signified an act of identification, and it was a proof that he was putting his whole soul into the work of supplication. If we are to prevail in interceding for another, we must make his or her case ours, taking his need or burden upon our own spirit, and then spreading it before God.

"Then he returned, and walked in the house to and fro" (2 Ki 4:35). Let it be noted that even the prayer of an Elisha did not meet with an immediate and full answer. Why then should we be so soon disheartened when heaven appears to be tardy in responding to our crying! God is sovereign in this, as in everything else; by this we mean that He does not deal uniformly with us. Sometimes our request is answered immediately, at the first time of asking, but often He calls for perseverance and persistence, requiring us to wait patiently for Him. We have seen how many rebuffs the faith of the mother met with, and now the faith of the prophet is tested too. It is true that he had been granted an encouragement by the waxing warm of the child's body — as the Lord is pleased to often give us "a token for good" (Ps 86:17) before the full answer is received; but as yet there was no sign of returning consciousness, and the form of the little one still lay silent and inert before him. And that also has been recorded for our instruction.

"Then he returned, and walked in the house to and fro; and went up, and stretched himself upon him" (v. 35). This pacing up and down seems to denote a measure of mental perturbation, for the prophets were "subject to like passions as we are" (Ja 5:17) and compassed with the same infirmities. But even if Elisha was now at his wit's end, he did not give way to despair and regard the situation as hopeless. No, he continued clinging to Him who is the giver of every good and perfect gift, and again stretched himself upon the child. Let us take this important lesson to heart and put it into practice, for it is at this point so many fail. It is the perseverance of faith which wins the day (see Mt 7:7).

Scott has pointed out,

> It is instructive to compare the manner in which Elijah and Elisha wrought their miracles, especially in raising the dead, with that of Jesus Christ. Every part of their conduct expressed a consciousness of inability and an entire dependence upon Another, and earnest supplication for His intervention; but Jesus wrought by His own power: He spake, and it was done: "Young man, I say unto thee arise; Talitha cumi; Lazarus come forth."

In all things He has the preeminence.

Sixth, the Marvel of the Miracle

The marvel of this was nothing less than the quickening of the child, the restoring of "a dead body to life" (2 Ki 8:5). After the prophet had again stretched himself upon the child, we are told that "the child sneezed seven times, and the child opened his eyes" (2 Ki 4:35). See how ready God is to respond to the exercise of real faith in Himself! In this case neither the mother nor the prophet had any definite or even indefinite promise they could plead, for the Lord had not said the child should be preserved in health or recovered if he fell ill. But though they had no promise, they laid hold of the known character of God. Since He had given the child unasked, Elisha did not believe He would now withdraw His gift and leave his benefactress worse off than she was before. Elisha knew that with the Lord there is "no variableness, neither shadow of turning" (Ja 1:17), and he clung to that. True, it makes prayer easier when there is some specific promise we can claim, yet it is a higher order of faith that lays hold of God Himself.

There was no promise that God would pardon a penitent murderer, and no sacrifice was appointed for such a sin, yet David appealed not in vain to the multitude of His tender mercies (Ps 51:1).

"And the child opened his eyes" (2 Ki 4:35). See what a prayer-hearing, prayer-answering God is ours! Hopeless as our case may be so far as all human aid is concerned, it is not too hard for the Lord. But we must "ask in faith, nothing wavering. For he that wavereth is like a wave of the sea driven with the wind and tossed," and therefore is it added, "Let not that man think that he shall receive anything from the Lord" (Ja 1:6-7). No, rather it is the one who declares with Jacob, "I will not let thee go, except thou bless me" (Gen 32:26) who obtains his request. What must have been Elisha's delight when he saw the child revive and obtained this further experience of God's grace in answer to his petition, delivering him from his grief! How great must have been his joy as he called for Gehazi and bade him summon the mother, and when he said to her, "Take up thy son!" Blessed is it to behold her silent gratitude — too full for words — as she "fell at his feet," and in worship to God, "bowed herself to the ground." Then, she "took up her son, and went out" (2 Ki 4:37), to get alone with God and pour out her heart in thanksgiving to Him.

Seventh, the Meaning of the Miracle

Some help is obtained here by noting that this passage opens with the connective conjunction (v. 18). That "And" not only intimates the continuity of the narrative and notes a striking contrast between the two principal divisions of it, but it also indicates there is an intimate relation between them. As we have pointed out on previous occasions, the word "and" is used in Scripture sometimes with the purpose of linking two things together, but at other times with the object of placing two objects or incidents in juxtaposition in order to display the contrasts between them. In the present instance it appears to be used for both reasons. As we hope to show, light is thrown on the typical significance of this miracle by carefully noting how it is immediately linked to the one preceding it. When we look at the respective incidents described, we are at once struck with the antitheses presented. In the former we behold Elisha journeying to Shunem; in the latter it is the woman who goes to him herself. First, it was the woman befriending the prophet; here he is seen befriending her. Previously a son is miraculously given to her; in this he is taken away.

The typical meaning of that does not appear on the surface, and therefore it will not be a simple matter for us to make it clear to the reader. Only the regenerate will be able to follow us intelligently, for they alone have experienced spiritually that which is here set forth figuratively. That which is outstanding in this incident is the mysteriousness of it: that a child should be miraculously given to this woman, and then that the hand of death should be laid upon him! That was not only a sore trial to the poor mother, but a most perplexing providence. To carnal reason it seemed as though God was mocking her. But is there not also something equally tragic, equally baffling, in the experience of the Christian? In the previous miracle we were shown a picture of the fruit of redemption, and here death appears to be written on that fruit. Ah, my reader, let it be clearly understood that we are as dependent upon God for the maintenance of that fruit as we were for the actual gift of it.

And what is the "fruit of redemption" as it applies to the individual? From the side which looks Godward: reconciliation, justification, sanctification, preservation. But from the selfward side, what a list might be drawn up. Peace, joy, assurance, fellowship with God and His people, delight in His Word, liberty in prayer, separation from the world, affections set upon things above. Oh the inexpressible sweetness of our "espousals" (Jer 2:2) and of our "first love" (Rev 2:4). But, in many cases, how soon is that joy dampened and that love is left! How wretched then is the soul; like Rachel mourning for her children, we refused to be comforted. How sore the perplexity! How Satan seeks to take advantage and persuade

such an one that God has ceased to be gracious. How strange that
such a blight should have fallen upon the fruit of the spirit! How
deeply mysterious the deadness which now rests upon the garden of
God's planting, causing the soul to say with the poet,

> Where is the blessedness I knew
> When first I saw the Lord;
> Where is the soul-refreshing view
> Of Jesus and His Word?
>
> What peaceful hours I once enjoyed!
> How sweet their memory still,
> But now I feel an aching void
> The world can never fill.

Yes, it does indeed seem inexplicable that the child of God's own
workmanship should pine away, and in a sense, lie cold and lifeless.
Ah, but we must not stop there. We must not sit down in despair
and conclude that all is lost. The incident before us does not end at
that point; the death of the child was not the final thing! There is
"good hope" for us here, important instruction to heed. That
"great woman" did not give away to dejection and assume that all
hope was gone. Very far from it. And if the Christian who is aware
of spiritual decays, of languishing graces, of his dire need of being
renewed in the inner man, would experience a gracious reviving,
then he should emulate this mother and do as she did. And again
we would point out that she did not faint in the day of trouble and
indulge in self-pity; she did not bemoan her helplessness and say,
What can I do in the presence of death? And if she did not, why
should you!

Mark attentively what this stricken woman did. (1) She regarded this inexplicable and painful event as a testing of her faith,
and she acted accordingly. (2) She moved promptly. Without delay she carried the child upstairs and laid him on the prophet's bed,
in anticipation of the Lord's showing Himself strong on her behalf.
(3) She vigorously bestirred herself, going to some trouble in order
to obtain relief, starting out on an arduous journey. (4) She refused to be deterred when her own husband half-discouraged her.
(5) She sought the One who had promised the son in the first instance. The soul must turn to God and cry "quicken thou me according to thy word" (Ps 119:25). (6) She clung to the original

promise and refused to believe that God had ceased to be gracious (2 Ki 4:28). (7) She declined to be put off by the unavailing intervention of an unregenerate minister (vv. 29-30). (8) She persisted in counting upon the power of Elisha, who was to her the representative of God. And gloriously was her faith rewarded.

Regarding the illustrative value of this miracle in connection with Elisha himself, it teaches us the following points. (1) The servant of God must not be surprised if those in whose conversion he has been instrumental should later experience a spiritual decay, especially when he is absent from them. (2) If he would be used to their restoration, no half measures will avail, nor may he entrust the work to a delegate. (3) Believing, expectant, fervent prayer, must be his first recourse. (4) In seeking to revive a languishing soul, he must descend to the level of the one to whom he ministers (v. 34) and not stand as on some pedestal, as though he were a superior being. (5) He must not be discouraged because there is not an immediate and complete response to his efforts, but should persevere. (6) No cold and formal measures will suffice; he must throw himself into this work heart and soul. (7) The order of recovery was: renewed circulation (v. 34), sneezing, eyes opened. We can draw a three-fold application here for the steps of spiritual renewal: the affections warmed, the head cleared (understanding restored), vision.

Chapter 12

EIGHTH MIRACLE
MEAL-HEALED POTTAGE

THE PASSAGE which is before us (2 Ki 4:38-41) has in it practical instruction as well as spiritual lessons for us, for the Scriptures make known the evils and dangers which are in this world as well as the glory and bliss of the world to come. Elisha was visiting the school of the prophets at Gilgal, instructing them in the things of God. At the close of a meeting he gave orders that a simple meal should be prepared for them; for though he was more concerned about their spiritual welfare, he did not overlook their physical. It was a time of "dearth" or famine, so one went out into the field to gather herbs, that they might have a vegetable stew. He found a wild vine with gourds. Securing a goodly quantity, he returned and shred them into the pot of pottage, quite unconscious that he was making use of a poisonous plant. Not until after the broth was poured out was the peril discovered, for when they began eating the men cried out, "There is death in the pot." How little we realize the many and varied forms in which death menaces us, and how constantly we are indebted to the preserving providence of God.

The effects of the curse which the Lord God pronounced upon the sin of Adam have been by no means confined unto the human family. "Cursed is the ground for thy sake" (Gen 3:17) was part of the fearful sentence, and as Romans 8:22 informs us, "The whole creation groaneth and travaileth in pain together until now." No matter where one looks, the observant eye can behold the consequences of the fall. No section of creation has escaped; even the fields and the woods bring forth not only thistles and thorns, but that which is noxious and venomous. Some of the most innocent-looking herbs and berries produce horrible suffering and death if eaten by man or beast. Yet for the most part, in fact with rare exceptions, God has mercifully provided adequate protection against such evils. The instinct of the animals and the intelligence of men causes each of them to leave alone that which is harmful. Either the eye discovers, the nostril detects, or the palate perceives their evil qualities, and thereby we are guarded against them.

It scarcely needs to be pointed out that what we have alluded to above in the material world suggests that which we find in the religious realm. Among that which is offered for intellectual and spiritual food, how much is unwholesome and vicious. The fields of Christendom have many "wild gourds" growing in them, the use of which necessarily entails "death in the pot," for fatal doctrine acts upon the soul as poison does upon the body. This is clear from that apostolic declaration, "Their word will eat as doth a canker" or "gangrene" (2 Ti 2:17), where the reference is to the evil doctrine of heretical teachers. But just as God has mercifully endowed the animals with instincts and man with sufficient natural intelligence to avoid what is physically injurious, so He has graciously bestowed upon His people spiritual "senses" which, if exercised, "discern both good and evil" (Heb 5:14). Thus they instinctively warn against unsound writings and preachers, so that "a stranger will they not follow, but will flee from him: for they know not the voice of strangers" (Jn 10:5).

The mercy of the Creator appears not only in the protecting "senses" with which He has endowed His creatures, but also in providing them with suitable remedies and effective antidotes. If there be herbs which are injurious and poisonous, there are others which are counteracting and healing. If the waters of Marah are bitter and undrinkable, there is a tree at hand which when cut down and cast into the waters renders them sweet (Ex 15:25). If we read at the beginning of the Scriptures of a tree the eating of whose fruit involved our race in disaster and death, before that volume is closed we are told of another tree, the leaves of which are "for the healing of the nations" (Rev 22:2). This fact, then, holds good in both the physical and the spiritual realms: for every evil, God has provided a remedy, for every poison an antidote, for every false doctrine a portion of the truth which exposes and refutes it. With these introductory observations, we may now consider the details of Elisha's eighth miracle.

First, the Location of the Miracle

"And Elisha came again to Gilgal: and there was a dearth in the land" (2 Ki 4:38). It will be remembered that it was from this place that Elisha had started out with his master on their final journey together before Elijah was raptured to heaven (2 Ki 2:1), where his sincerity had been put to the proof by the testing, "Tarry here, I pray thee." From Gilgal they had passed to Bethel (2:2), and from there to Jericho, and finally to the Jordan. It is striking to note that our hero wrought a miracle at each of these places in inverse order of the original journey. At the Jordan he had divided its waters so that he passed over dry-shod before the wondering gaze of the young prophets (2:14-15). At Jericho he had healed the evil waters (2:19-22). At Bethel he had cursed the profane children in the name of the Lord and brought about their destruction (2:23-25). And now here at Gilgal Elisha again exercises the extraordinary powers with which God had endowed him. Wherever he goes, the servant of God should, as opportunity affords, use his ministerial gifts.

"And Elisha came again to Gilgal: and there was a dearth in the land" (v. 38). Gilgal was to the east of Jericho, close to the Jordan, where there would be more moisture and vegetation than further inland. It was a place made memorable from the early history of Israel. It was there that the nation had set up twelve stones as a monument to God's gracious intervention, when He had caused them to pass through the river dry-shod (Jos 4:18-24). It was there too that they had circumcised those who had been born in the wilderness wanderings, thereby rolling away the reproach of Egypt from off them. This evidenced their separation from the heathen, as being God's peculiar people, who made the circumcision of the heart (Jer 4:4; Ro 2:29), which is the distinguishing mark of God's spiritual children. It was there also that they had first partaken of "the old corn of the land" (Jos 5:11) so that miraculous supplies of manna ceased. Yet even such a favored spot as this was affected by the dearth, for great wickedness had also been perpetrated there (1 Sa 15:21-23 and cf. Ho 9:15).

Second, the Occasion of the Miracle

"There was a dearth in the land." The Hebrew word for "dearth" (*raab*) signifies a famine, and is so rendered in 1 Kings 18:2. This

is one of the "four sore judgments" which the Lord sends when He
expresses His displeasure against a people: "the sword, and the famine, and the noisome beast, and the pestilence" (Eze 14:21). In
our day the "famine" with which a righteous God afflicts a land is
one far more solemn and serious than that of dearth of material food,
as that threatened in Amos 8:11: "Behold, the days come, saith the
Lord GOD, that I will send a famine in the land, not a famine of
bread, nor a thirst for water, but of hearing the words of the LORD."
Such a "famine" is upon Christendom today. It has not yet become
quite universal, but almost so. Thousands of places dedicated to divine worship have become social centers, political clubs, ritualistic
playhouses, and today they are heaps of rubble. The vast majority
of those still standing provide nothing for people desiring spiritual
food, and even in the very few where the Word of God is ostensibly
ministered, it is no longer so in the power and blessing of the Spirit.
It is this which gives such pertinence to our present passage.

"And Elisha came again to Gilgal: and there was a dearth in the
land; and the sons of the prophets were sitting before him" (2 Ki
4:38). What a blessed and beautiful conjunction of things was this.
How instructive for the under-shepherd of Christ and for His sheep
in a day like this. Though God was acting in judgment, the prophet
did not consider that that warranted him ceasing his labors until conditions became more favorable. So far from it, he felt it was a time
when he should do all in his power to "strengthen the things that
remain, that are ready to die" (Rev 3:2), and encourage those who
are liable to give way to dejection because of the general apostasy.
"Preach the word; be instant in season, out of season" (2 Ti 4:2)
is the injunction which God has laid upon His ministers. In seasons
of "dearth" the servant of Christ needs to be particularly attentive to
the spiritual needs of young believers, instructing them in the holiness and righteousness of a sin-hating God when His scourge is upon
the nation; and also making known His faithfulness and sufficiency
unto "His own" in the darkest hour, reminding them that "God is
our refuge and strength, a very present help in trouble" (Ps 46:1).

See here what a noble example Elisha has left those called by God
to engage in proclaiming His truth. The prophet was not idle; he
did not wait for needy souls to come to him, but took the initiative
and went to them. Times of national distress and calamity do not
exempt any from the discharge of spiritual duties nor justify any

slackness in employing the appointed means of grace. Nor did these "sons of the prophets" raise the objection that Elisha sought them at an inopportune time and make the excuse they must busy themselves looking after their temporal interests. No, they gladly availed themselves of their golden opportunity, making the most of it by attentively listening to the instructions of Elisha. Their "sitting before him" showed respect and attentiveness. It reminds us of Mary who "sat at Jesus' feet, and heard his word" (Lk 11:39), which Christ designated that "good part," the one thing "needful" (v. 42). And though many today no longer may hear the Word preached, they can still sit and read it. Be thankful for the printed page, if it contains that which strengthens faith and promotes closer walking with God.

Third, the Beneficiaries of the Miracle

"And he said unto his servant, Set on the great pot, and seethe [boil or concoct] pottage for the sons of the prophets" (2 Ki 4: 38). The order of action in this verse is significant, for it shows how the needs of the soul take precedence over those of the body. Elisha saw to it that they had spiritual food set before them before arranging for material food. On the other hand, the prophet did not conduct himself as a fanatic and disdain their temporal needs. Here, as everywhere in Scripture, the balance is rightly preserved. Attention to and enjoyment of fellowship with God must never be allowed to crowd out the discharge of those duties pertaining to the common round of life. As Christ thought of and ministered to the bodily needs of the hungry multitudes after He had broken unto them the bread of life, so His servant here was concerned about the physical well-being of these students: a plain and simple meal in either case; in the one, bread and fish; in the other, vegetable stew.

"And one went out into the field to gather herbs, and found a wild vine, and gathered thereof wild gourds his lap full, and came and shred them into the pot of pottage: for they knew them not" (v. 39). Apparently this person took it upon himself to go out and gather herbs in the field; no doubt his intention was good, but so far as the narrative is concerned, it records no commission from Elisha to act thus — a clear case where the best intentions do not warrant us to act unless we have a definite word from God, and to use only those means He has appointed. It is possible this person may have returned thanks to God when his eye fell upon those gourds and felt that his steps had been directed by Him to the place where they were growing. If so, we have a warning how easily we may misunderstand the divine providences when we are acting in self-will and interpret them in a way which justifies and apparently sanctifies the course we have taken. When Jonah fled from the command the Lord had given him, to "flee unto Tarshish" and went down to Joppa, he "found a ship going" to that very place (Jon 1:3)!

Seasons of "death" are peculiarly dangerous ones. Why so? Because in times of famine, food is scarce, and, because there is less to select from, we are very apt to be less particular and act on the principle of "beggars cannot be choosers." Certainly there is a warning here to be careful about what we eat at such times, and especially of that which grows wild. The Hebrew word here rendered "wild" means uncultivated, and is generally connected with "wild beasts," which were not only ceremonially unclean under the Mosaic law but unfit for human consumption. It is to be duly noted that there was a plentiful supply of these "wild gourds" even though there was a "dearth" in the land. So it is spiritually; when there is a "famine" of hearing the words of the Lord, Satan sees to it that there is no shortage of spurious food. Witness the number of tracts from cultists and pornographic booklets which are so freely circulated, to say nothing of the vile literature in which the things of God are openly derided.

Yet though these gourds were "wild," they must have borne a close resemblance to wholesome ones; or he who gathered them would not have been deceived by them, nor would it be said of those who stood by while he shred them into the pot of pottage that "they knew them not." This too has a spiritual counterpart, as the enemy's "tares" sown among the wheat intimates. Satan is a subtle imitator. Not only does he transform himself "into an angel of light" but his "deceitful workers" transform themselves "into the apostles of Christ" (2 Co 11:13-14). They come preaching Jesus and His gospel, but as the Holy Spirit warns us, it is "another Jesus" and "another gospel" than the genuine one (2 Co 11:4). Those who looked on while this person was shredding the wild gourds into the pot raised no objection, for they were quite unsuspicious, instead of carefully examining what they were to eat. What point this gives to the apostolic exhortation, "Prove all things; hold fast that which is good" (1 Th 5:21); and if we refuse to do so, who is to blame when we devour that which is injurious?

Fourth, the Necessity of the Miracle

"So they poured out for the men to eat. And it came to pass, as they were eating of the pottage, that they cried out, and said, O thou man of God, there is death in the pot. And they could not eat thereof" (2 Ki 4:40). It was not until the eleventh hour that they discovered their peril, for the deadly danger of these "wild gourds" was not exposed until they had begun eating them; not only had the gourds' appearance deceived them, but they had no offensive or suspicious odor while cooking. The case was particularly subtle, for seemingly it was one of their own number who had gathered the poisonous herbs. Ah, note how the apostle commended the Bereans for carefully bringing his teaching to the test of Holy Writ (Ac 17:11). Much more do we need to do so with the preachings and writings of uninspired men. We need to "consider diligently" what is set before us by each ecclesiastical ruler (Pr 23:1 and cf. Mt 24:45), for though they be "dainties" and "sweet words," yet they may be "deceitful meat" (Pr 23:2, 8). How we need to make Psalm 141:4 our prayer!

It was when the sons of the prophets began to eat the pottage that they discovered its deadly character. Ah, my reader, are you able to discriminate between what is helpful to the soul and what is harmful? Is your spiritual palate able to detect error from truth, Satan's poison from "the sincere [pure] milk of the word?" Do you really endeavor so to do, or are you lax in this matter? "Hear my words, O ye wise men, and give ear unto me, ye that have knowledge. For the ear trieth words, as the mouth tasteth meat" (Job 34:2-3). But let us not miss the moral link between what is said in 2 Kings 4:40 and that which was before us in verse 38. It was those who had just previously been sitting at the feet of Elisha who now discovered the poisonous nature of these gourds. Is not the lesson plain and recorded for our learning? It is those who are instructed by the true servant of God who have most spiritual discernment and better judgment than others not so favored. Then "take heed what ye hear" (Mk 4:24) and what ye read.

Fifth, the Nature of the Miracle

"They cried out, and said, O thou man of God, there is death in the pot. And they could not eat thereof." What made them aware of their peril we know not. Nor is the child of God always conscious of it when some secret repression or unseen hand prevents him from gratifying his curiosity and turns his feet away from some synagogue of Satan where there is "death in the pot" being served in that place. Have not all genuine Christians cause to say with the apostle, "Who delivered us from so great a death, and doth deliver: in whom we trust that he will yet deliver us" (2 Co 1:10). From that pot of death, Elisha, under God, delivered them.

Sixth, the Means of the Miracle

"But he said, Then bring meal. And he cast it into the pot; and he said, Pour out for the people, that they may eat. And there was no harm [or 'evil thing'] in the pot" (2 Ki 4:41). The "meal" we regard as the Word of God: either the written or the personal Word. One of the great types of Christ is seen in the meat (i.e., meal) offering of Leviticus 2. It is only by the Word we are safeguarded from evil. See how graciously God provided for "His own." Though there was a "dearth in the land," yet these sons of the prophets were not without "meal"! How thankful we should be for the Word of God in our homes in such a day as this. Though someone else fetched the meal, "he [Elisha] cast it into the pot"!

Seventh, the Meaning of the Miracle

Much of this has been intimated in what has already been pointed out. Let it not be overlooked that verse 38 of 2 Kings 4, begins with "And": after a reviving, be careful where you go for your food! If you are suspicious of the soundness of a religious publication, take counsel of a competent "man of God." Let not a time of spiritual "dearth" render you less careful of what you feed upon. In seasons of famine the servant of God should be diligent in seeking to strengthen the hands of young believers. Only by making the Word of God our constant guide shall we be delivered from the evils surrounding us.

Chapter 13

NINTH MIRACLE
TWENTY LOAVES OF BARLEY

IT SEEMS STRANGE so few have perceived that a miracle is recorded in 2 Kings 4:42-44, for surely a careful reading of those verses makes it evident that they describe the wonder-working power of the Lord. How else can we explain the feeding of so many with such a little and then a surplus remaining? It is even more strange that scarcely any appear to have recognized that we have here a most striking foreshadowment of the only miracle wrought by the Lord Jesus which is narrated by all the four evangelists, namely, His feeding of the multitude from a few loaves and fishes. In all of our reading, we have not only never come across a sermon thereon, but so far as memory serves, not so much as a quotation from or allusion to this striking passage. Thomas Scott dismisses the incident with a single paragraph, and though Matthew Henry is a little fuller, he too says nothing about the supernatural character of it. We wonder how many of our readers, before turning to this article, could have answered the question, Where in the Old Testament is described the miracle of the feeding of a multitude through the hands of a man?

First, the Occasion of the Miracle

Though there was a "dearth [famine] in the land" (2 Ki 4:38) yet we learn from the first verse of our passage that it was not a total or universal one: some barley had been grown in Baal-shalisha. In this we may perceive how in wrath the Lord remembers mercy. Even where the crops of an entire country are a complete failure — an exceedingly exceptional occurrence — there is always food available in adjoining lands. Therein we behold an exemplification of

God's goodness and faithfulness. He declared, "While the earth remaineth, seedtime and harvest, and cold and heat, and summer and winter, and day and night shall not cease" (Gen 8:22). Though more than four thousand years have passed since then, each returning one has furnished clear evidence of the fulfillment of that promise — a demonstration both of the divine veracity and of God's continuous regulation of the affairs of earth. As we have said, it is very rare for there to be a total failure of the crops in any single country, for as the Lord declares, "I caused it to rain upon one city, and caused it not to rain upon another city: one piece was rained upon, and the piece whereon it rained not withered" (Amos 4:7).

Second, the Contributor to the Miracle

"And there came a man from Baal-shalisha, and brought the man of God bread of the firstfruits" (2 Ki 4:42). Let us begin by observing how naturally and artlessly the conduct of this unnamed man is introduced. Here was one who had a heart for the Lord's servant in a time of need, who thought of him in this season of scarcity and distress, and who went to some trouble to minister to him. Shalisha adjoined Mount Ephraim (1 Sa 9:4), and probably a journey of considerable distance had to be taken in order to reach the prophet. Ah, but there was more behind this man's action than meets the eye; we must look deeper if we are to discover the springs of his deed. It is written, "The steps of a good man are ordered by the LORD" (Ps 37:23). And thus it was in the case before us. This man now befriended Elisha because God had worked in him "both to will and to do of his good pleasure" (Phil 2:13). It is only by comparing scripture with scripture we can discover the fullness of meaning in any verse.

Before passing on let us pause and make application to ourselves of the truth to which attention has just been called. It has an important bearing on each of us, and one which needs to be emphasized in this day of practical atheism. The whole trend of things in our evil generation is to be so occupied with what are termed "the laws of Nature," that the operations of the Creator are lost sight of; man and his doings are so eulogized and deified that the hand of God in providence is totally obscured. It should be otherwise with the saint. When some friend comes and ministers to your need, while being grateful to him, look above him and his kindness to the One who has sent him. I may pray, "Give us this day our daily bread" and then, because I am so absorbed with secondary causes and the instruments which He may employ, fail to see my Father's hand as He graciously answers my petition. God is the giver of everything temporal as well as spiritual, even though He uses human agents in the conveying of them.

"And there came a man from Baal-shalisha." This town was originally called "Shalisha" but the evil power exerted by Jezebel had stamped upon it the name of her false god, as was the case with other places (cf. "Baal-hermon," 1 Ch 5:23). But even in this seat of idolatry there was at least one who feared the Lord, who was regulated by His law, and who had a heart for His servant. This should be a comfort to the saints in a time of such fearful and widespread declension as now prevails. However dark things may get, and we believe they will yet become much darker before there is any improvement, God will preserve to Himself a remnant. He always has, and He always will. In the antediluvian world there was a Noah, who by grace was upright in his generations and walked with God. In Egypt, when the name of Jehovah was unknown among the Hebrews, a Moses was raised up, who refused to be called the son of Pharaoh's daughter. So now there is one here and there as a voice in the wilderness. Though the name of this man from Shalisha is not given, we doubt not it is inscribed in the Book of Life.

"And there came a man from Baal-shalisha, and brought the man of God bread of the firstfruits." Again we point out that there is more here than meets the careless eye or is obvious to the casual glance. Other passages which make mention of the "firstfruits" must be compared if we are to learn the deeper meaning of what is here recorded and discover that this man's action was something more than one of thoughtfulness and kindness to Elisha. "The first of the firstfruits of thy land thou shalt bring into the house of the LORD thy God" (Ex 23:19, 34:26). The "firstfruits," then, belonged to the Lord, being an acknowledgment both of His goodness and proprietorship; a fuller and very beautiful passage is found in Deuteronomy 26:1-11. From Numbers 18:8-13 we learn that these became the portion of the priests. "Whatsoever is first ripe in the land, which they [the people] shall bring unto the LORD, shall be thine [Aaron's and his sons]; every one that is clean in thine house shall eat of it" (v. 13). The same holds good in the rebuilt temple. "The first of all the firstfruits . . . shall be the priest's" (Eze 44:30).

This man from Shalisha then, was, in principle, acting in obedience to the divine law. We say "in principle," because it was enjoined that the firstfruits should be taken into "the house of the LORD" and that they became the priest's portion. But this man belonged to the kingdom of Israel and not of Judah; he lived in Samaria and had no access to Jerusalem, and even had he gone there, entrance to the temple had been forbidden. In Samaria there were none of the priests of the Lord, only those of Baal. But though he rendered not obedience to the letter, he certainly did so to the spirit, for he recognized that these firstfruits were not for his own use; and though Elisha was not a priest he was a prophet, a servant of the Lord. It is for this reason, we believe, that it is said he brought the firstfruits not to "Elisha" but to "the man of God." That designation occurs first in Deuteronomy 33:1 in connection with Moses, and is descriptive not of his character but of his office — one wholly devoted to God, his entire time spent in His service. In the Old Testament it is applied only to the prophets and extraordinary teachers (1 Sa 2:27, 9:6; 1 Ki 17:18); but in the New Testament it seems to belong to all of God's servants (1 Ti 6:11; 2 Ti 3:17).

What has been pointed out above should throw light on a problem which is now troubling many conscientious souls and which should provide comfort in these evil days. The situation of many of God's people is now much like that which prevailed when our present incident occurred. It was a time of apostasy, when everything was out of order. Such is the present case of Christendom. It is the clear duty of God's people to render obedience to the letter of His Word wherever that is possible; but when it is not, they may do so in spirit. Daniel and his fellow Hebrews could not observe the Passover feast in Babylon, and no doubt that was a sore grief to them. But that very grief signified their desire to observe it, and in such cases God accepts the will for the deed. For many years past, this writer and his wife have been unable to conscientiously celebrate the Lord's supper; yet (by grace) we do so in spirit, by remembering the Lord's death for His people in our hearts and minds. "Not forsaking the assembling of ourselves together" (Heb 10:25) is very far from meaning that the sheep of Christ should attend a place where the "goats" predominate, or where their presence would sanction what is dishonoring to their Master.

Before passing on, we should point out another instructive and encouraging lesson here for the humble saint. This man from Shalisha, acting in the spirit of God's law, journeying with his first-fruits to where Elisha was, could have had no thought in his mind that by this action he was going to be a contributor to a remarkable miracle. Yet such was actually the case, for those very loaves of his became the means, by the wonder-working power of God, of feeding a large company of people. And this is but a single illustration of a principle which, under the government of God, is of frequent occurrence, as probably most of us have witnessed. Ah, my reader, we never know how far-reaching may be the effects and what fruits may issue for eternity from the most inconspicuous act done for God's glory or for the good of one of His people. How often has some obscure Christian, in the kindness of his heart, done something or given something which God has been pleased to bless and multiply in a manner and to an extent which never entered his (or her) mind.

"And brought the man of God bread of the firstfruits, twenty loaves of barley, and full ears of corn in the husk thereof." How it appears that it delighted the Holy Spirit to describe this offering in detail. Bearing in mind that a time of serious "dearth" then prevailed, may we not see in the varied nature of this gift thoughtfulness and consideration on the part of him that made it. Had the whole of it been made up in the form of "loaves," some of it might have become moldy before the whole of it was eaten. At best it would need to be consumed quickly; to obviate that, part of the barley was brought in the husk. On the other hand, had all been brought in the ear, time would be required for the grinding and baking, and in the meanwhile the prophet might be famished and fainting. By such a division, both disadvantages were prevented. From the whole, we are taught that in making gifts to another or in ministering to his needs we should exercise care in seeing that it is in a form best suited to his requirements. The application of this principle pertains to spiritual things as well as temporal.

Third, the Generosity of the Miracle

Before noting the use to which Elisha put this offering, let us observe that gifts sometimes come from the most unexpected quarters. Had this man come from Bethel or Shunem there would be no occasion for surprise, but that one from Baal-shalisha should bring God's servant an offering of his firstfruits was certainly not to be

looked for. Ah, does not each of God's servants know something of
this experience! If on the one hand some on whose cooperation he
had reason to count, failed and disappointed him, others who were
strangers befriended him. More than once or twice have the writer
and his wife had this pleasant surprise. We cherish their memory,
while seeking to forget the contrasting ones. Joseph might be envied
and mistreated by his brethren, but he found favor in the eyes of
Potiphar. Moses may be despised by the Hebrews, but he received
kindly treatment in the house of Jethro. Rather than have Elijah
starve by the brook Cherith, the Lord commanded the ravens to
feed him. Our supplies are sure, though at times they may come from
strange quarters.

"And he said, Give unto the people, that they may eat" (2 Ki 4:
42). In the preceding miracle this same trait is manifest: nothing is
there said of Elisha partaking of the pottage, nor even of the young
prophets in his charge, but rather "the people." Such liberality will
not go unrewarded by God, for He has promised "Give, and it shall
be given unto you" (Lk 6:38). Such was the case here, for the
very next thing recorded after his "Pour out for the people that they
may eat" (2 Ki 4:41) is the receiving of these twenty loaves. And
what use does he now make of them? His first thought was not for
himself, but for others. We must not conclude from the silence of
this verse that the prophet failed either to perceive the hand of God
in this gift or that he neglected to return thanks unto Him. Had the
Scriptures given a full and detailed account of such matters, they
would run into many volumes. According to the law of analogy we
are justified in concluding that he did both. Moreover, what follows
shows plainly that his mind was stayed upon the Lord.

The situation which confronted Elisha is one that in principle has
often faced God's people. What the Lord gives to one is not to be
used selfishly but is to be shared with others. Yet sometimes we are
in the position that what is on hand does not appear sufficient for
that purpose. My supply may be scanty and the claims of a growing
family have to be met. If I contribute to the Lord's cause and minister to His servants and people, may not my little ones go hungry?
Here is where the exercise of faith comes in. Lay hold of such promises as Luke 6:38 and 2 Corinthians 9:8; act on them and you
shall prove that "the liberal soul shall be made fat" (Pr 11:25).
Especially should the ministers of Christ set an example in this respect; if they be close-handed, it will greatly hinder their usefulness.

Elisha made practical use of what was designed as an offering to the Lord, as David did not hesitate to take the "shewbread" and give to his hungry men.

Fourth, the Opposition to the Miracle

"And his servitor said, What! should I set this before an hundred men?" (2 Ki 4:43). Ah, the servant of God must not expect others to be equally zealous in exercising a gracious spirit or to cooperate with him in the works of faith. No, not even those who are his assistants — none can walk by the faith of another. (When Luther announced his intention of going to Worms, even his dearest brethren sought to dissuade him.) But was not such an objection a natural one? Yes, but certainly not spiritual. It shows how shallow and fleeting must have been the impression made on the man by the previous miracles. It was quite in keeping with what we read elsewhere of this "servitor," Gehazi. His language expressed incredulity and unbelief. Was he thinking of himself? Did he resent his master's generosity and think, We shall need this food for ourselves? And this, after all the miracles he had seen God work through Elisha! Ah, it takes something more than the witnessing of miracles to regenerate a dead soul, as the Jews made evident when the Son of God was in their midst.

Fifth, the Means of the Miracle

Faith in God and His Word was the only human means involved. "He said again, Give the people, that they may eat: for thus saith the LORD, They shall eat, and shall leave thereof" (2 Ki 4:43). Where there is real faith in God it is not stumbled by the unbelief of others; but when it stands in the wisdom of men, it is soon paralyzed by the opposition it encounters. When blind Bartimaeus began to cry out, "Jesus, thou son of David, have mercy on me," and many charged him that he should hold his peace, "he cried the more a great deal" (Mk 10:46, 48). On the other hand, one with a stony-ground hearer's faith endures for a while, "for when tribulation or persecution ariseth because of the word, by and by [quickly] he is offended" (Mt 13:21). When Elisha had first said, "Give unto the people, that they may eat," it was the language of faith. 2 Kings 4:41 seems to show that the people had been seeking the prophet in the extremity of their need. His own barrel of meal had probably run low, and it is likely he had been praying for its replenishment. And here was God's answer — yet in such a form or measure as to further test his faith! Elisha saw the hand of God in this gift and counted upon His making it sufficient to meet the needs of the crowd. Elisha regarded those twenty loaves as an "earnest" of greater bounties.

Do we regard such providences as "a token for good," or are we so wrapped up in the token itself that we look no further? It was a bold and courageous faith in Elisha; he was not afraid the Lord would put him to confusion and cause him to become a laughing-stock to the people. At first his faith was a general (yet sufficient) one in the character of God. Then it met with a rebuff from Gehazi, but he refused to be shaken. And now it seems to us that the Lord rewarded His servant's faith by giving him a definite word from Himself. The way to get more faith is to use what has already been given us (Lk 8:18), for God ever honors those who honor Him. Trust Him fully and He will then bestow assurance. The minister of Christ must not be deterred by the carnality and unbelief of those who ought to be the ones to strengthen his hands and cooperate with him. Alas, how many have let distrustful deacons quench their zeal by the difficulties and objections which they raise. How often the children of Israel opposed Moses and murmured against him, but "by faith . . . he endured, as seeing him who is invisible" (Heb 11:27).

Sixth, the Antitype of the Miracle

There is no doubt whatever in our minds that the above incident supplies the Old Testament foreshadowment of our Lord's miracle in feeding the multitude, and it is both interesting and instructive to compare and contrast the type with its antitype. Note, then, the following parallels: (1), in each case there was a crowd of hungry people; (2), Elisha took pity on them, and Christ had compassion on the needy multitude (Mt 14:14); (3), a few "loaves" formed the principal article of diet, and in each case they were barley ones (Jn 6:9); (4), in each case, the order went forth "give [not 'sell'] the people that they may eat" (cf. Mk 6:37); (5), in each case an unbelieving attendant raised objection (Jn 6:7); (6), Elisha fed the crowd through his servant (2 Ki 4:44) and Christ through His apostles (Mt 14:19); (7), in each case a surplus remained after the people had eaten (v. 44 and cf. Mt 14:20).

And now observe wherein Christ has the preeminence: (1), He fed a much larger company, over five thousand (Mk 14:21) instead of one hundred; (2), He employed fewer loaves — 5 (Mt 14:17), instead of twenty; (3), He supplied a richer feast, fish as well as bread; (4), He wrought by His own power.

Seventh, the Meaning of the Miracle

It will suffice if we just summarize what we have previously dwelt upon. (1) The servant of God who is faithful in giving out to others will not himself be kept on short rations. (2) The more one obtains from God, the more should he impart to the people: "Freely ye have received, freely give." (3) God ever makes His grace abound to those who are generous. (4) A true servant of God has implicit confidence in the divine character. (5) Though he encounters opposition, he refuses to be stumbled thereby. (6) Though other ministers ridicule him, he acts according to God's Word. (7) God does not fail him, but honors his trust.

Chapter 14

TENTH MIRACLE
NAAMAN THE LEPER

THE HEALING OF NAAMAN is the best known one of all the wonders wrought through Elisha. It has been made the subject of numerous sermons in the past, supplying as it does a very striking typical picture of salvation. Not in all its varied aspects — for salvation is many-sided — but as portraying the condition of him who is made its subject, his dire need because of the terrible malady of which he was the victim, the sovereign grace which met with him, the requirements he had to comply with, his self-will therein, and how his reluctance was overcome. Yet there is not a little in this incident which is offensive to our supercilious age, inclining present-day preachers to leave it alone, so that much that has been said about it in the past will be more or less new to the present generation. As it has pleased the Holy Spirit to enter into much more detail upon the attendant circumstances of this miracle, this will require us to give it a fuller consideration.

It is their spiritual import which renders the Old Testament Scriptures of such interest to us upon whom the ends of the ages are come: "For whatsoever things were written aforetime were written for our learning" (Ro 15:4). That which is set before us more abstractly in the epistles is rendered easier to understand by means of the concrete and personal illustrations supplied under the previous dispensations, when figures and symbols were employed more freely. Noah and his family in the ark preserved from the flood which swept away the world of the ungodly; the Hebrews finding security under the blood of the pascal lamb when the angel of death slew all the firstborn of the Egyptians; healing being conveyed by faith's look at the brazen serpent on the pole; the cities of refuge affording asylum to the manslayer who fled for refuge from the avenger of blood, are so many examples of simple yet graphic pre-figurations of different aspects of the redemption which is found in Christ Jesus. Another is before us here in 2 Kings 5.

Before taking up the spiritual meaning of what is recorded of Naaman, one thing mentioned about him deserves separate notice, and we will look at it now so that our main line of thought may not be broken into later on. In the opening verse of chapter five, it is stated that Naaman was "a great man with his master, and honour-able, because by him the LORD had given deliverance [victory] unto Syria." This teaches us that there can be no success in any sphere of life unless God gives it, for "the way of man is not in him-self: it is not in man that walketh to direct his steps" (Jer 10:23), still less to insure their outcome. "Except the LORD build the house, they labour in vain that build it [as was made evident when God brought to nought the lofty ambitions of those erecting the tower of Babel!]: except the LORD keep the city, the watchman waketh but in vain" (Ps 127:1) — as Belshazzar discovered, when the Medes surprised and overcame his sentinels and captured Babylon.

Not only can there be no success in any human undertaking un-less the Lord is pleased to prosper the same, but He exercises His own sovereignty in the instruments or agents employed in the carry-ing out of His purposes, whether it be in the communicating of blessings or the execution of judgments. It is therefore to be duly observed that it was not because Naaman was a good man that the Lord caused his military efforts to thrive; far from it, for he was an idolator, a worshiper of Rimmon. Moreover, not only was he a stranger to God spiritually but he was a leper, and therefore cere-monially unclean, shut out by the Mosaic law. From this we may learn that when the Most High is pleased to do so, He makes use of the wicked as well as the righteous — a truth which needs pressing on the attention of the world today. Temporal success is far from be-ing an evidence that the blessing of God rests upon either the person or the nation enjoying it. All men are in God's hands to employ as and where He pleases — as truly so in the political and military realms as in the churches.

First, the Subject of the Miracle

Six things (the number of man) are here recorded about Naa-man. (1) He was "captain of the host of the king of Syria." In modern language this would be commander-in-chief of the king's army. Whether or not he had risen from the ranks we cannot be sure, though the reference to his "valour" suggests that he had been promoted from a lower office. Whether that was so or not, he now occupied a position of prominence, being at the summit of his profession.

(2) He was "a great man with his master." It has been by no means always the case that the head of the military forces was greatly esteemed by his master. History records many instances where the reigning monarch has been jealous of the popularity enjoyed by the general, fearful in some cases that he would use his powerful influence against the interests of the throne. But it was quite otherwise in this case, for as the sequel goes on to show, the king of Syria was warmly devoted to the person of his military chieftain.

(3) "And honourable." Far from the king's slighting Naaman and keeping him in the background, he stood high in the royal favor. Naaman had furthered the interests of his kingdom securing notable victories for his forces, and his master was not slow to show his appreciation and reward his valorous general. The brilliant exploits of many a brave officer have passed unnoticed by the powers that be, but not so here.

(4) His military success is here directly ascribed to God, for our passage goes on to say, "by him the LORD had given deliverance unto Syria." The blessing of heaven had attended him and crowned his efforts, and therein he was favored above many. Not that this intimated he personally enjoyed the approbation of God, but that divine providence made use of him in accomplishing His will.

(5) He was naturally endowed with qualities which are highly esteemed among men, being possessed of great bravery and fortitude, for we are told, "he was also a mighty man in valour" — daring and fearless — and thus well equipped for his calling.

It might well be asked, What more could any man desire? Did he not possess everything which is most highly prized by the children of this world? What he not what they would designate "the darling of fortune," having all that the human heart could wish? He had, as men express it, "made good in life." He occupied a most enviable position. He possessed those traits which were admired by his fellows. He had served his country well and stood high in the king's regard and favor.

Even so there was a dark cloud on his horizon. There was something which not only thoroughly spoiled the present for him, but took away all hope for the future. For, (6) "he was a leper." Here was the tragic exception. Here was that which cast its awful shadow over everything else. He was the victim of a loathsome and incurable disease. He was a pitiful and repulsive object, with no prospect whatever of any improvement in his condition.

Yes, my reader, the highly-privileged and honored Naaman was a leper, and as such he portrayed what you are and what I am by nature. God's Word does not flatter man: it lays him in the dust — which is one reason why it is so unpalatable to the great majority of people. It is the Word of truth, and therefore instead of painting flattering pictures of human nature, it represents things as they actually are. Instead of lauding man, it abases him. Instead of speaking of the dignity and nobility of human nature, it declares it to be leprous — sinful, corrupt, depraved, defiled. Instead of eulogizing human progress, it insists that "every man at his best state is altogether vanity" (Ps 39:5). And when the Holy Scriptures define man's attitude toward and relationship with God, they insist that "There is none righteous, no, not one: There is none that understandeth, there is none that seeketh after God" (Ro 3:10-11). They declare that we are His enemies by our wicked works (Col 1:21), and that consequently we are under the condemnation and curse of God's law, and that His holy wrath abides on us (Jn 3:36).

The Word of truth declares that by nature all of us are spiritual lepers, foul and filthy, unfit for the divine presence: "being alienated from the life of God" (Eph 4:18). You may occupy a good position in this world, even an eminent station in the affairs of this life; you may have made good in your vocation and wrought praiseworthy achievements, by human standards; you may be honorable in the sight of your fellows, but how do you appear in the eyes of God? A leper, one whom His law pronounces unclean, one who is utterly unfit for His holy presence. That is the first outstanding thing; the dominant lesson taught by our present passage. As it was with Naaman, so it is with you: a vast difference between his circumstances and his condition. There was the horrible and tragic exception: "a great man . . . but a leper"!

We would not be faithful to our calling were we to glide over that in God's Word which is distasteful to proud flesh and blood. Nor would we be faithful to our readers if we glossed over their frightful and fatal natural condition. It is in their souls' interests they should face this humiliating and unpleasant fact: that in God's sight they are spiritual lepers. But we must individualize it. Have you, my reader, realized this fact in your own case? Have you seen yourself in God's light? Are you aware that your soul is suffering from a disease that neither you nor any human being can cure? It is so, whether you realize it or not. The Scriptures declare that from the sole of your foot to the crown of your head there is no soundness in you, yes, that in the sight of the holy one, you are a mass of "wounds, and bruises, and putrifying sores" (Is 1:6). Only as you penitently accept that divine verdict is there any hope for you.

All disease is both the fruit and the evidence of sin, as was plainly intimated to Israel. Under the Levitical law God might well have required separate purifications for every form of disease. But He did not, and thereby He displayed His tenderness and mercy. Had such a multiplicity of ceremonial observances been required it would have constituted an intolerable burden. He therefore singled out one disease as a standing object lesson, one that could not fail to be a fit representation and most effective symbol of sin. This disease was white leprosy, described with much minuteness of detail in Leviticus 13 and 14. Leprosy, then, was not only a real but a typical disease, corresponding in a most solemn and striking manner to that fearful malady — sin — with which we are infected from the center to the circumference of our being. While it is true that the type is only intelligible in the light of its antitype, the shadow in the presence of its substance, yet the former is often an aid to the understanding of the latter.

That the disease of leprosy was designed to convey a representation of the malady of sin appears from these considerations. (1) The ceremonial purification whereby the stain of leprosy was cleansed pointed to the Lord Jesus as making atonement for the cleansing of His people. (2) It was not a physician but the high priest who was the person specifically appointed to deal with the leper. (3) There was no prescribed remedy for it; it could only be cured by a direct miracle. (4) The leper was cut off from the dwelling place of God and the tabernacle of His congregation, being put "outside the camp." Thus it will be seen from these circumstances that leprosy was removed from the catalog of ordinary diseases, and had stamped upon it a peculiar and typical character. It was a visible sign of how God regarded the sinner: as one unsuited to the presence of Himself and His people. How unspeakably blessed then, to discover that, though not the first He performed, yet the first individual miracle of Christ's recorded in the New Testament is His healing of the leper (Mt 8:2-4).

For the particular benefit of young preachers and for the general instruction of all, we will close this chapter with an outline.

1. *Leprosy has an insignificant beginning.* To the nonobservant eye it is almost imperceptible. It starts as "a rising, a scab, or bright spot" (Lev 13:2). It is so trivial that usually no attention is paid to it. Little or no warning is given of the fearful havoc it will work. Was it not thus with the entrance of sin into this world? To the natural man the eating of the forbidden fruit by our first parents appears a very small matter, altogether incommensurate with the awful effects it produced. The unregenerate discern not that sin is deserving of and exposes them to eternal destruction. They regard it as a trifle, unduly magnified by preachers.

2. *Leprosy is inherited.* It is a communicable disease. It poisons the blood, and so is readily transmitted from parent to child. It is so with sin. "By one man sin entered into the world, and death by sin; and so death passed upon all men, for that all sinned" (Ro 5:12). None has escaped this dreadful entail. "Behold, I was shapen in iniquity; and in sin did my mother conceive me" (Ps 51:5) is equally true of every member of Adam's race. None is born spiritually pure; depravity is communicated in every instance from sire to son, from mother to daughter. Human nature was corrupted at its fountainhead, and therefore all the streams issuing therefrom are polluted.

3. *Leprosy works insidiously and almost imperceptibly.* It is a disease which is attended by little pain; only in its later stages, when its horrible effects reveal themselves, is it unmistakeably manifest. And thus it is with that most awful of all maladies. Sin is subtle and sly, so that for the most part its subjects are quite unconscious of its workings. Hence we read of "the deceitfulness of sin" (Heb 3:13). It is not until the Spirit convicts, that one is made aware of the awfulness and extent of sin, and begins to feel "the plague of his own heart" (1 Ki 8:38). Yes, it is not until a person is born again that he learns his very nature is depraved. Only as the

sinner grows old in sin does he discover what a fearful hold his lusts have upon him.

4. *Leprosy spreads with deadly rapidity.* Though it begins with certain spots in the skin which are small at first, they gradually increase in size; slowly but surely the whole body is affected. The corruption extends inwardly while it spreads outwardly, vitiating even the bones and marrow. Like a locust on the twig of a tree, it continues eating its way through the flesh, till nothing but the skeleton is left. This is what sin has done in man; it has corrupted every part of his being, so that he is totally depraved. No faculty, no member of his complex constitution has escaped defilement. Heart, mind, will, conscience — spirit and soul and body — are equally poisoned. "I know that in me (that is, in my flesh,) dwelleth no good thing" (Ro 7:18).

5. *Leprosy is highly infectious.* Inherited inwardly, contagious outwardly. The leper communicates his horrible disease to others wherever he goes. That is why he was quarantined under the Mosaic law, and when he saw anyone approaching, he was required to give warning by crying, "Unclean, unclean." The analogy continues to hold good. Sin is a malady which is not only inherited by nature, but it is developed by association with the wicked. "Evil communications corrupt good manners" (1 Co 15:33). That is why the righteous are bidden, "Enter not into the path of the wicked, and go not in the way of evil men. Avoid it [as a plague], pass not by it, turn from it, and pass away" (Pr 4:4-5). Such repetition bespeaks our danger and intimates how slow we are to be warned against it. "Shun profane and vain babblings: . . . their word will eat as doth a canker" (2 Ti 2:16-17).

6. *Leprosy is peculiarly loathsome.* There is nothing more repellent to the eye than to look upon one on whom this awful disease has obtained firm hold. Except with the most callous, despite one's pity, he or she is obliged to turn away from such a nauseating sight with a shudder. Under Judaism there was no physician who ministered to the leper, and hence it is said of his putrifying sores that "they have not been closed, neither bound up, neither mollified with ointment" (Is 1:6). The leper may well appropriate to himself the language of Job, "All my inward [or 'intimate'] friends abhorred me: and they whom I love are turned against me" (19:19). All of which is a figure of how infinitely more repellent is the sinner in the sight of Him who is "of purer

eyes than to behold evil, and canst not look on iniquity" (Hab 1: 13).

7. *Leprosy is a state of living death.* There is a discoloration of the skin, loss of sensation, and spreading ulceration. The fingers, toes, and nose atrophy. Vision is impaired and sometimes blindness results. As one has said, "The leper is a walking sepulchre." And this is precisely what sin is: a state of spiritual death — a living on the natural side of existence, but dead to all things spiritual. Thus we find an apostle declaring "she that liveth in pleasure is dead while she liveth" (1 Ti 5:6). The natural man is "dead in trespasses and sins" (Eph 2:1); he is alive sinward and worldward but dead Godward.

8. *Leprosy was dealt with by banishment.* No leper was allowed to remain in the congregation of Israel. The terms of the Mosaic law were most explicit: "he shall dwell alone; without the camp shall his habitation be" (Lev 13:46). In the center of the camp was Jehovah's abode, and around His tabernacle were grouped His covenant people. From them the leper was excluded. How rigidly that was enforced may be seen from the fact than even Miriam, the sister of Moses (Num 12:10-15), and Uzziah the king (2 Ki 15:5) were not treated as exceptions. The leper was deprived of all political and ecclesiastical privileges, dealt with as one dead, excluded from fellowship. It is a visible sign of how God regards the sinner, for sin shuts out from His presence (Is 59:2; 2 Th 1:9).

9. *Leprosy makes its victim an object of shame.* It could not be otherwise. Robbing its subject of the bloom of health, replacing it with that which is hideous. Excluding him from God and His people, placing him outside the pale of decency. Consequently the leper. was required to carry about with him every mark of humiliation and distress. The law specified that "his clothes shall be rent, and his head bare, and he shall put a covering upon his upper lip, and shall cry, Unclean, unclean" (Lev 13:45). What a spectacle! What a picture of abject misery! What a solemn portrayal of the natural man! Sin has marred the features of God's image, in whose likeness man was originally made, and stamped upon him the marks of the devil.

10. *Leprosy was incurable so far as the Old Testament was concerned.* One really stricken with this disease was beyond all human aid. The outcome was inevitably fatal. Modern medical science has reported some cured cases; and by lengthy treatment with sul-

fone drugs, the tubercular form is usually arrestable. But there is no sure cure; research still goes on. In like manner sin is beyond human cure; it cannot be eradicated. No power of will or effort of mind can cope with it. Neither legislation nor reformation is of any avail. Education and culture are equally impotent. Sooner can the Ethiopian change his skin or the leopard his spots than those do good who are accustomed to do evil (Jer 13:23).

But what is beyond the power of man is possible with God. Where the science of the ages stands helpless, the Saviour manifests His sufficiency. "He is able also to save them to the uttermost that come unto God by him" (Heb 7:25). To the leper He said, "I will; be thou clean. And immediately his leprosy was cleansed" (Mt 8: 3). Blessed, thrice blessed is that! In view of the ten points above, how profoundly thankful every Christian should be that "the blood of Jesus Christ his Son cleanseth us from all sin" (1 Jn 1:7).

Chapter 15

TENTH MIRACLE
A LITTLE JEWISH MAID

IN THE PRECEDING ARTICLE our attention was confined to
the subject of this miracle, namely Naaman, the Syrian, who was
stricken with the horrible disease of leprosy — a striking type of the
natural man, corrupted by sin, unfit for the presence of a holy God.
The most fearful thing of all was that leprosy was incurable by the
hand of man. Naaman was quite incapable of ridding himself of his
terrible burden. No matter what plan he followed, what attempts
he made, no help or relief was to be obtained from self-efforts.
(Have you realized the truth of this, in its spiritual application, my
reader? There is no deliverance from sin, no salvation for your soul
by anything that you can do.) There was no physician in Syria
who could effect a cure; no matter what fee Naaman offered, what
quack he applied to, none was of any avail. And such is the case of
each of us by nature. Our spiritual malady lies deeper than any human hand can reach; our condition is too desperate for any religious practitioner to cure. Man can no more deliver himself, or
his fellows, from the guilt and defilement of sin than he can create
a world.

Most solemnly was the fact shadowed forth under the system of
Judaism. No remedy was provided for this fearful disease under the
Mosaic law; no directions were given to Israel's priesthood to make
use of any application, either outward or inward. The leper's healing was left entirely to God. All the high priest of the Hebrews could
do was to examine closely the various symptoms of the complaint,
have the leper excluded from his fellows, and leave him to the disposal of the Lord. Whether the sufferer was healed or not, whether
he lived or died, was wholly to be decided by the Almighty. So it is
in grace. There is no possible salvation for any sinner except at the

hands of God. There is no other possible alternative, no other prospect before the sinner than to die a wretched death and enter a hopeless eternity unless distinguishing mercy intervenes, unless a sovereign God is pleased to work a miracle of grace within him. It is entirely a matter of His will and power. Again we ask, do you realize that fact, my reader? God is your Maker, and He is the determiner of your destiny. You are clay in His hands to do with as He pleases.

Second, the Contributor to the Miracle

"And the Syrians had gone out by companies, and had brought away captive out of the land of Israel a little maid; and she waited on Naaman's wife" (2 Ki 5:2). In one of the many periods in which the name of Jehovah was blasphemed among the heathen, through the unfaithfulness of His ancient people, a little Jewish maid was taken captive by the Syrians. In the dividing of the spoils, she fell into the hands of Naaman the commander of the Syrian forces. Observe the series of contrasts between them. He was a Gentile, she a hated Jew. He was a "great man," she but "a little maid." He was "Naaman," she was left unnamed. He was "captain of the host of Syria," while she was captive in the enemy's territory. But he was a leper; while strange to say, she was made a contributing instrument unto his healing. It has ever been God's way to make use of the despised and feeble, and often in circumstances which seem strange to human wisdom. Let us take note how this verse teaches us a most important lesson in connection with the mysteries of divine providence.

"And had brought away captive out of the land of Israel a little maid." Visualize the scene. One fair morning the peace of Samaria was rudely broken. The tramp of a hostile army was heard in the land. A cruel foe was at hand. The Syrians had invaded the country, and heaven was silent. No scourge from God smote the enemy; instead, he was permitted to carry away some of the covenant people. Among the captives was "a little maid." Ah, that may mean little to us today, but it meant much to certain people at that day. A home was rendered desolate! Seek to enter into the feelings of her parents as their young daughter was ruthlessly snatched from them. Think of the anguish of her poor mother, wondering what would become of her. Think of her grief-stricken father in his helplessness, unable to rescue her. Endeavor to contemplate what would be the state of mind of the little girl herself as she was carried away by heathen to a strange country. Bring before your mind's eye the whole painful incident until it lives before you.

Do you not suppose, dear friend, that both the maid and her parents were greatly perplexed? Must they not have been sorely tried by this mysterious providence? Why, oh why? must have been asked by them a hundred times. Why had God allowed the joy of their home to be shattered? If the maiden had reflected at all, must she have thought her lot strange. Why was she, a favored daughter of Abraham, now a servant in Naaman's household? Why this enforced separation from her parents? Why this cruel captivity? Such questions she might have asked at first, and asked in vain. Ah, does the reader perceive the point we are leading up to? It is this: God had a good reason for this trial. He was shaping things in His own, unfathomable way for the outworking of His good and wise purpose. Nothing happens in this world by mere chance. A predestinating God has planned every detail in our lives. "My times are in thy hand" (Ps 31:15). He "hath determined the times before appointed, and the bounds of their habitation" (Ac 17:26). What a resting place for our poor hearts does that grand truth supply!

It was God who directed that this little maid of Israel should become a member of Naaman's household. And why? That she might be a link in the chain which ended not only in the healing of his leprosy, but also most probably in the salvation of his soul. Here then is the important lesson for us to take to heart from this incident. Here is the light which it casts upon the mysterious ways of God in providence: He has a wise and good reason behind each of the perplexing and heart-exercising trials which enter our lives. The particular reason for each trial is frequently concealed from us at the time it comes upon us; if it were not, there would be no room for the exercise of faith and patience in it. But just as surely as God had a good reason for allowing the happiness of this Hebrew household to be darkened, so He has in ordering whatever sorrow has entered your life. It was the sequel which made manifest God's gracious design; and it is for the sequel you must quietly and trustfully wait. This incident is among the things recorded in the Old Testament "for our learning, that we through patience and comfort of the scriptures might have hope" (Ro 15:4).

"And she said unto her mistress, Would God my lord were with the prophet that is in Samaria! for he would recover him of his leprosy" (2 Ki 5:3). This is surely most striking and blessed. It would have been natural for this young girl to have yielded to a spirit of enmity against the man who had snatched her away from her own home, to have entertained hatred for him, and to have been maliciously pleased that he was so afflicted in his body. The fall not only alienated man from God but it radically changed his attitude toward his fellowmen, evidenced at a very early date by Cain's murder of his brother Abel. Human depravity has poisoned every relationship; in their unregenerate state God's own people are described as "hateful, and hating one another" (Titus 3:3). But instead of cherishing ill feelings against her captor, this little maid was concerned about his condition and solicitous about his welfare. Apparently she had been brought up in the nurture of the Lord, and the seeds planted by godly parents now sprang up and bore fruit in her young life. Beautiful is it to here behold grace triumphing over the flesh.

How this little maid puts us to shame! How sinfully have we conducted ourselves when the providence of God crossed our wills and brought us into situations for which we had no liking! What risings of rebellion within us, what complaining at our circumstances. So far from being a blessing to those with whom we came into contact, we were a stumblingblock to them. Has not both writer and reader much cause to bow his head in shame at the recollection of such grievous failures! Was not this child placed in uncongenial circumstances and a most trying situation? Yet there was neither murmuring against God nor bitterness toward her captor. Instead, she bore faithful testimony to the God of Israel and was moved with compassion toward her leprous master. What a beautiful exemplification of the sufficiency of divine grace! She remembered the Lord in the house of her bondage and spoke of His servant the prophet. How we need to turn this into earnest prayer, that we too may glorify the Lord "in the fires" (Is 24:15).

No position would seem more desolate than this defenseless maiden in the house of her proud captors, and no situation could promise fewer openings for usefulness. But though her opportunities were limited, she made the most of them. She despised not the day of small things, but sought to turn it to advantage. She did not conclude it was useless for her to open her mouth, nor argue that an audience of only one person was not worth addressing. No, in a simple but earnest manner, she proclaimed the good news that there was salvation for even the leper, for the very name "Elisha" meant "the salvation of God."

"And one went in, and told his lord, saying, Thus and thus said the maid that is of the land of Israel" (2 Ki 5:4). A very incidental and apparently trivial statement is this, yet being a part of God's eternal truth it is not to be passed over lightly and hurriedly. We are ever the losers by such irreverent treatment of the Word. There is nothing meaningless in that Holy volume; each single verse in it sparkles with beauty if we view it in the right light and attentively survey it. It is so here.

First, this verse informs us that the little maid's words to her mistress did not pass unheeded. They might have done so, humanly speaking, for it would be quite natural for those about her — a mere child, a foreigner in their midst — to have paid no attention to her remarks. Even had they done so, surely such a statement as she had made must have sounded like foolish boasting. If the best physicians in Syria were helpless in the presence of leprosy, who would credit that a man of another religion, in despised Samaria, should be able to heal him! But strange as it may seem, her words were heeded.

Second, in this we must see the hand of God. "The hearing ear, and the seeing eye, the LORD hath made even both of them" (Pr 20: 12) — true alike both physically and spiritually. Yet how little is this realized today, when the self-sufficiency of man is proclaimed on every side and the operations of the Most High are so much ignored. All around us are those who pay no heed to the declarations of Holy Writ and who perceive no beauty in Christ that they should desire Him. Who then has given to thee an ear that responds to the truth and an eye that perceives its divine origin? And every real Christian will answer, The God of all grace. As it was the Lord who opened the heart of Lydia that she "took unto her [Greek] the things which were spoken" (Ac 16:14), so He caused those about her to listen to the words of this little maid. Ah, my reader, make no mistake upon this point: the most faithful sermon from the pulpit falls upon deaf ears unless the Holy Spirit operates; whereas the simplest utterance of a child can become effectual through God.

Third, this made manifest the effect of the maid's words upon her mistress. She communicated it to another, and this other went in and acquainted the king of the same. Thus 2 Kings 5:4 reveals to us one of the links in the chain that eventually drew Naaman to Elisha and resulted in his healing. It also shows how our words are heard and often reported to others, thereby both warning and encouraging us of the power of the tongue. This will be made fully manifest in the day to come. Nothing which has been done for God's glory will be lost. When the history of this world is completed, God will make known before an assembled universe what was spoken for Him (Mal 3:16; Lk 12:3).

Finally, we are shown here how God is pleased to make use of "little" and despised things. A maid in captivity. Who would expect her to do service for the Lord? Who would be inclined to listen to her voice? Her age, her nationality, her position were all against her. Yet because she used her opportunity and bore witness to her mistress, her simple message reached the ears of the king of Syria. The Lord grant us to be faithful wherever He has placed us.

"And the king of Syria said, Go to, go, and I will send a letter unto the king of Israel" (2 Ki 5:5). Here also we must see the hand of the Lord. Had He not worked upon the king too, the message would have produced no effect on his majesty. Why should that monarch pay any attention to the utterance of a kitchen maid? Ah, my reader, when God has a design of mercy, He works at both ends of the line. He not only gives the message to the messenger, but He opens the heart of its recipient to heed it. He who bade Philip take a journey into the desert, also prepared the Ethiopian eunuch for his approach (Ac 8:26-31). He who overcame Peter's scruples to go unto the Gentiles, also inclined Cornelius and his household to be "present before God, to hear all things that were commanded him of God (Ac 10:33). "The king's heart is in the hand of the Lord, as the rivers of water: he turneth it whithersoever he will" (Pr 21:1). Strikingly did that receive illustration here. Yet though God wrought, in the instance now before us, it did not please Him to use the king as an instrument.

Third, the Misapprehension of the Miracle

"Go to, go, and I will send a letter unto the king of Israel" (2 Ki 5:5). As will appear in the sequel, the Lord had a reason for permitting the king to act this way. Poor Naaman was now misdirected by the carnal wisdom of his master. The little maid had said nothing about "the king of Israel," but had specified "the prophet that is in Samaria." It would have been much better for the leper to have heeded more closely her directions; he would have been spared needless trouble. Yet how true to life is the picture here presented. How often is the sinner, who has been awakened to his desperate condition, wrongly counselled and turned aside to cisterns which hold no water! Rarely does a troubled soul find relief at once. More frequently his experience is like that of the old woman in Mark 5:26 who tried "many physicians" in vain before she came to Christ; or like the prodigal son when he "began to be in want" and went and joined himself to a citizen of the far country and got nothing better than "the husks that the swine did eat" (Lk 15:14-18), before he sought his father.

"And he departed, and took with him ten talents of silver, and six thousand pieces of gold, and ten changes of raiment" (2 Ki 5:5). It has been computed that the value of these things would be at least seventy thousand dollars today. The Hebrew maid has said nothing of the need for silver and gold; but knowing nothing of the grace of God, Naaman was prepared to pay handsomely for his healing. Again we exclaim, how true to life is this picture. How many there are who think the "gift of God" may be purchased (Ac 8:20) — if not literally with money, yet by works of righteousness and religious performances. And even where that delusion has been removed, another equally erroneous often takes its place: the idea that a heavily-burdened conscience, a deep sense of personal unworthiness, accompanied by sighs and tears and groans, is the required qualification for applying to Christ and the ground of peace before God. Fatal mistake. "Without money and without price" (Is 55:1) excludes all frames, feelings, and experiences, as truly as it does the paying of a priest.

Fourth, the Foil of the Miracle

"And he brought the letter to the king of Israel, saying, Now when this letter is come unto thee, behold, I have therewith sent Naaman my servant to thee, that thou mayest recover him of his leprosy. And it came to pass, when the king of Israel read the letter, that he rent his clothes, and said, Am I God, to kill and to make alive, that this man doth send unto me to recover a man of his leprosy? wherefore consider, I pray you, and see how he seeketh a quarrel against me" (2 Ki 5:6-7).

How this made manifest the apostate condition of Israel at that time and shows why God had moved the Syrians to oppress them! There was some excuse for the king of Syria acting as he did, for he was a heathen; but there was none for the king of Israel. Instead of getting down on his knees and spreading this letter before the Lord, as a later king of Israel did (Is 37:14), he acted like an infidel; instead of seeing in this appeal an opportunity for Jehovah to display His grace and glory, he thought only of himself.

What a contrast was there here between the witness of the little maid and the conduct of the king of Israel. Yet his meanness served as a foil to set off her noble qualities. She was in lowly and distressing circumstances, whereas he was a monarch upon the throne. Yet she was concerned about the welfare of her master, while he thought only of himself and kingdom. She had implicit confidence in God and spoke of His prophet, whereas neither God nor His servant had any place in the king's mind. Some may think from a first reading of verse 7 that the king's language sounds both humble and pious, but a pondering of it indicates it was but the utterance of pride and unbelief. Knowing not the Lord, he saw in this appeal of Benhadad's nothing but a veiled threat to humiliate him, and he was filled with fear. Had he sought God, his terror would have soon been quieted and a way of relief shown him; but he was a stranger to Him, and evidenced no faith even in the idols he worshiped. Yet this made the more illustrious the marvel of the miracle which followed.

Perhaps the Christian reader is tempted to congratulate himself that there is nothing for him in verse 7. If so, such complacency may be premature. Are you quite sure, friend, that there has been no parallel in your past conduct to that of Israel's king? Were you never guilty of the thing wherein he failed? When some heavy demand was made upon you, some real test or trial confronted you, did you never respond by saying, I am not sufficient for this; it is quite beyond my feeble powers? Possibly you imagined that was a pious acknowledgment of your weakness, when in reality it was a voicing of your unbelief. True, the Christian is impotent in himself; so, too is the non-Christian. Is then the saint no better off than the ungodly? If the Christian continues impotent, the fault is his. God's grace is sufficient, and His strength is made perfect in our weakness. Feeble knees and hands bring no glory to God. He has bidden us, "Be strong in the Lord, and in the power of his might"

(Eph 6:10). Then cease imitating this defeatist attitude of Israel's king, and, "Be strong in the grace that is in Christ Jesus" (2 Ti 2:1).

Chapter 16

TENTH MIRACLE
PRIDE IN THE WAY

IN THE PREVIOUS ARTICLE we emphasized the secret operations of God in inclining one and another to pay attention to the message of the little Hebrew maid. It was God who gave the hearing ear to both Naaman's wife and the king of Syria. Perhaps some have thought that such was not the case with the king of Israel! No, it was not. Instead of sharing her confidence and cooperating with her effort, he was skeptical and antagonistic. Therein we may perceive God's sovereignty. He does not work in all alike, being absolutely free to do as He pleases. He opens the eyes of some but leaves others in their blindness. This is God's high and awful prerogative: "Therefore hath he mercy on whom he will have mercy, and whom he will he hardeneth" (Ro 9:18). This is what supplies the key to God's dealings with men and which explains the course of evangelical history. Clearly is that solemn principle exemplified in the previous chapter, and we should be unfaithful as an expositor if we deliberately ignored it as so many now do.

"And it came to pass when the king of Israel had read the letter, that he rent his clothes, and said, Am I God, to kill and to make alive, that this man doth send unto me to recover a man of his leprosy?" (2 Ki 5:7). So utterly skeptical was Jehoram that he considered it not worthwhile even to send for Elisha and confer with him. The prophet meant nothing to Israel's unbelieving king, and therefore he slighted him. Perhaps this strikes the reader as strange, for the previous miracles Elisha had wrought must have been well known. One would have thought his restoring of a dead child to life would thoroughly authenticate him as an extraordinary man of God. But did not the Lord Jesus publicly raise a dead man to life?

130

And yet within a few days both the leaders of the nation and the common people clamored for His crucifixion! And is it any different in our day? Have we not witnessed providential marvels, divine interpositions both of mercy and judgment? and what effect have they had on our evil generation? Jehoram's conduct is easily accounted for: "the carnal mind is enmity against God" (Ro 8:7), and that enmity evidenced itself by his slighting God's accredited servant.

"And it was so, when Elisha the man of God had heard that the king of Israel had rent his clothes, that he went to the king, saying, Wherefore has thou rent thy clothes? let him come now to me, and he shall know that there is a prophet in Israel" (2 Ki 5:8). The slighted Elisha pocketed his pride and communicated with the king, rightly concluding that his own feelings were not worth considering where the glory of God was concerned.

> Naaman came into the land of Israel, expecting relief from a prophet of the God of Israel, and Elisha would by no means have him go back disappointed, lest he should conclude that Jehovah was like the gods of the nations, and as unable to do good or evil as they were. On the contrary he would have it known that God has "a prophet in Israel" by whom He performed such cures as none of the heathen prophets, priests, or physicians could effect; and which were far beyond all the power of the mightiest monarchs (Scott).

The "counsel of the LORD, that shall stand," whatever devices were in Jehoram's heart to the contrary (Pr 19:21).

"The righteous are bold as a lion." Elisha not only rebuked the king for his unbelieving fears but summarily gave him instructions concerning Naaman. However unwelcome might be his interference, that deterred him not. The real servant of God does not seek to please men, but rather to execute the commission he has received from on high. It is true that the prophets, like the apostles, were endowed with extraordinary powers, and therefore they are not in all things models for us today; nevertheless the gospel minister is not to cringe before anyone. It is his duty to denounce unbelief and to proclaim that the living God is ever ready to honor those who honor Him and to work wonders in response to genuine faith. As God overruled the king of Syria's misdirecting of Naaman, so He now overcame the skepticism of the king of Israel by moving him to respond to Elisha's demand — thereby demonstrating that the words of the little maid were no idle boast and her confidence in God no misplaced one.

"So Naaman came with his horses and with his chariot, and stood at the door of the house of Elisha" (2 Ki 5:9). Naaman before the prophet's abode may be regarded as a picture of the natural man in his sins, not yet stripped of his self-righteousness, nor aware that he is entirely dependent on divine mercy, having no title or claim to receive any favor at God's hand. The fact that he rode in a chariot mitigated his terrible condition not one iota. No matter how rich the apparel that covered his body, though it might hide from human view his loathsome disease, it availed nothing for the removal of it. And as the valuables he had brought with him could not procure his healing, neither can the cultivation of the most noble character nor the performance of the most praiseworthy conduct in human esteem merit the approbation of God. Salvation is wholly of divine grace and cannot be earned by the creature: "Not by works of righteousness which we have done, but according to his mercy he saved us, by the washing of regeneration, and renewing of the Holy Ghost; which he shed on us abundantly through Jesus Christ our Saviour" (Titus 3:5-6).

However much it might be in accord with the principles and sentiments which regulate fallen human nature, there was surely something most incongruous in the scene now before us. Here was a poor creature stricken with a most horrible disease, and yet we behold him seated in a chariot. Here was one smitten by a malady no physician could heal, surrounded by official pomp. Here was one entirely dependent upon the divine bounty, yet one whose horses were laden with silver and gold. Do we not behold in him, then, a representative not only of the natural man in his sins, but one filled with a sense of his own importance and bloated with pride! Such is precisely the case with each of us by nature. Totally depraved though we be, alienated from God, criminals condemned by His holy law, our minds at enmity with Him, dead in trespasses and sins, yet until a miracle of grace is wrought within and the abcess of our pride is lanced, we are puffed up with self-righteousness, refuse to acknowledge we deserve anything but eternal punishment, and imagine we are entitled to God's favorable regard.

Not only does Naaman here fitly portray the self-importance of the natural man while unregenerate, but as hinted above he also illustrates the fact that the sinner imagines he can gain God's approbation and purchase his salvation. The costly things which the Syrian had brought with him were obviously designed to ingratiate himself in the eyes of the prophet and pay for his cure. Following such a policy was of course quite natural, and therefore it shows what is the native thought of every man. He supposes that a dutiful regard of religious performances will obtain for him the favorable notice of God, that his fastings and prayers, church-attendance and contributing to its upkeep, will more than counterbalance his demerits. Such an insane idea is by no means confined to Buddhists and Romanists but is common to the whole human family. It is for this reason we have to be assured, "By grace are ye saved through faith; and that not of yourselves: it is the gift of God: not of works, lest any man should boast" (Eph 2:8-9). Spiritually speaking, every man is bankrupt, a pauper, and salvation is entirely gratis, a matter of charity.

"But the natural man receiveth not the things of the Spirit of God: for they are foolishness unto him: neither can he know them, because they are spiritually discerned" (1 Co 2:14). This is true alike of the most cultured and the thoroughly illiterate. No amount of education or erudition fits one for the apprehension of spiritual things. Man is blind, and his eyes must be opened before he can perceive either the glory of God and His righteous claims or his own wretchedness and deep needs. Not until a miracle of grace humbles his heart will he take himself to the throne of grace in his true character; not until the Holy Spirit works effectually within him will he come to Christ as an empty-handed beggar.

It is recorded that a famous artist met with a poor tramp and was so impressed with his woebegone appearance and condition that he felt he would make an apt subject for a drawing. He gave the tramp a little money and his card and promised to pay him well if he would call at his house on the following day and sit while he drew his picture. The next morning the tramp arrived, but the artist's intention was defeated. The tramp had washed and shaved and so spruced himself that he was scarcely recognizable!

Similarly does the natural man act when he first attempts to respond to the gospel call. Instead of coming to the Lord just as he is in all his want and woe, as one who is lost and undone, he supposes he must first make himself more presentable by a process of reformation. Thus he busies himself in mending his ways, improving his conduct, and performing pious exercises, unaware that Christ "came not to call the righteous, but sinners to repentance" — to take their place in the dust before Him. What we have just been dwelling upon receives striking illustration in the chapter before us. Instead of sending Naaman directly to Elisha, Benhadad gave him a letter of introduction to the king of Israel; and instead of casting himself on the mercy of the prophet, he sent a costly fee to pay for the healing of his commander-in-chief. We have seen the futility of his letter — the effect it had upon its recipient; now we are to behold how his lavish outlay of wealth produced no more favorable response from Elisha. Naaman had to learn the humiliating truth that, where divine grace is concerned, the millionaire stands on precisely the same level as the pauper.

Fifth, the Requirement of the Miracle

"And Elisha sent a messenger unto him, saying, Go and wash in Jordan seven times, and thy flesh shall come again to thee, and thou shalt be clean" (2 Ki 5:10). As the representative of Him who deigned to wash the feet of His disciples, the minister of the gospel must not decline the most menial service nor despise the poorest person. Elisha has set us an example of both, for he scorned not to minister to the physical needs of Elijah by washing his hands (3:11), and refused not to help the impoverished widow (4:2). On the other hand, the servant of Christ is to be no sycophant, toadying to those of affluence; nor is he to feed the pride of the self-important. From the sequel it is evident Naaman considered that he, as a "great man," was entitled to deference, and probably felt that the prophet ought to consider a favor or honor was now being shown him. But, officially, Elisha was an ambassador of the King of kings; and with becoming dignity, he let Naaman know that he was at no man's beck and call, though he failed not to inform him of the way in which healing was to be obtained.

"And Elisha sent a messenger unto him, saying, Go and wash in Jordan seven times, and thy flesh shall come again to thee, and thou shalt be clean." Here we see no servile obeisance nor owning of the mightiness of Naaman. The prophet did not even greet him, nor so much as go out of his house to meet him in person. Instead, he sent him a message by a servant. Ah, my reader, God is no respecter of persons, nor should His ministers be. Incalculable harm has been wrought in churches by pastors pandering to those in high places, for not only are the haughty injured thereby, but the lowly are stumbled; and in consequence, the Holy Spirit is grieved and quenched.

God will not tolerate any parading of fleshly distinctions before Him: "That no flesh should glory in his presence" (1 Co 1:29) is the unrepealable decision. The most eminent and gifted of this world are due no more consideration from the Most High than the most lowly, for "there is no difference: For all have sinned and come short of the glory of God" (Ro 3:22-23). All alike have broken the law; all alike are guilty before the supreme judge; all alike must be saved by sovereign grace, if they be saved at all.

But there is another way in which we may regard the prophet's conduct on this occasion; not only did he maintain his official dignity, but he evidenced personal humility and prudence, having his eye fixed on the glory of God. It is not that he was indifferent to Naaman's welfare. No, the fact that he sent his servant out to him with the needful directions evidenced the contrary. But Elisha knew full well that the all-important thing was not the messenger, but the message. It mattered nothing who delivered the message — himself or his servant; but it mattered everything that the God-given word should be faithfully communicated. Elisha knew full well that Naaman's expectation lay in himself, so like a true "man of God" he directed attention away from himself. What a needed lesson for us in this person-exalting day. How much better would preachers serve souls and honor their Master if, thus hidden, they occupied them with the gospel instead of with themselves. It was in this self-effacing spirit that Paul rebuked the person-worshipping Corinthians when he said, "Who then is Paul, and who is Apollos, but ministers by whom ye believed?" (1 Co 3:5). So too our Lord's forerunner who styled himself "the voice [heard but not seen!] of one crying in the wilderness" (Jn 1:23).

What was the force of "Go wash in Jordan seven times"? Let us give first a general answer in the words of another.

When Naaman stood with his pompous retinue, and with all his silver and gold at the door of Elisha, he appears before us as a marked illustration of a sinner building on his own efforts after righteousness. He seemed furnished with all that the heart could desire, but in reality all his preparations were but a useless incumberance, and the prophet soon gave him to understand this. "Go wash" swept away all confidence in gold, silver, raiment, retinue, the king's letter, everything. It stripped Naaman of everything, and reduced him to his true condition as a poor defiled leper needing to be washed. It put no difference between the illustrious commander-in-chief of the hosts of Syria, and the poorest and meanest leper in all the coasts of Israel. The former could do nothing less; the latter needed nothing more. Wealth cannot remedy man's ruin, and poverty cannot interfere with God's remedy. Nothing that a man has done need keep him out of heaven; nothing that he can do will ever get him in. "Go wash" is the word in every case.

But let us consider this "Go wash" more closely and ponder it in the light of its connections. As one stricken with leprosy, Naaman pictures the natural man in his fallen estate. And what is his outstanding and distinguishing characteristic? Why, that he is a depraved creature, a sinner, a rebel against God. And what is sin? From the negative side, it is failure to submit to God's authority and be subject to His law; positively, it is the exercise of self-will, a determination to please myself; "we have turned every one to his own way" (Is 53:6). If then a sinner inquires of God's servant the way of recovery, what is the first and fundamental thing which needs to be told him? That self-will and self-pleasing must cease; that he must submit himself to the will of God. And that is only another way of saying that he must be converted, for "conversion" is a turning round, a right about-face. And in order for conversion, repentance is the essential requisite (Ac 3:19). And in its final analysis, "repentance" is taking sides with God against myself, judging myself, condemning myself, bowing my will to His.

Again, sin is not only a revolt against God, but a deification of self. It is a determination to gratify my own inclinations, it is saying, "I will be lord over myself." That was the bait which the serpent dangled before our first parents when he tempted Eve to eat of the forbidden fruit: "Ye shall be as gods" (Gen 3:5). Casting off allegiance to God, man assumed an attitude of independence and self-sufficience. Sin took possession of his heart; he became proud, haughty, self righteous. If, then, such a creature is to be recovered and restored to God, it must necessarily be by a process of humbling him. The first design of the gospel is to put down human pride, to lay man low before God. It was predicted by Isaiah when speaking of gospel times, "The lofty looks of man shall be humbled, and the haughtiness of men shall be bowed down" (2:11). And again, "every mountain and hill shall be made low: and the crooked shall be made straight" (40:4); and therefore did our Lord begin His Sermon on the Mount by saying, "Blessed are the poor in spirit: for their's is the kingdom of heaven" (Mt 5:3). That was the basic truth which the prophet pressed upon Naaman: that he must abase himself before the God of Israel.

"Go wash in Jordan seven times" was but another way of saying to the conceited Syrian, "God resisteth the proud, but giveth grace unto the humble. Submit yourselves therefore to God. . . . Cleanse your hands, ye sinners; and purify your hearts, ye double minded. Be afflicted, and mourn, and weep: let your laughter be turned to mourning, and your joy to heaviness. Humble yourselves in the sight of the Lord, and he shall lift you up" (Ja 4:6-10). Naaman must come down from off his "high horse" and take his proper place before the Most High. Naaman must descend from his "chariot" and evidence a lowly spirit. Naaman must "wash," or "bathe" as the word is often translated, in the waters of the Jordan; not once or twice but no less than seven times, and thus completely renounce self. And the requirement which God made of Naaman, my reader, is precisely the same as His demand upon you, upon me: pride has to be mortified, self-will relinquished, self-righteousness repudiated. Have we complied with this? Have we renounced self-pleasing and surrendered to the divine scepter? Have we given ourselves to the Lord (2 Co 8:5) to be ruled by Him? If not, we have never been savingly converted.

In its ultimate significance, the "Go wash in Jordan seven times" had a typical import, and in the light of the New Testament there is no difficulty whatever in perceiving what that was. There is one provision, and one only, which the amazing grace of God and the wondrous love of His Son has made for the healing of spiritual lepers. It is that blessed "fountain" which has been opened for sin and for uncleanness (Zec 13:1). That holy "fountain" had its rise at Calvary, when from the pierced side of Christ "forthwith came there out blood and water" (Jn 19:34). That wondrous "fountain" which can cleanse the foulest was provided at the incalculable cost of the crucifixion of Immanuel, and hence the washing in "Jordan" which speaks of a point, beyond which there is no return. Here, then, dear friend, is the evangelical significance of what has been before us. If you have been made conscious of your depravity, ready to deny self, willing to humble yourself into the dust before God, here is the divine provision: a bath into which you may plunge by faith, and thereby obtain proof that "the blood of Jesus Christ his Son cleanseth us from all sin" (1 Jn 1:7). If by grace you have already done so, then join the writer in exclaiming, "Unto him that loved us, and washed us from our sins in his own blood . . . to him be glory and dominion for ever and ever. Amen" (Rev 1:5-6).

Chapter 17

TENTH MIRACLE
TOO SIMPLE A REMEDY

IN OUR LAST CHAPTER we dwelt mainly upon the requirement which was made upon Naaman when he reached the prophet's abode: "Go and wash in Jordan seven times," seeking to supply answers to, Why was he so enjoined? What was the implication in his case? What bearing has such a demand upon men generally today? What is its deeper significance?

We saw that it was a requirement which revealed the uselessness and worthlessness of Naaman's attempt to purchase his healing. We showed that it was a requirement which demanded the setting aside of his own will and submitting himself to the will of Israel's God. We pointed out that it was a requirement which insisted that he must get down off his "high horse" (descend from his chariot), humbling and abasing himself. We intimated that it was a requirement which, typically, pointed to that amazing provision of the grace of God for spiritual lepers, namely, the "fountain opened . . . for sin and for uncleanness" (Zec 13:1), and by which alone defilement can be cleansed and iniquities blotted out.

"But Naaman was wroth, and went away, and said, Behold, I thought, He will surely come out to me, and stand, and call on the name of the LORD his God, and strike his hand over the place, and recover the leper" (2 Ki 5:11). In his own country he was a person of consequence, a "great man," commander-in-chief of the army, standing high in the favor of the king. Here in Israel the prophet had treated him as a mere nobody, paying no deference to him, employing a servant to convey his instructions. Naaman was chagrined; his pride was wounded, and because his self-importance had not been ministered to, he turned away in a huff. Elisha's "Go and wash in Jordan seven times" was not intended to signify the means of cure, but was designed as a test of his heart, and strikingly did it serve its purpose. It was a call to humble himself before Jehovah. It required the repudiation of his own wisdom and the renunciation of self-pleasing; and that is at direct variance with the inclinations of fallen human nature, so much so that no one ever truly complied with this just demand of God's until He performed a miracle of grace in the soul.

Even the most humiliating providences are not sufficient in themselves to humble the proud heart of man and render him submissive to the divine will. One would think that a person so desperately afflicted as this poor leper would have been meekened and ready to comply with the prophet's injunction. Ah, my reader, the seat of our moral disease lies too deep for external things to reach it. So fearful is the blinding power of sin that it causes its subjects to be puffed up with self-complacency and self-righteousness and to imagine they are entitled to favorable treatment even at the hands of the Most High. And does not that very spirit lurk in the hearts of the regenerate! And it not only lurks there, but at times it moves them to act like Naaman! Has not the writer and the Christian reader ever come before the Lord with some pressing need and sought relief at His hands, and then been angry because He responded to us in quite a different way from what we expected and desired? Have we not had to bow our heads for shame as He gently reproved us with His "Doest thou well to be angry?" (Jon 4:4). Yes, there is much of this Naaman spirit that needs to be mortified in each of us.

"Behold, I thought" said Naaman. Herein he supplies a true representation of the natural man. The sinner has his own idea of how salvation is to be obtained. It is true that opinions vary when it comes to the working out of detail, yet all over the world fallen man has his own opinion of what is suitable and needful. One man thinks he must perform some meritorious deeds in order to obtain forgiveness. Another thinks the past can be atoned for by turning over a new leaf and living right for the future. Yet another, who has obtained a smattering of the gospel, thinks that by believing in Christ he secures a passport to heaven, even though he continues to indulge the flesh and retain his beloved idols. However much they may differ in their self-concocted schemes, this one thing is common to them all: "I thought." And that "I thought" is put over against the Word and way of God. They prefer the way that "seemeth right" to them; they insist on following out their own theorizings; they pit their prejudices and presuppositions against a "thus saith the Lord." Reader, you perceive here the folly of Naaman, but have you seen the madness of setting your own thoughts against the authority of the living God!

And what was it that this foolish and haughty Syrian "thought"? Why this: "He will surely come out to me, and stand, and call on the name of the LORD his God, and strike his hand over the place, and recover the leper." He was willing to be restored to health, but it must be in his own way—a way in which his self-respect might be retained and his importance acknowledged. He desired to be healed, provided he should also be duly honored. He had come all the way from Syria to be rid of his leprosy, but he was not prepared to receive cleansing in the manner of God's prescribing. What madness! What a demonstration that the carnal mind is enmity against God! What proof of the fearful hold which Satan has over his victims until a stronger one delivers them from his enthralling power!

Naaman had now received what the king of Israel had failed to give him—full directions for his cure. There was no uncertainty about the prescription nor of its efficacy, would he but submit to it. "Go and wash in Jordan seven times . . . and thou shalt be clean." But he felt slighted. Such instructions suited not his inclinations; the divine requirement accorded not with the conceits of his unhumbled heart.

What right had Naaman, a leper, to either argue or prescribe? He was a petitioner and not a legislator; he was suing for a favor, and therefore was in no position to advance any demands of his own. If such were the case and situation of Naaman, how infinitely less has any depraved and guilty sinner the right to make any terms with God! Man is a criminal, justly pronounced guilty by the divine law. Mercy is his only hope, and it is therefore for God to say in what way mercy is to be shown him and how salvation is to be obtained. For this reason the Lord says not only, "Let the wicked forsake his way," but also adds "and the unrighteous man his thoughts" (Is 55:7). Man must repudiate his own ideas, abandon his own prejudices, turn away from his own schemes, and reject his own preferences. If we are to enter the kingdom of heaven, we must "become as little children" (Mt 18:3). Alas, of the vast majority of our fellowmen it has to be said, that they, "going about to establish their own righteousness, have not submitted themselves unto the righteousness of God" (Ro 10:3). They "will not come to Christ that they might have life" (Jn 5:40).

C. E. Stuart wrote,

> In Naaman's mind all was arranged. He pictured the scene to himself, and made himself the foremost figure in the group — the Gentile idolator waited on by the prophet of God. The incongruity of this he did not then see. We see it. God would visit him in grace, but as one who had no ground of his own to stand on. As a sinner He could meet him. As a leper He could heal him. As the captain of the hosts of the king of Syria He would not receive him. What place has a sinner before God save that of one to whom mercy can be shown? What place is suited to the leper save that outside the camp? Naaman has to learn his place. He may be wroth with the prophet, but he cannot move him. Before him he is only a leper, whatever he may appear before others. Learning his place, he has to learn his vileness. He imagined Elisha would have struck his hand over the place. A sign, a scene, he expected — not a mere word. He did not know what a defiling object he was. The priest looked on the leper to judge whether he was leprous or not. He touched him only when he was clean (Lev 14). Of Naaman's leprosy there was no doubt, for he had come to be healed of it. To touch him ere he was clean would only have defiled the prophet! But further, if he had been able to touch him, and so have healed him, would not man have thought there was virtue in the prophet? By sending him to the Jordan to wash, it would be clearly seen the cure was direct from God. Man has no virtue in himself — he can only be the channel of God's grace to others. God must have all the glory of the cure, and Naaman must be taught his own condition and vileness.

"Are not Abana and Pharpar, rivers of Damascus, better than all the waters of Israel? may I not wash in them, and be clean? So he turned and went away in a rage" (2 Ki 5:12). Naaman was incensed not only because he thought that insufficient respect had been shown to his own person, but also because he felt his country had been slighted. If it was merely a matter of bathing in some river, why could not those of his own land have sufficed? This was tantamount to dictating to Jehovah, for it was the word of His prophet he now challenged. Shall the beggar insist on his right to choose what form the supply of his need must take! Shall the patient inform the physician what remedy will be acceptable to him! Is the guilty culprit to have the effrontery to dictate to the judge what shall be done to him! Yet a worm of the earth deems himself competent to pit his wits against the wisdom of God. A hell-deserving sinner is impudent enough to draw up terms on which he considers heaven is due him. But if we are to be cleansed, it can only be by the way of God's appointing and not by any of our own devising. Matthew Henry said,

> He thinks this too cheap, too plain, too common, a thing for so great a man to be cured by; or he did not believe it would at all effect the cure, or, if it would, what medicinal virtue was there in Jordan more than in the rivers of Damascus? But he did not consider (1) That Jordan belonged to Israel's God, from whom he was to expect the cure, and not from the gods of Damascus; it watered the Lord's land, the holy land, and in a miraculous cure, relation to God was much more considerable than the depth of the channel or the beauty of the stream. (2) That Jordan had more than once before this obeyed the commands of Omnipotence: it had of old yielded a passage to Israel, and of late to Elijah and Elisha, and therefore was fitter for such a purpose than those rivers which had only observed the common law of their creation, and had never been thus distinguished; but above all, Jordan was the river appointed, and if he expected a cure from the Divine power he ought to acquiesce in the Divine will, without asking why or wherefore. It is common for those that are wise in their own conceits to look with contempt on the dictates and prescriptions of Divine wisdom, and to prefer their own fancies before them.

"So he turned and went away in a rage." How true to life; how accurate the picture! The flesh resents the humbling truth of God and hates to be abased. And let us say here for the benefit of young preachers who are likely to read these lines: you must expect some of your hearers to turn from you in anger if you faithfully minister the Word of God in its undiluted purity. It has ever been thus. If the prophets of the Lord incensed their hearers, can you expect your message will be palatable to the unregenerate? If the incarnate Son of God had to say, "Because I tell you the truth, ye believe me not" (Jn 8:45), can you expect the truth to meet with a better welcome from your lips? If the chief of the apostles declared, "For if I yet pleased men, I should not be the servant of Christ" (Gal 1:10), do you expect to be popular with them? There is but one way to avoid displeasing your hearers, and that is by unfaithfulness to your trust, by carnal compromise, by blunting the sharp edge of the sword of the Spirit, by keeping back what you know will prove unacceptable. In such an event, God will require their blood at your hand and you will forfeit the approbation of your Master.

"So he turned and went away in a rage." In this we may see the final effort of Satan to retain his victim before divine grace delivered him. The rage of Naaman was but the reflection of Satan, who was furious at the prospect of losing him. It reminds us of the case recorded in Luke 9:37-42. A father of a demon-possessed child had sought for help from the apostles, which they had been unable to render. As the Saviour came down from the mount, the poor father approached Him and He gave orders, "bring they son hither." We are told, "And as he was yet a coming, the devil threw him down, and tare him" (v. 42). But Jesus rebuked the unclean spirit, and healed the child, and delivered him again to his father. It is frequently thus; the conflict which is waged in the soul is usually worst just before peace is found. Lusts rage, unbelief seeks to wax supreme, the truth of sovereign grace when first apprehended is obnoxious, and to be told our righteousnesses are as filthy rags stirs up enmity. Satan fills the soul with rage against God, against His truth, against His servant. Often that is a hopeful sign, for it at least shows that the sinner has been aroused from the fatal sleep of indifference.

"And his servants came near, and spake unto him, and said, My father, if the prophet had bid thee do some great thing, wouldest thou not have done it? how much rather then, when he saith to thee, Wash, and be clean?" (2 Ki 5:13). Let us consider first the surface teaching of this verse. This gentle remonstrance was "a word spoken in season." Had Naaman remained calm and reasonable he would have perceived that what was required of him was simple and safe, and neither difficult nor dangerous. Had the prophet prescribed some laborious and lengthy task, or ordered a drastic operation or painful remedy, probably Naaman would have complied without a murmur. So why not do this when no other sacrifice was demanded of him but the humbling of his pride? "When sinners are under serious impressions, and as yet prejudiced against the Lord's method of salvation, they should be reasoned with in meekness and love, and persuaded to make trial of its simplicity" (Thomas Scott). If it is necessary to rebuke their petulence and point out to them the foolishness of their proud reasoning, we should make it evident that our rebuke proceeds from a desire for their eternal welfare.

> It is a great mercy to have those about us that will be free with us, and faithfully tell us our faults and follies, though they be our inferiors. Masters must be willing to hear reason from their inferiors: Job 31:13, 14. As we should be deaf to the counsel of the ungodly though given by the greatest and most venerable names, so we should have our ears open to good advice, though brought to us by those who are much below us: no matter who speaks, if it be well said . . . The reproof was modest and respectful: they call him "father" — for servants must honor and obey their masters with a kind of filial affection (Matthew Henry).

How few ministers of the gospel now proclaim the divine injunction, "Let as many servants as are under the yoke count their own masters worthy of all honour, that the name of God and his doctrine be not blasphemed" (1 Ti 6:1).

It may be those servants had heard quite a lot from the Hebrew maid of the wondrous miracles that had been wrought by Elisha, and hence they were very desirous that Naaman should try out his directions. Or, perhaps it was because they were deeply devoted to their master, holding him in high esteem, and felt he was forsaking his own mercies by permitting his wounded vanity to now blind his better judgment. At any rate, they saw no sense in coming all the way from Syria and now leaving Samaria without at least making a trial of the prophet's prescription. Such are the suggestions made by the commentators to explain this action of Naaman's attendants. Personally, we prefer to look higher and see the power of the Most High in operation, working in them both to will and to do if His good pleasure, employing them as one more link in the chain which brought about the accomplishment of His purpose; "For of him, and through him, and to him, are all things: to whom be glory for ever. Amen" (Ro 11:36).

What has been before us here is in full accord with the other things already contemplated. It seemed quite unlikely that any serious attention should be paid to the simple statement of the captive Hebrew maid, but God saw to it that her words did not fall to the ground. It appeared very much as though Naaman's mission was blocked when the skeptical king of Israel failed to cooperate, but God moved Elisha to intervene and caused his royal master to carry out his order. And now that Naaman himself turned away from the prophet in a rage, it certainly looked as though the quest would prove unsuccessful. But that could not be. The Almighty had decreed that the Syrian should be healed of his leprosy and brought to acknowledge that the God of Israel was the true and living God; and all the powers of evil could not prevent the fulfillment of His decree. Yet just as He is generally pleased to work, so here; He used human instruments in the accomplishing of His purpose. It may be concluded that, naturally and normally, those attendants would have their place and distance, and would not have dared to remonstrate with their master while he was in such a rage. Behold the secret power of God working within them, subduing their fears, and moving them to appeal to Naaman.

The little maid was not present to speak to her august master and plead with him to further his best interests. The prophet of the Lord had issued his instructions, only for them to be despised. What, then? Shall Naaman return home unhealed? No, such a thing was not possible. He was to learn there was a God in Israel and that He had thoughts of mercy toward him. But he must first be abased. Mark, then how God acted. He moves in a mysterious way, His wonders to perform — oftentimes unperceived and unappreciated by us. He inclines Naaman's own followers to admonish him and show him the folly of his proud reasoning. Remarkable and significant is it to observe the particular instruments the Lord here employed. It was first the servant maid whom He used to inform Naaman that there was a prophet in Israel by whom he could obtain healing. Then it was through his servant that Elisha gave the Syrian the needed instructions. And now it was Naaman's own servants who prevailed upon him to heed those instructions. All of this was intended for the humbling of the mighty Naaman. And, we may add, for our instruction. We must take the servant's place and have the servant spirit if we would hope for God to employ us.

See here too the amazing patience of the Lord. Here was one who was wrothful against His faithful prophet: what wonder then that He struck him down in his tracks. Here was a haughty creature who refused to humble himself and, in effect, impudently dictated to God how he should receive healing. Had he been on his knees supplicating the divine favor, his attitude would have been a becoming one; instead, he turned his back upon God's servant and moved away in a rage. Yet it was then that God acted — not against him, but for him, so that where sin abounded, grace did much more abound. And why? Because sovereign mercy had ordained him a vessel unto honor from all eternity.

Let the Christian reader join with the writer in looking back to the past, recalling when we too kicked against the pricks. How infinite was the forbearance of God toward us! Though we had no regard for Him, He had set His heart upon us; and perhaps at the very time when our awful enmity against Him was most high-handedly operative, He moved someone of comparative obscurity to reason with us and point out to us the folly of our ways and urge us to submit to God's holy requirements.

Chapter 18

TENTH MIRACLE
COMPLETE SUBMISSION

WE DEVOTED MUCH of our attention in previous chapters to
the requirement made upon Naaman, because that demand and his
compliance therewith are the hinge on which this miracle turns, as
the response made by the sinner to the call of the gospel settles
whether or not he is to be cleansed from his sin. This does not denote that the success or failure of the gospel is left contingent upon
the will of men, but rather announces that order of things which God
has instituted: an order in which He acts as moral governor and in
which man is dealt with as a moral agent. In consequence of the
fall, man is filled with enmity against God and is blind to his eternal interests. His will is opposed to God's, and the depravity of his
heart causes him to forsake his own mercies. Nevertheless he is still
a responsible creature, and God treats him as such. As his moral
governor, God requires obedience from him; and in the case of His
elect He obtains it, not by physical compulsion but by moral per-
suasion, not by mere force but by inclining him to free concurrence.
He does not overwhelm by divine might, but declares, "I drew them
with cords of a man, with bands of love" (Ho 11:4).

What has just been pointed out above receives striking illustration
in the incident before us. When God's requirement was made to
Naaman it pleased him not; he was angry at the prophet and rebellious against the instructions given him. "Go and wash in Jordan
seven times" was a definite test of obedience, calling for the surrender of his will to the Lord. Everything was narrowed down to that
one thing: would he bow before and submit to the authoritative
Word of God? In like manner every person who hears it is tested by
the gospel today. The gospel is no mere "invitation" to be heeded or

148

not as men please, and grossly dishonoring to God is it if we consider it only as such. The gospel is a divine proclamation, demanding the throwing down of the weapons of our warfare against heaven. God "now commandeth all men every where to repent" (Ac 17:30). And again we are told, "And this is His commandment, That we should believe on the name of his Son Jesus Christ" (1 Jn 3:23). The gospel is "for obedience to the faith" (Ro 1:5), and Christ is "the author of eternal salvation unto all them that obey him" (Heb 5:9). To those "that obey not the gospel," the Lord Jesus will come in flaming fire, taking vengeance (2 Th 1:7-8). If men will not bow to Christ's scepter, they shall be made His footstool.

It was this very obedience that Naaman was reluctant to render, so much so that he was on the point of returning to Syria unhealed. Yet that could not be. In the divine decree he was marked out to be the recipient of God's sovereign grace. As yet Naaman might be averse to receiving grace in the way of God's appointing, and the devil might put forth a supreme effort to retain his victim; but whatever be the devices of the human heart or the malice of its enemy, the counsel of the Lord must stand. When God has designs of mercy toward a soul, He sets in operation certain agencies which result in the accomplishment of His purpose. The flesh may resist and Satan may oppose, but it stands written, "Thy people shall be willing in the day of thy power" (Ps 110:3). That "day" had now arrived for Naaman, and speedily was this made manifest. It pleased God to exercise His power by moving the Syrian's servants to remonstrate with him and by making effectual their plea. "My father," they said, "if the prophet had bid thee do some great thing, wouldst not thou have done it? how much rather then, when he saith to thee, Wash and be clean? Then went he down, and dipped himself seven times in Jordan, according to the saying of the man of God" (2 Ki 5:13-14). "Then went he down." That was something which he had to do; and until he did it, there was no cleansing for him. The sinner is not passive in connection with God's blotting out his iniquities. He has to repent (Ac 3:19), and believe in Christ (Ac 10:43) in order to obtain forgiveness of his sins. It was a voluntary act on the part of Naaman. Previously he had been unwilling to comply with the divine demand, but the secret power of God has worked in him — by means of the pleading of his attendants — overcoming his reluctance. It was an act of self-abasement. "He went down and dipped" signifies three things: he descended from his chariot, he waded into the waters, he was submerged beneath them, and thus did he own his vileness before God. No less than "seven times" must he plunge into that dark stream, thereby acknowledging his total uncleanness. A person only slightly soiled may be cleansed by a single washing, but Naaman must dip seven times to make evident how great was his defilement. The seven times also intimated that God required complete submission to His will. Nothing short of full surrender to Him is of any avail.

"Then went he down, and dipped himself seven times in Jordan, according to the saying of the man of God." It is of deep importance that we grasp the exact implication of this second clause; otherwise, we shall miss one of the principal lines in this gospel picture. Note well then that it was not according to the pleading of his attendants, the last thing mentioned in the context. Had Naaman acted simply to please them, he might have dipped himself in Jordan seventy times and been no better off for it. "According to the saying of the man of God" signifies according to the declaration of God Himself through His prophet. Naaman heeded the Word of God and rendered faith obedience (Ro 1:5) to it. Repentance is not sufficient to procure cleansing; the sinner must also believe. And this is what Naaman now did. His heart laid hold of the divine promise, "Go and wash in Jordan seven times, and thy flesh shall come again to thee, and thou shalt be clean." He believed that "shalt" and acted upon it. Have you done similarly, my reader? Has your faith definitely appropriated the gospel promise, "Believe on the Lord Jesus Christ, and thou shalt be saved"? If not, you will never be saved until it has. Faith is the indispensable requirement, for without faith it is impossible to please God (Heb 11:6).

"And his flesh came again like unto the flesh of a little child, and he was clean" (2 Ki 5:14). Of course it did. It could not be otherwise, for "he is faithful that promised" (Heb 10:23). None has ever laid hold of a divine promise and found it to fail, and none ever will. That which has been spoken through the prophets and apostles is the Word of Him "that cannot lie" (Titus 1:2). He cannot falsify His Word. He cannot depart from it, alter it, or break it. "For ever, O Lord, thy word is settled in heaven" (Ps 119:89). Forever, too, is it settled on earth: "My covenant will I not break, nor alter the thing that is gone out of my lips" (Ps 89:34). God has promised to receive, welcome, own, justify, preserve, and bring to heaven, all who will take Him at His simple Word; who will rely upon it unconditionally and without reservation, setting to their seal that He is true. The warrant for us to believe is contained in the promise itself, as it was for Naaman. The promise says, "you may"; the promise says, "You must"; the promise says, "You are shut up to faith" (Gal 3:23). And I, I say, "Lord, I believe." Faith is taking God at His Word — His undeceiving and infallible Word — and trusting in Jesus Christ as my Saviour. If you have not already done so, delay no longer, but trust Him now, and wash in that "fountain" which has been opened "for sin and for uncleanness" (Zec 13:1).

"And his flesh came again like unto the flesh of a little child, and he was clean." Let it be duly noted that there was no lengthy interval between the faith-obedience of Naaman and his healing, in fact no interval at all. There was no placing of him upon probation before his disease was removed. His cleansing was instantaneous. Nor was his cleansing partial and effected only by degrees; he was fully and perfectly healed there and then, so that not a single spot of his leprosy remained. And that is exactly what the glorious gospel of God announces and promises: "the blood of Jesus Christ his Son cleanseth us from all sin" (1 Jn 1:7). The moment a sinner claims Christ as his own, His perfect righteousness is placed to his account. The moment any sinner really takes God at His Word and appropriates the gospel promise, he is — without having to wait for anything further to be done for him or in him — entitled to and fit for heaven, just as was the dying thief. If he is left here another hundred years, he may indeed enter into a fuller understanding of the riches of divine grace, but he will not become one iota more fit for glory. "Giving thanks unto the Father, which hath made us meet [not 'is now doing so'] to be partakers of the inheritance of the saints in light" (Col 1:12).

"And he returned to the man of God, he and all his company, and came, and stood before him: and he said, Behold, now I know that there is no God in all the earth but in Israel: now therefore, I pray thee, take a blessing of thy servant" (2 Ki 5:15). When a work of grace is wrought upon a person, it is soon made evident by him. Notice the radical and blessed transformation which had been produced in Naaman's heart as well as in his body. He might have hastened back at once to Syria, but he did not. Previously he had turned his back upon Elisha in a rage, but now he sought his face in gratitude. Formerly he had despised the "waters of Israel" (v. 12); now he acknowledged the God of Israel. All was completely changed. The proud and haughty Syrian was humbled, terming himself the prophet's "servant." The bitterness of his legalistic heart which had resented a way of deliverance that placed him on the same level as paupers had received its death wound. The enmity of his carnal mind against God and his hatred of His prophet, together with his leprosy, were all left beneath Jordan's flood, and he emerged a new creature — cleansed and lowly in heart. No longer did he expect the prophet to seek him out and pay deference to him. Instead he at once went to Elisha and honored him as God's servant — a lovely figure of a saved sinner desiring fellowship with the people of God.

Sixth, the Sequel of the Miracle

Let us look more closely at the actions of the cleansed Naaman. First, he "returned to the man of God." Nor did he seek him in vain. This time Elisha came forth in person, there being no longer any need to communicate through his servant.

Second, Naaman was the first to speak, and he bore testimony to the true and living God: "Behold, now I know that there is no God in all the earth, but in Israel." He had listened to no lectures on evidences of the divine existence, nor did he need to; effectively is a soul taught when it is made partaker of saving grace. Naaman was as sure now as Elisha himself that Jehovah alone is God.

Third, this testimony of Naaman was not given in private to the prophet, but openly before "all his company." Have you, my reader, made public profession of your faith? "I am not ashamed of the gospel of Christ" (Ro 1:16); does a like witness issue from your lips, or are you attempting to be a "secret disciple" of His?

Fourth, Naaman now wished to bestow a present on Elisha as an expression of his gratitude. Are you ministering to the temporal needs of God's servants?

Yes, my reader, where a work of divine grace has been wrought, its subject soon makes the fact evident to those around him. One who has fully surrendered to God cannot hide the fact from his fellows, nor will he wish to. A new life within cannot help but be made manifest in a new life without. When Zaccheus was made a partaker of God's "so great salvation," he gave half his goods to the poor and made fourfold restitution to those he had robbed (Lk 19: 8). When Saul of Tarsus was converted, he at once said, "Lord, what wilt thou have me to do?" and henceforth a walk of loving obedience to Him marked the grand transformation. No sooner was the Philippian jailor made savingly acquainted with Christ than he who had made fast in the stocks the feet of the sorely-beaten apostles "washed their stripes" and, after being baptized, "brought them into his house" and "set meat before them" (Ac 16). Is it thus with you? Does your everyday conduct testify what Christ has done for you? Or is your profession only like a leafy tree without any fruit on it?

"But he said, As the LORD liveth, before whom I stand, I will receive none. And he urged him to take it; but he refused" (2 Ki 5: 16). Naaman was now taught the freeness of God's grace. This freeness is pictured by Joseph, when he gave orders for the sacks of his brethren to be filled with corn and their money to be returned and placed in their sacks (Gen 42:25). When God gives to sinners, He gives freely. It was for a truly noble reason then that Elisha declined the blessing from Naaman's hand: he would not compromise the blessed truth of divine grace. "He would have Naaman return to Syria with this testimony, that the God of Israel had taken nothing from him but his leprosy! He would have him go back and declare that his gold and silver were useless in dealing with One who gave all for nothing" (*Things New and Old*). God delights in being the giver. If you wish to please Him, continue coming before Him as a receiver. Listen to David, "What shall I render unto the LORD for all his benefits toward me? I will take the cup of salvation, and call upon his name" (Ps 116:12-13). In other words, he would "render" to Him by receiving more!

By his response Elisha showed Naaman that the servant of God looks upon the wealth of this world with holy contempt.

> Gratitude to the Lord will dictate liberality to the instruments of His mercies. But different circumstances will render it necessary for them to adopt different measures. The "man of God" will never allow himself to covet any one's gold or silver, or apparel; but be content with daily bread, and learn to trust for tomorrow. Yet sometimes he will understand that the proffered kindness is the Lord's method of supplying his necessities, that it will be fruit abounding to the benefit of the donor, and that there is a propriety in accepting it as a token of love; but as others, the gift will be looked on as a temptation, and he will perceive that the acceptance of it would degrade his character and office, dishonor God, and tend exceeding to the injury of the giver. In this case he will decidedly refuse it. This is particularly to be adverted to in the case of the great, when

they first turn their thoughts to religious subjects. From knowledge of the world, they are apt to suspect all their inferiors of mercenary designs, and naturally suppose that ministers are only carrying on a trade like other men; while the conduct of too many so-called confirms them in the sentiment. There is but one way of counteracting this prejudice, and that is by evidencing a disinterested spirit, and not asking anything, and in some cases refusing to accept favors from them, until they have attained a further establishment in the faith; and by always persevering in an indifference to every personal interest (Scott).

"And Naaman said, Shall there not then, I pray thee, be given to thy servant two mules' burden of earth? for thy servant will henceforth offer neither burnt-offering nor sacrifice unto other gods, but unto the LORD" (2 Ki 5:17). Once the true God is known (v. 15), all false ones are repudiated. Observe carefully his "be given" and "thy servant." He does not offer to purchase this soil, nor does he as "captain of the hosts" of Syria's victorious army demand it as a right. Grace had now taught him to be a recipient and conduct himself as a servant. Beautiful is it to see the purpose for which he wanted this earth; it was not from a superstitious veneration of the soil, but that he might honor God. This exhibits, once more, the great and grand change which had been wrought in Naaman. His chief concern now was to be a worshiper of the God of all grace, the God of Israel, and to this end he requests permission to take home with him sufficient soil of the land of Israel to build an altar. And is not the application of this to ourselves quite apparent? When a soul has tasted that the Lord is gracious, the spirit of worship possesses him, and he will reverently pour out his heart's adoration unto Him.

The order of truth we have been considering is deeply instructive. First, we have a cleansed leper, a sinner saved by grace, (v. 14). Then an assured saint: "I know" (v. 15); and now a voluntary worshiper (v. 17). That is the unchanging order of scripture. No one that ignores the cleansing blood of Christ or "the washing of water by the word" (Eph 5:26) can obtain any access to the thrice holy God. And none who doubts his acceptance in the beloved can offer unto the Father that praise and thanksgiving which are His due. Therefore believers are bidden to "draw near with a true heart in full assurance of faith, having our hearts sprinkled from an evil conscience" (Heb 10:22). As we have passed from one detail to another, we have sought to make definite application to ourselves. Let us do so here. Naaman was determined to erect an altar unto the Lord in his own land. Reader, are you the head of a household, and do you claim to be a Christian? Then gather this family around you each day and conduct worship. If you do not, you have good reason to call into question the genuineness of your profession. If God has His due place in your heart, He will have it in your home.

"In this thing the LORD pardon thy servant, that when my master goeth into the house of Rimmon to worship there, and he leaneth on my hand, and I bow myself in the house of Rimmon: when I bow down myself in the house of Rimmon, the LORD pardon thy servant in this thing" (2 Ki 5:18). This presents a real difficulty; for as the verse reads, it quite mars the typical picture and seems utterly foreign to all that precedes. It is true that Naaman was a converted heathen; and he had himself acknowledged that "there is no God in all the earth, but in Israel," so however great his previous ignorance, he was now enlightened. His desire to erect an altar unto Jehovah would appear to preclude the idea that he should in the next breath suggest that he play the part of a compromiser and then presumptuously count on the Lord's forgiveness. One who is fully surrendered to the Lord makes no reservation. He cannot, for His requirement is, "Thou shalt worship the LORD thy God, and him only shalt thou serve;" and again, "Touch not the unclean thing, and I will receive you." And still more difficult is it for us to understand Elisha's, "Go in peace" (v. 19), if he had just been asked to grant a dispensation for what Naaman himself evidently felt to be wrong.

Is there then any legitimate method of removing this difficulty? Though he does not adopt it himself, Scott states that many learned men have sought to establish an alternative translation: "In this thing the Lord pardon thy servant: that when my master went into the house of Rimmon to bow down himself there, that I bowed down myself there — the Lord pardon thy servant in this thing." We do not possess sufficient scholarship to be able to pass judgment on this rendition, but from what little we do know of the Hebrew verb (which has no present tense), it strikes us as likely. In this case, Naaman's words look backward, evidencing a quickened conscience, confessing a past offence, rather than forward and seeking a dispensation for a future sin. But if that translation is a cutting of the knot rather than an untying of it, then we must suppose that Elisha perceived that Naaman was convinced that the thing he anticipated was not right. So, instead of rebuking him, Elisha left that conviction to produce its proper effect, assured that in due course when Naaman's faith and judgment matured, he would take a more decided stand against idolatry.

We will take up, seventh, the meaning of this miracle, in the next chapter.

Chapter 19

ELEVENTH MIRACLE
A WAYWARD SERVANT

Seventh, the Meaning of the Miracle

THE ELEVENTH MIRACLE of Elisha is so closely connected with the tenth that it will scarcely be out of place for us to bring forward the final division of the foregoing and use it as the introduction to this one. Though we dwelt at more than customary length with the healing of Naaman and pointed out much as we went along that was typical, yet there still remain several details of interest which deserve separate notice.

First, the cleansing of Naaman supplied a striking display of the sovereignty of God. This was emphasized by the Lord Jesus in His first public discourse in the synagogue at Nazareth, when He reminded His hearers, "Many lepers were in Israel in the time of Eliseus [Elisha] the prophet; and none of them was cleansed, saving Naaman the Syrian" (Lk 4:27). It is ever thus with Him whose thoughts are so different from and whose ways are so high above ours that, acting in the freeness of His grace, He passes by others and singles out the most unlikely to be the recipients of His high favors (1 Co 1:26-29).

Second, the cleansing of Naaman afforded a blessed foreshadowment of the divine mercy reaching out to the Gentiles, for Naaman was not an Israelite but a Syrian. Nevertheless he was made to learn the humbling lesson that if divine grace were to be extended to him, it could only proceed from the God of Abraham. That was why he must wash in the Jordan; the waters of "Abana and Pharpar" (2 Ki 5:12) were of no avail — he must wash in one of Israel's streams. This truth is written boldly across the pages of Holy Writ. The harlot of Jericho was to be spared when her city was destroyed, but it could only be by her heeding the instructions of the two Hebrew spies. The widow of Zarephath was preserved through the famine, but it was by receiving Elijah into her home. The Ninevites were delivered from impending wrath, but at the preaching of Jonah. The king of Babylon received a dream from God, but for its interpretation he must turn to Daniel. To the Samaritan adulteress Christ declared, "Salvation is of the Jews" (Jn 4:22). Then let us heed the warning of Romans 11:18-25.

Third, the cleansing of Naaman provided a full picture of "the way of salvation" or what is required of the sinner in order for his cleansing. First we have a picture of how fallen man appears in the eyes of the holy God: a leper, one condemned by His law, a loathsome object, unfit for the divine presence, a menace to his fellowmen. Then we behold man's self-righteousness and self-importance, as Naaman came expecting to purchase his healing and was angry at the prophet's refusal to show him deference. Next we learn of the demand made upon him; he must descend from his chariot and go and wash seven times in the Jordan. There must be the setting aside of his own thoughts and desires, the humbling of proud self, the acknowledgment of his total depravity, full surrender to God's authority, and faith's laying hold of the promise "and thy flesh shall come again to thee, and thou shalt be clean." Finally, we behold the immediate and complete transformation: "and his flesh came again like unto the flesh of a little child," with a corresponding change of heart and conduct toward Elisha and his God.

Before passing from this most fascinating incident, let us consider further the particular waters into which Naaman was required to dip. It was not in the river Kishon or the pool of Bethesda, but the Jordan. Why? The answer to that question reveals the striking accuracy of our type. As leprosy (emblem of sin) was in question, the curse must be witnessed to. Sin has called down the curse of the One against whom it has raised its defiant head (Gen 3). The curse is God's judgment upon sin, and that judgment is death. It is this of which the Jordan ever speaks. It was not because its waters possessed any magical properties or healing virtues; the very name Jordan means "judgment." Those who heeded our Lord's forerunner "were baptized of him in the river Jordan, confessing their sins" (Mk 1:5); immersion beneath its waters was the acknowledgment that death was their due. Therefore did the Saviour allude to His death as a "baptism" (Lk 12:50), for at the cross He was overwhelmed by the judgments of God (Ps 42:7; 88:7). When a sinner believes the gospel and appropriates Christ as his substitute, God regards him as having passed through His judgment of sin, so that he can now say, "I am crucified with Christ," and in his baptism as a believer there is a symbolic showing forth of that fact.

The miracle which is now to engage our attention is of quite another order, the differences between them being most striking. We will therefore consider, first, its contrasts.

First, the Contrasts of this Miracle

The subject of the foregoing miracle was a heathen idolater; now it is the prophet's own servant. Naaman sought the prophet for relief; the other pursued the relieved one and virtually demanded tribute from him. There we beheld Elisha teaching Naaman the grand truth of the freeness of divine grace; here we see Gehazi casting a dark cloud over the same. In the one Naaman is represented as expressing deep gratitude for his recovery and urging the man of God to receive a present at his hands; now the avaricious Gehazi is portrayed as coveting that which his master so nobly refused. There it was a poor creature healed of his leprosy; here it is one being smitten with that dread disease. There we beheld God's goodness acting in mercy; here we see His severity acting in holy justice. The former closes with the recipient of divine grace returning home as a devout worshiper; the latter ends with a pronouncement of God's curse on the transgressor and on his seed forever.

Second, the Subject of the Miracle

The one on whom this solemn miracle was wrought is Gehazi, the servant of Elisha. He has come before us several times previously, and nowhere was he seen to advantage. First, when the woman of Shunem sought the man of God on behalf of her dead son and cast herself at his feet, "Gehazi came near to thrust her away" (2 Ki 4: 27), and his master told him to "let her alone." Then the prophet instructed his servant to go before him and lay his staff upon the face of the child (v. 29). Elisha could successfully smite the waters of Jordan with Elijah's mantle because "the spirit of Elijah" rested upon him (2:15); but being devoid of the Spirit, Gehazi found the prophet's staff of no avail in his prayerless hands (4:31). In 4:43 we beheld his selfishness and unbelief: "What, should I set this before an hundred men" when Elisha was counting upon God to multiply the loaves. Thus his character and conduct is consistent and in keeping with his name which significantly enough means "denier."

Third, the Occasion of the Miracle

"But Gehazi, the servant of Elisha the man of God, said, Behold, my master hath spared Naaman this Syrian, in not receiving at his hands that which he brought: but, as the LORD liveth, I will run after him, and take somewhat of him" (2 Ki 5:20). It will be remembered that before Naaman left Syria for the land of Samaria that he provided himself with a costly treasure, consisting of "ten talents of silver, and six thousand pieces of gold, and ten changes of raiment" (v. 5). No doubt a part of this was designed for traveling expenses for the retinue of servants who accompanied him, but the major portion of it he evidently intended to bestow upon his benefactor. But Elisha had firmly refused to receive anything (vv. 15-16), and so he was now returning home with his horses still laden with the treasure. This was more than the covetous heart of Gehazi could endure, and he determined to secure a portion of it for himself. The honor of Jehovah and the glory of His grace counted nothing with him.

Every word in the above verse repays careful attention. The ominous "But" intimates the solemn contrast between the two miracles. Gehazi is here termed not only "the servant of Elisha" but "of Elisha the man of God" — the added words bring out the enormity of his sin. First, they call attention to the greatness of the privilege he had enjoyed, being in close attendance on so pious a master. This rendered his wicked conduct the more excuseless, for it was not the act of an ignorant person, but of one well instructed in the ways of righteousness. Second, it emphasizes the enormity of his offence, for it reflected seriously on the official character of the one who employed him. The sins of those in the sacred office or of those associated with them are far graver than those of others (Ja 3:1). But just as Gehazi had no concern for the glory of God, so he cared nothing for the reputation of Elisha.

What has just been pointed out definitely refutes one of the wide-spread delusions of our day, namely, that it is their unfavorable surroundings which are responsible for the degenerate conduct of so many of the present generation: social improvement can only be effected by improving the wages and homes of the poor. And is the behavior of the rich any better? Is there less immorality in the west end of London than in the east? It is drunken and thriftless people who make the slums, and not the slums which ruin the people. God's Word teaches it is "out of the heart" of fallen man (Mk 7:21-23) and not from his faulty environment that all proceeds which defiles human nature. Nor it is any more warrantable for any person to attempt to throw the blame for his downfall on his being obliged to mingle with evil characters. Gehazi was isolated from all bad companions, placed in the most favorable circumstances, dwelling with a "man of God," but his soul was depraved! While "the heart of the sons of men is fully set in them to do evil" (Ec 8:11), the gospel and not more social reforms is the only remedy.

Neither his close association with the man of God nor the witnessing of the miracles performed by him effected any change within Gehazi. The state of his heart is revealed by each expression recorded in verse 20 of 2 Kings 5. "Behold, my master hath spared Naaman." Incapable of appreciating the motives which had actuated Elisha, he felt that he had foolishly missed a golden opportunity. Gehazi regarded Naaman as legitimate prey, as a bird to be plucked. Contemptuously, he refers to him as "this Syrian." There was no pity for the one who had been such a sufferer, and no thankfulness that God had healed him. He was determined to capitalize on the situation: "I will run after him, and take somewhat of him." His awful sin was deliberately premeditated. What was worse, he made use of an impious oath: "As the LORD liveth I will run after him." There was no fear of God before his eyes; instead, he defiantly took His holy name in vain.

"So Gehazi followed after Naaman. And when Naaman saw him running after him, he lighted down from the chariot to meet him, and said, Is all well?" (v. 21). It is solemn to observe that God put no hindrance in the way of him who had devised evil. He could have moved Naaman to quicken his pace and to outdistance Gehazi. But He did not, an indication that God had given Gehazi up to his heart's lusts. It is ever a signal mark of divine mercy when the Lord interferes with our plans and thwarts our carnal designs. When we purpose doing anything wrong and a providential obstacle blocks us, it is a sign that God has not yet abandoned us to our madness. The graciousness of Naaman in alighting from his chariot and the question he asked gave further evidence of the change which had been wrought in him.

Fourth, the Aggravation of the Miracle

"And he said, All is well. My master hath sent me, saying, Behold, even now there be come to me from mount Ephraim two young men of the sons of the prophets: give them, I pray thee, a talent of silver, and two changes of garments" (v. 22). Here we see the wicked Gehazi adding sin to sin, thereby treasuring up to himself wrath against the day of wrath (Ro 2:5). First, his greedy heart cherished a covetous desire; then he deliberately and eagerly (as his "running" shows) proceeded to realize the same; and now he resorts to falsehoods. Liars can tell a plausible tale, especially when asking for charity. The thievish knave pretended it was not for himself, but for others in need that he was seeking relief — ever a favorite device employed by the unscrupulous when seeking to take advantage of unwary victims. Worse still, he compromised his master by saying he had sent him. To what fearful lengths will a covetous heart carry its subjects!

"And Naaman said, Be content, take two talents. And he urged him, and bound two talents of silver in two bags, with two changes of garments, and laid them upon two of his servants, and they bare them before him" (2 Ki 5:23). Naaman was quite unsuspicious. He not only complied with Gehazi's request but gave him more than he asked for. After the prophet's firm and repeated refusals to accept his gifts, he should have been more on his guard. There is a warning here for us to beware of crediting every beggar we encounter, even though he is a religious one. There have always been religious leeches who consider the righteous are legitimate prey for them to fatten upon. While it is a Christian duty to relieve the genuinely poor, yet we are not to encourage idleness or let ourselves be deceived by those with a smooth tongue. Investigate their case.

"And when he came to the tower, he took them from their hand, and bestowed them in the house: and he let the men go, and they departed" (v. 24). He took pains to carefully conceal his ill-gotten gains in a secret place, no doubt congratulating himself on his shrewdness. This reminds us of our first parents hiding themselves (Gen 3:8) and of Achan's sin (Jos 7:21). "But he went in, and stood before his master" (2 Ki 5:25). Pretending to be a faithful and dutiful servant, he now appeared before Elisha to await his orders. The most untruthful and dishonest often assume a pious pose in the company of the saints! "And Elisha said unto him, Whence comest thou, Gehazi?" An opportunity was thus given him to confess his sins, but instead of so doing, he added lie to lie: "And he said, Thy servant went no whither." There was no repentance, but a daring brazenness.

Fifth, the Justice of the Miracle

"And he said unto him, Went not mine heart with thee, when the man turned again from his chariot to meet thee? Is it a time to receive money, and to receive garments, and oliveyards, and vineyards, and sheep, and oxen, and menservants, and maidservants? The leprosy therefore of Naaman shall cleave unto thee, and unto thy seed for ever. And he went out from his presence a leper as white as snow" (vv. 26-27). Though Christians are not endowed with the extraordinary powers of the prophets, yet if they be truly walking with God they will discern a liar when he confronts them (1 Co 2:15). Elisha put his finger on the worst feature of the offence: "Is it a time to receive money [and thus stain God's free grace]?" From the words that follow, Elisha indicated that he knew how Gehazi planned to use the money: he intended to leave his service and set up as a farmer. His punishment was an appropriate one: he had coveted something of Naaman's — he should have that which would henceforth symbolically portray the polluted state of his soul.

Sixth, the Significance of the Miracle

That Gehazi fully deserved the frightful punishment which was visited upon him and that the form it took was a case of what is termed "poetic justice" will be evident to every spiritual mind. Nevertheless there was a severity of dealing with him which is more noticeable than in other cases. Nor is the reason far to seek. God was incensed at his having so grievously compromised the display of His free grace. The Lord is very jealous of His types. Observe how He moved Joseph to restore the money to the sacks of his brethren when they came to obtain food from Egypt (Gen 42:25), because he was there foreshadowing Christ as the bread of life — given to us "without money and without price."

The failure of Moses was far more than a losing of his temper: it was a marring of a blessed type. Note, "smite the rock" in Exodus 17:6, but only "speak" to it in Numbers 20:8 — Christ was to be "smitten" (Is 53:4) but once! As Moses suffered a premature death for his sin, so Gehazi was smitten with leprosy for his.

Seventh, the Lesson of the Miracle

We shall mention only three of the lessons we can draw from this miracle. First, there is a sharply pointed example here of the bitter fruits borne by the nourishing of a covetous spirit, and a fearful exemplification of that word, "For the love of money is the root of all evil: which while some coveted after, they have erred from the faith, and pierced themselves through with many sorrows" (1 Ti 6:10). How we need to pray, "Turn away mine eyes from beholding vanity" (Ps 119:37).

Second, there is a most solemn warning against putting a stumblingblock in the way of a babe in Christ. Naaman had only recently come to know Jehovah as the God of all grace and that was another reason why He dealt so severely with Gehazi (see Mt. 18:6)!

Third, there is a searching test for those of us who are engaged exclusively in God's service: though delivered from the love of money, we may seek the good opinion and praise of men.

Chapter 20

TWELFTH MIRACLE
FLOATING IRON

As WE POINTED OUT in our Introduction, the larger part of what is recorded of the life of this prophet is devoted to a description of the miracles performed by him and the circumstances or occasions which gave rise to them. Excepting that which occupied our attention in the first two or three chapters, when we contemplated the preparing and enduing of him for his work, very little indeed has been said about Elisha's mission or ministry up to the point we have now reached in his history. Yet here and there brief hints have been given us about that which engaged most of his energies. Those hints center around the several brief mentions made of "the sons of the prophets" and the relation which Elisha sustained to them, a further reference to whom is found in the passage which is now before us. As we pointed out in a previous book on Elijah, Israel had fallen on bad times, and spirituality was at a low ebb. Idolatry was rampant and God's judgments fell frequently upon them — in the form of letting the surrounding nations invade their land (1 Ki 20:1, 26; 22:1; 2 Ki 1:1; 5:2).

From the brief allusion made to them, it would seem that Elisha devoted much of his time and attention to the training of young preachers, who were formed into schools and designated "the sons of the prophets," which in the Hebrew language would emphasize the nature of their calling and contain no reference to their ancestry. There was one group of them at Bethel and another at Jericho (2 Ki 2:3, 5) and yet another at Gilgal (4:38). It is from the last reference we learn that Elisha was accustomed to sojourn with them for a time and preach or lecture to them, as their "sitting before him" signifies (Deut 33:3; Lk 2:46; 10:39). From the repeated mention of "the people" in this connection (2 Ki 4:41-42), we gather that these seminaries also served as more general places of assembly where the pious in Israel gathered together for the worship of Jehovah and to receive edification through His servant. That Elisha acted as rector or superintendent of these schools is evident from the young prophets owning him as "thou man of God" (4: 40) and "master" (6:5).

First, the Connection of the Miracle

"And the sons of the prophets said unto Elisha, Behold now, the place where we dwell with thee is too strait for us" (2 Ki 6:1). By means of the opening "And," the Holy Spirit has linked together the miracle recorded at the end of chapter 5 and the one we are now to consider. As in previous instances it suggests both comparisons and contrasts. Each miracle concerned those who were intimately connected with Elisha — in the one case his personal attendant, in the other his students. Each occurred at the same place — in the immediate vicinity of the Jordan. Each was occasioned by dissatisfaction with the position its subjects occupied — the one reprehensible, the other commendable. But first it was the unfaithful Gehazi, while here it is the devoted sons of the prophets. In the one, Gehazi took matters into his own hands; in the other they deferentially ask permission of their master. In the former an act of theft was committed; in the latter a borrowed article was recovered. In one a curse descended upon the guilty one; in this, an article was retrieved from the place of judgment.

Second, the Occasion of the Miracle

"And the sons of the prophets said unto Elisha, Behold now, the place where we dwell with thee is too strait for us" (v. 1). There does not appear to us to be anything in this verse which justifies the conclusion that some have drawn from it, namely, that these young men were discontented with their quarters and requested something more congenial. Charity always requires us to place the best construction on the projects and actions of our fellows. The motives which prompt them lie beyond our understanding and therefore are outside of our province; and actions are to be condemned only when it is unmistakably clear that they are evil in their nature or tendency. Had these students given expression to a covetous desire, surely Elisha would have reproved them; certainly he would not have encouraged their plan, as the sequel shows he did.

We are not told which particular school of the prophets this one was, but from its proximity to the Jordan there can be little doubt that it was the one situated either at Jericho or Gilgal — most probably the latter, because the reference in 2 Ki 4:38 seems to indicate that it was there that Elisha made his principal headquarters. This appears to be confirmed by the language used by the students "where we dwell with thee"; they would have said "sojourn" had he been merely on a temporary visit to them. From their statement, we gather that under the superintendency of Elisha their school had flourished, that there had been such an increase of their numbers that the accommodation had become too cramped for them. Accordingly, they respectfully called the attention of their master to what seemed a real need. It is to be observed that they did not impudently take matters into their own hands and attempt to spring a surprise upon Elisha, but instead pointed out to him the exigency of the situation.

"Let us go, we pray thee, unto Jordan, and take thence every man a beam, and let us make us a place there, where we may dwell" (2 Ki 6:2). Had their desire for more spacious quarters proceeded from carnal ambition, they would have aspired to something more imposing than a wooden building. Nor is it at all likely that in such a case they would volunteer to do the work themselves. Instead they would have suggested going around soliciting gifts from the people, so that they might have the money to hire others to erect a more commodious seminary for them.

> They were humble men who did not affect that which was gay or great. They did not speak of sending for cedars, and marble stones and curious artificers, but only of getting every man a beam, to run up a plain hut or cottage with. It becomes the sons of the prophets, who profess to look for the great in the other world to be content with mean things in this (Henry).

Alas that Protestants have so often aped the heathen in making a show before the world.

"And he answered, Go ye" (v. 2), which he surely would not have done if they were seeking something more agreeable to the flesh. That reply of Elisha's was something more than a bare assent to their proposal or permission for them to execute the same; it was also a real testing of their hearts. Those who are accustomed to judge others harshly might infer that these young men had grown tired of the strict discipline which Elisha must have enforced, and had found irksome the pious and devotional type of life he required from them, and that this idea of making for the Jordan was but a cover for their determination to get away from the man of God. In such a case they promptly would have availed themselves of his grant, bidden him farewell, and taken their departure.

But we may learn something more from this answer, "Go ye"; it gives us a sidelight on the prophet's own character, manifesting as it does his humility. He at once perceived the reasonableness of their request and concurred with them therein. A proud and haughty man would quickly resent any suggestion coming from those under his charge or care. Thus an important practical lesson is here taught: superiors ought not to consider themselves above receiving and weighing ideas from their underlings; and when discerning the wisdom of the same and recognizing they could be carried out to advantage, they should not hesitate to adopt them. It is the mark of a little mind, and not of a great one, which considers it has a monopoly of intelligence and is independent of help from others. Many a man has paid dearly for disdaining the counsel of his wife or employees.

"And one said, Be content, I pray thee, and go with thy servants" (v. 3). Very blessed is this, revealing as it does the happy relations which existed between them and of the veneration and love these students had for their master. Such meekness and graciousness on the part of superiors as we have alluded to above is not unappreciated by their subordinates. Nobly did they respond to the test contained in Elisha's "Go ye," by begging him to accompany them on their expedition. And how such a request on their part refutes the evil inference which some might draw from their original proposal — jumping to the conclusion that they were tired of Elisha's company and merely devised this plan as a pretext to get away from him. It is a warning to us not to surmize evil of our fellows, giving point to Christ's admonition, "Judge not according to the appearance, but judge righteous judgment" (Jn 7:24).

Third, the Location of the Miracle

"And he answered, I will go. So he went with them to the Jordan." And a good thing it was that he did so, as the sequel shows.

"And when they came to Jordan, they cut down wood" (2 Ki 6:4). Very commendable was this. But how unlike some of the young people of our generation, who have been encouraged to expect that someone else will do everything for them, that they should be waited on hand and foot by their seniors. These young men were willing and ready to put their own shoulder to the work. They did not seek to shelter behind a false conception of their sacred calling and indulge in foolish pride over their office by concluding that such a thing was beneath their dignity. No, instead of hiring others to do it, they performed the task themselves.

"But as one was felling a beam, the axe head fell into the water: and he cried, and said, Alas, master! for it was borrowed" (v. 5). An accident now happened. In one sense it is perfectly true that there are no accidents in a world that is presided over by the living God; but in another sense it is equally true that accidents do occur in the human realm.

This calls for a defining of our term. What is an accident? It is when some effect is produced or some consequence issues from an action undesigned by its performer. From the divine side of things, nothing occurs in this world but what God has ordained; but from the human side, many things result from our actions which were not intended by us. It was no design of this man that he should lose the head of his ax; that he did so was accidental on his part.

Fourth, the Objective of the Miracle

"And he cried and said, Alas, master! for it was borrowed." The objective, then, was to recover the borrowed article now lost. How strange that such a thing should happen while in the performance of duty! Yet the Lord had a wise and good reason for permitting it, and mercifully prevented the death of another (Deu 19:5). It is to be noted that the student did not regard Elisha as being too great a man to be troubled about such a trifling matter, but rather as an honest person deeply concerned over the loss; and assured of his master's sympathy, he at once informed him. His "alas" seems to denote that he regarded his loss as final and had no expectation it would be retrieved by a miracle. The lesson for us is plain: even though (to our shame) we have no faith of His showing Himself strong on our behalf, it is ever our duty and privilege to spread before our Master everything that troubles us.

> Not one concern of ours is small
> If we belong to Him,
> To teach us this, the Lord of all
> Once made the iron to swim.
>
> John Newton

Fifth, the Means of the Miracle

"And the man of God said — " Observe the change in verse 6 of 2 Kings 6 from verse 1: not simply "Elisha" here, because he was about to act officially and work a miracle. "Where fell it?" This was designed to awaken hope. "And he shewed him the place. And he cut down a stick, and cast it in thither; and the iron did swim" (v. 6). There was no proportion between the means and the end — to demonstrate that the power was of God! The Hebrew word for "stick" is a generic one. It is rendered "tree" 162 times, being the same word as in Deuteronomy 21:23 — quoted in Galatians 3:13! It is also translated "wood" 103 times, as in Genesis 6:14, the shittim "wood" used in connection with the frame and furniture of the tabernacle, and in verse 4 of 2 Kings 6. Evidently it was a small tree or sapling Elisha cut down.

Sixth, the Meaning of the Miracle

The incident which has been before us may, we consider, be justly regarded as broadly illustrating what is portrayed by the law and the gospel. It serves to give us a typical picture of the sinner's ruin and redemption. As the result of being dissatisfied with the position God originally assigned us — subjection to His authority — we (in Adam) appropriated what was not ours, and in consequence suffered a fearful fall. The inanimate iron falling into the Jordan — the place of "judgment" — is an apt figure of the elect in their natural state: dead in trespasses and sins, incapable of doing anything for their deliverence. The way and means which God took for our recovery was for Christ to come right down to where we were, and to be "cut off" (Dan 9:26), yes, "cut off out of the land of the living" (Is 53:8), enduring judgment on our behalf, thereby recovering us to God (1 Pe 3:18).

This incident may also be taken to inform the believer of how lost blessings may be restored to him. Are there not among our readers some who no longer enjoy the liberty they once had in prayer, or the satisfaction they formerly experienced in reading the Scriptures? Are there not some who have lost their peace and assurance, and are deeply concerned about being so deprived? If so, the devil will say the loss is irrecoverable and you must go mourning the rest of your days. But that is one of his many lies. This passage reveals how your situation may be retrieved. (1) Acquaint your Master with your grief (2 Ki 6:5); unbosom yourself freely and frankly unto Him. (2) Let His "where fell it?" (v. 6) search you. Examine yourself: review the past, ascertain the place or point in your life where the blessing ceased, discover the personal cause of your spiritual loss, judge yourself for the failure and confess it, acknowledging the blame to be entirely yours. (3) Avail yourself and make use of the means for recovery: cast in the "stick" or "tree" (v. 6): that is, plead the merits of Christ's cross (1 Pe 2:24). (4) Stretch forth the hand of faith (v. 7); that is, count upon your Master's infinite goodness and grace, expect His effectual intervention, and the lost blessing shall be restored to you.

This incident may also be viewed as making known to us how we may grow in grace. (1) There must be the desire and prayer for spiritual expansion (2 Ki 6:1) — a longing to enter into and possess the "large place" (Ps 118:5) God has provided for us. (2) The recognition that to enter therein involves effort from us (v. 2), labor on our part. (3) Seek the oversight of a servant of God in this (v. 3), if one is available. (4) Observe very carefully the particular place to which we must take ourselves if such spiritual enlargement is to be ours. We are to be buried under the Jordan. We can only enter into an enriched spiritual experience by dying more and more unto the flesh, that is, by denying self, and mortifying our lusts (Ro 8:13; Col 3:5). (5) Expect to encounter difficulties (2 Ki 6:5). (6) Use the appointed means (v. 6) for overcoming the obstacle of the flesh (Gal 6:14). (7) Stretch forth the hand of faith (2 Ki 6:7) and appropriate what God has given us in Christ.

Seventh, the Lessons of the Miracle

(1) See the value of requesting our Master's presence even when you are about to engage in manual labor. (2) Be conscientious about borrowed articles — books, for example! We should be more careful about things lent us than those which are our own. (3) Despise not those engaged in manual labor; Elisha did not. (4) Let

not the servant of God disdain what may seem trifling opportunities to do good. (5) Remember your Father cares for His people in their minutest concerns. (6) Is anything too hard for Him who made the iron to swim? (7) What encouragement is here for us to heed (Phil 4:6)!

Chapter 21

THIRTEENTH MIRACLE
EYES WITH NEW SIGHT

IN THIS INCIDENT we see Elisha discharging a different line of duty. No longer do we see him engaged in ministering to the young prophets, but instead we find him faithfully rendering valuable assistance to his sovereign. Once more the lust of blood or booty moved the king of Syria to war against Israel. Following the advice of his military counsellors, he decided to encamp in a certain place through which the king of Israel was apt to pass, expecting to catch him and his retainers. God acquainted Elisha with his master's peril, and accordingly the prophet went and warned him. By heeding him, the king was preserved from the snare set for him. It is required of us, as we have opportunity, to "do good unto all men" (Gal 6:10). True, the Christian is not endowed with the extraordinary gifts of Elisha; nevertheless he has a responsibility toward his king or ruler. Not only is he divinely commanded to "Honour the king" (1 Pe 2:17), but "I exhort therefore, that, first of all, supplications, prayers, intercessions, and giving of thanks, be made for all men: For kings, and for all that are in authority" (1 Ti 2:1-2). We come now to the thirteenth miracle.

First, the Connection of the Miracle

"Then the king of Syria warred against Israel, and took counsel with his servants, saying, In such and such a place shall be my camp" (2 Ki 6:8). Clearly, the opening "Then" bids us pay attention to the connection. From a literary viewpoint we regard our present incident as the sequel to what is mentioned in chapter 5, taking 2 Kings 6:1-7 as a parenthesis, thereby emphasizing the base ingratitude of the Syrian monarch for the miraculous healing of his commander-in-

173

chief in the land of Israel. There he had written a personal letter to Israel's king (5:5-6) to recover Naaman from his leprosy; but here he has evil designs upon him. That he should invade the land of Samaria so soon after such a remarkable favor had been rendered to him, made worse his offence and made more manifest his wicked character. It is wrong for us to return evil for evil, for vengeance belongeth alone unto the Lord; but to return evil for good is a sin of double enormity; yet how often have we treated God thus!

But there is another way in which this opening "Then" may be regarded, namely, by linking it unto the typical significance of what is recorded in verses 1-7. We suggested a threefold application of that miracle. First, this miracle supplies a picture of the sinner's redemption. Viewing it thus, what is the next thing he should expect to meet with? Why, the rage of the enemy, and this is illustrated by the attack of the king of Syria.

Second, this miracle may also be regarded as showing the Christian how a lost blessing is to be retrieved. And when the believer has peace, joy, and assurance restored to him, what is sure to follow? This, "Then the king of Syria warred against Israel." Nothing so maddens Satan as the sight of a happy saint — blessed is it to see in what follows how his evil designs were thwarted.

Third, this miracle can also be viewed as portraying how the Christian may grow in grace — by mortifying his members which are upon the earth. And if he does, and enters into an enlarged spiritual experience, then he may expect to be an object of the enemy's renewed assaults; yet he shall not be overcome by him.

"Then the king of Syria warred against Israel." Yes, my reader, there were wars in those days; human nature has been the same in each generation and in all countries. So far from war being a new thing, the history of nations — both ancient and modern, civilized and uncivilized — is little more than a record of animosities, intrigues, and fightings. "Their feet are swift to shed blood" (Rom 3:15) is one of the solemn indictments which God has made against the whole human family. There is no hint anywhere that Ben-hadad had received any provocation from Israel; it was just his own wicked greed and bloodthirstiness which moved him. And this in spite of a serious defeat he had suffered on a previous occasion (1 Ki 20:1, 26-30). "The heart of the sons of men is fully set in them to do evil" (Ec 8:11), and nothing but the restraining hand of God can stop them from executing their desires and devices. Neither solemn warnings nor kindly favors — as this man had recently received — will soften their hearts, unless the Lord is pleased to sanctify the same unto them.

"Then the king of Syria warred against Israel, and took counsel with his servants" (2 Ki 6:8). He asked not counsel of the Lord, for He was a stranger to him. We are glad to see no mention is made here of Naaman. It was with his "servants" rather than "the captain of the host" (5:1) he now conferred. We would hope that it was against the remonstrance of Naaman rather than with his approval that the king now acted. Yet what daring impiety to attack a people whose God wrought such marvels! If he had been impressed by the healing of his general, the impression speedily faded. "Saying, In such and such a place shall be my camp" (6:8). From the sequel it would appear that this particular "place" was one through which the king of Israel had frequent occasion to pass; thus Ben-hadad evidently laid a careful ambush for him there.

Thus it is with the great enemy of our souls: he knows both our ways and our weaknesses, and where he is most likely to gain an advantage over us. But as carefully as he made his plans, this king reckoned without the Most High.

Second, the Occasion of the Miracle

"And the man of God sent unto the king of Israel, saying, Beware that thou pass not such a place; for thither the Syrians are come down" (2 Ki 6:9). Yes, the king of Syria had left the living God out of his calculations. God is fully acquainted with the thoughts and intents of His enemies and, with the utmost ease, can bring them to naught. The methods which He employs in providence are as varied as His works in creation. On this occasion He did not employ the forces of nature, as He did at the Red Sea when He overthrew Pharoah and his hosts. Nor did He bid the king of Israel engage Ben-hadad in battle and enable him to vanquish his enemy. Instead, He prompted His servant to give his royal master warning and made the king believe him. The lesson for us is important. God does not always use the same method in His interpositions on our behalf. The fact that He came to my relief for deliverance in a certain manner in the past is no guarantee that He will follow the same course or use the same means now. This is to lift our eyes above all secondary causes to the Lord Himself.

Observe that it was "the man of God" not merely "Elisha" who went with this warning. "The Lord GOD . . . revealeth his secret unto his servants the prophets" (Amos 3:7). Thus it was in his official character that he went to the king with this divine message. Just previously he had used his extraordinary powers to help one of his students; here he befriended his sovereign. Whatever gift God has bestowed on his servants, it is to be used for the good of others. One of their principal duties is to employ the spiritual knowledge they have received in warning those in peril. How merciful God is in warning both sinners and saints of the place of danger! How thankful we should be when a man of God puts us on our guard against an evil which we suspected not! How many disastrous experiences shall we be spared if we heed the cautions given us by the faithful messengers of Christ. It is at our peril and to our certain loss if, in our pride and self-will, we disregard their timely "beware that thou pass not . such a place."

The course which the Lord took in delivering the king of Israel from the ambush set for him may not have flattered his self-esteem, any more than Timothy's was when Paul bade him "flee youthful lusts"; yet we may perceive the wisdom of it. God was enforcing the king's responsibility. He gave him fair warning of his danger; if he disregarded it then his blood was on his own head. So it is with us. The particular locality of peril is not named. The Syrian had said, "In such and such a place shall be my camp," and, "Beware that thou pass not such a place" was the prophet's warning. That the king would identify it in his mind is clear from the sequel. Yet since there is nothing meaningless in Scripture, there must be a lesson for us in its not being specifically named. We are plainly informed in the Word that our arch foe lies in wait to ensnare us. Sometimes a particular danger is definitely described; at others it is (as here) more generally mentioned — that we may ever be on our guard, pondering "the path of our feet" (Pr 4:26).

Though Satan may propose, God will both oppose and dispose. Before passing on to the sequel, let us link up what has just been before us with the typical teaching of the previous miracle — as the opening "Then" of verse 8 of 2 Kings 6 and the connecting "And" of verse 9 require — and complete the line of thought set out in our third paragraph above. When a sinner has been delivered from the power of darkness and translated into the kingdom of God's dear Son, he at once becomes the object of the devil's enmity; but God has graciously made provision for his security and prevents the enemy from ever completely vanquishing him. Likewise when a believer has been enabled to regain his peace and joy, Satan will renew his efforts to encompass his downfall; but his attempts will be foiled, for since the believer is now in communion with God, he has light on his path and clearly perceives the place to be avoided. So also when by means of mortification the Christian enjoys an enlarged spiritual experience, Satan will lay a fresh snare for him; but it will be in vain, for such a one will receive and heed divine warning.

"And the king of Israel sent to the place which the man of God [not 'Elisha'!] had told him and warned him of, and saved himself there, not once nor twice" (v. 10). Here we see the king's skepticism (cf. 5:7). He had some respect for the prophet's message or he would have disregarded it, yet he had not full confidence therein or he would not have "sent" to investigate. It was well for him that he went to that trouble, for thereby he obtained definite corroboration and found the caution he had received was not groundless. Ah, my reader, the warnings of God's servants are not idle ones, and it is our wisdom to pay the most serious heed to them. But alas, while most of our fellow men will pay attention to warnings against physical and temporal dangers, they are deaf concerning their spiritual and eternal perils. There is a real sense in which we are required to emulate Israel's king here: we are to follow no preacher blindly, but we must test his warnings, investigating them in the light of Scripture: "Prove all things; hold fast that which is good" (1 Th 5:21) and thereby we shall obtain divine corroboration.

"Therefore the heart of the king of Syria was sore troubled for this thing; and he called his servants, and said unto them, Will ye not show me which of us is for the king of Israel" (2 Ki 6:11). It never crossed his mind that it was the Lord who was thwarting him. Being a stranger to Him, he had no place in his thoughts for God; and therefore he sought a natural explanation. Instead of recognizing that God was on the side of Israel and blaming himself, he was chagrined at the failure of his plan. He suspected a traitor in his camp and sought a scapegoat.

"And one of his servants said, None, my lord, O king: but Elisha, the prophet that is in Israel, telleth the king of Israel the words that thou speakest in thy bedchamber" (v. 12). Even the heathen are not in entire ignorance of God; they have sufficient light and knowledge of Him to render them "without excuse" (Rom 1:19-20, 2:14-15).

Much more so is this the case with unbelievers in Christendom. This verse also shows how the spirituality and power of a true servant of God is recognized even by his enemies. The spokesman here may have been one of those who formed the retinue of Naaman when he came to Elisha and was healed of his leprosy. Yet observe there was no recognition and owning of God here. There was no acknowledgment that He was the one who revealed such secrets to His servants, no terming of Elisha "the man of God," but simply "the prophet that is in Israel." He was regarded merely as a "seer," possessing magical powers. Neither God nor His servant is accorded His rightful place by any but His own people.

Third, the Location of the Miracle

This miracle occurred at Dothan, which was to the west of Jordan, in the northeast portion of Samaria. Significantly enough, Dothan means "double feast," and from Genesis 37:16-17 we learn it was the place where the flocks were fed. "And he said, Go and spy where he is, that I may send and fetch him. And it was told him, saying, Behold, he is in Dothan" (2 Ki 6:13). Even now, the Syrian monarch was unwilling to recognize that he was fighting against Jehovah, but determined to remove this obstacle in the way of a successful carrying out of his campaign, even though that obstacle was a prophet. God allowed him to have his own way up to this point, that he might discover he was vainly flinging himself against God's "brick wall" and be made to feel his own impotency.

This verse illustrates the persistence of our great adversary, who will not readily accept defeat. As the Syrian now sought to secure the one who had come between him and his desired victim, so the devil makes special efforts to silence those who successfully warn the ones he would like to take captive.

"Therefore sent he thither horses, and chariots, and a great host [of infantry]: and they came by night, and compassed the city about" (v. 14). That he had some realization of the power Elisha wielded is evident by the strength and size of the force he now sent forth to take him prisoner. Yet the fact that he did not deem him to be invincible is shown by the plan he put into operation. Though the wicked are rendered uneasy by the stirrings of conscience and their convictions that they are doing wrong and following a course of madness, yet they silence the one and treat the other as vain superstitions, and continue in their sinful career. The surrounding of Dothan "by night" illustrates the truth that the natural man prefers the darkness to the light, and signifies that our adversary follows a policy of stealth and secrecy, ever seeking to take us unawares, especially when we are asleep.

Fourth, the Subject of the Miracle

"And when the servant of the man of God was risen early, and gone forth, behold, an host compassed the city both with horses and chariots. And his servant said unto him, Alas, my master! how shall we do?" (v. 15). Notice its subject is termed a servant, not of "Elisha" but of "the man of God." It is in such small but perfect details that the devout student loves to see the handiwork of the Holy Spirit, evidencing as it does the verbal inspiration of the Scriptures — God guiding each penman in the selection of every word he employed. This man, the successor of Gehazi, was new in the prophet's service, and therefore he was now being tested and taught. When a young believer throws in his lot with the people of God he will soon discover they are hated by the world; but he is called upon to share their reproach. Let not his older brethren expect too much from him while he is young and inexperienced; not until he has learned to walk by faith will he be undaunted by the difficulties and perils of the way.

"Alas, my master! how shall we do?" See here a picture of a young, weak, timid, distracted believer. Is not the picture true to life? Cannot all of us recall its exact replica in our own past experience? How often have we been nonplussed by the trials of the way and the opposition we have encountered. Quite likely this "young man" (v. 17) thought he would have a smooth path in the company of the man of God, and yet here was a situation that frightened him. And did we never entertain a similar hope? And when our hope was not realized, did we never give utterance to an unbelieving "Alas!" How shall we act — shutting God completely out of our view, with no hope of deliverance, no expectation of His showing Himself strong on our behalf? If memory enables us to see here a past representation of ourself, then let compassion cause us to deal leniently and gently with others who are similarly weak and fearful.

It should be borne in mind that the young believer has become, constitutionally, more fearful than unbelievers. Why so? Because his self-confidence and self-sufficience has been shattered. He has become as "a little child," conscious of his own weakness. So far so good; the great thing now is for him to learn where his strength lies. It should also be pointed out that Christians are menaced by more numerous and more formidable foes than was Elisha's servant, "For we wrestle not against flesh and blood, but against principalities, against powers, against the rulers of the darkness of this world, against spiritual wickedness in high places" (Eph 6:12). Well might we tremble and be more distrustful of ourselves were we more conscious of the supernatural beings opposing us. "And he answered, Fear not: for they that be with us are more than they that be with them" (2 Ki 6:16). A realization of that will dispel our doubts and quiet our fears. "Greater is he that is in you, than he that is in the world" (1 Jn 4:4).

Fifth, the Means of the Miracle

"And Elisha prayed, and said, LORD, I pray thee, open his eyes, that he may see" (2 Ki 6:17). How blessed is this! "Thou wilt keep him in perfect peace, whose mind is stayed on thee: because he trusteth in thee" (Is 26:3). There was no trepidation on the part of Elisha; perfect peace was his, and therefore could he say, "Fear not" to his trembling companion. Note there is no scolding of his servant, but instead a turning to the Lord on his behalf. At first the writer was puzzled at the "Elisha prayed" rather than the "man of God"; but pondering this brought out a precious lesson. It was not in his official character that he prayed, but simply as a personal believer — to show us that God is ready to grant the petition of any child of His who asks in simple faith and unselfish concern for another.

Sixth, the Marvel of the Miracle

"And the LORD opened the eyes of the young man; and he saw: and, behold, the mountain was full of horses and chariots of fire round about Elisha" (2 Ki 6:17). Proof was this of his "they that be with us are more than they that be with them": the invisible guard was now made visible to the eyes of his servant. Blessed illustration is this that, "The angel of the LORD encampeth round about them that fear him, and delivereth them" (Ps 34:7). "Are they [angels] not all ministering spirits, sent forth to minister for them who shall be heirs of salvation?" (Heb 1:14). Doubtless the angels took the form of "horses and chariots" on this occasion because of the Syrian horses and chariots which "compassed Dothan" (2 Ki 6:14). What could horses of flesh and material chariots do against celestial ones of fire! That they were personal beings is clear from the "they" of verse 16; that they were angels may also be gathered from a comparison with Hebrews 1:7 and 2 Thessalonians 1:7-8.

Seventh, the Meaning of the Miracle

Here we are shown how to deal with a young and fearing Christian. The strong "ought to bear the infirmities of the weak" (Ro 15:1). Many of God's little ones are living far below their privileges, failing to apprehend the wondrous provisions which God has made for them. They are walking far too much by sight, occupied with the difficulties of the way and those opposing them. First, such are not to be browbeaten or upbraided; that will do no good, for unbelief is not removed by such a method. Second, their alarm is to be quietened with calm and confident "Fear not," backed up with, "For they that be with us are more than they that be with them," and, "If God be for us, who can be against us?" (Ro 8:31), showing their fears are needless. Third, definite prayer is to be made for the shrinking one that the Lord will operate on and in him, for God alone can open his spiritual eyes to see the sufficience of His provision for him.

Chapter 22

FOURTEENTH MIRACLE
SIGHTLESS EYES

First, the Connection of the Miracle

THAT WHICH ENGAGED OUR ATTENTION in the last chapter grew out of the determination of Ben-hadad to again wage war on Israel. After taking counsel with his servants, the Syrian laid an ambush for the king of Israel, but they had reckoned without Jehovah. God revealed to His servant, the prophet, the danger menacing his royal master, and accordingly he went and told the king, who, attending to the warning, was delivered from the trap set for him. The heart of the king of Syria was troubled at this thwarting of his design, and, suspecting a traitor in his own camp, made inquiry. Whereupon one of his attendants informed him that nothing could be concealed from the prophet that was in Israel, and that he had put the intended victim on his guard. After sending out spies to discover the whereabouts of Elisha and learning that he was in Dothan, the king of Syria sent a formidable force, consisting of "horses and chariots" and a "great host" of footmen to take him captive, determining to remove this obstacle from his path.

The miracle we are about to consider is a double one and, strictly speaking, comprises the fourteenth and fifteenth of the series connected with our prophet. But the record is so brief and the two miracles are so closely related that they scarcely warrant separate treatment. Therefore instead of taking them singly we propose to consider them jointly, viewing the second as the counterpart or complement of the former. It is a miracle which stands out from the last one which occupied our notice. That one concerned the opening of eyes; this the closing of them. There, only one person was involved; here a great host of men is concerned. In the one it was the proph-

182

et's own servant who was the subject; here it is the soldiers who had been sent to take him captive. In the former, he responded to an urgent appeal from his attendant; here he acts without any solicitation. Both miracles occurred at the same place. They were both wrought in answer to Elisha's prayer. They are both recorded for our learning and comfort.

In connection with the preceding miracle, Elisha had prayed to his Master for Him to open the eyes of his servant, and we are told, "And the LORD opened the eyes of the young man; and he saw: and, behold, the mountain was full of horses and chariots of fire round about Elisha" (2 Ki 6:17). That the prophet himself already saw this celestial convoy is clear; it was his own vision of them which moved him to ask that his servitor might also behold them. We may deduce the same from the immediate sequel. Far from being in a panic at the great host of Syrians which had come to take him captive, Elisha calmly stood his ground. "The wicked flee when no man pursueth: but the righteous are bold as a lion" (Pr 28:1), for since God is for them, who can be against them? There was no need for him to cry to the Lord for deliverance, for divine protection was present to his view. Therefore he quietly waited till the enemy actually reached him before he acted.

Before passing on, let us offer a further remark about this celestial guard which was round about Elisha. That it was composed of personal beings is clear from the pronoun *"they* that be with us are more than *they* that be with them." That they were angelic beings is evident from several passages: "Who maketh his angels spirits; his ministers a flaming fire" (Ps 104:4). At His second advent, we are told, "The Lord Jesus shall be revealed from heaven with his mighty angels, In flaming fire taking vengeance on them that know not God, and that obey not the gospel of our Lord Jesus Christ" (2 Th 1:7-8). The ministry of angels is admittedly a mysterious subject, one about which we know nothing except what it has pleased God to reveal to us. Yet it is a subject which holds by no means an inconspicuous place in Holy Writ. It would be outside our present scope to explore it at large; rather must we confine ourself to that aspect of it which is here presented unto us.

Angels are not only God's messengers sent on missions of mercy, but they are also His soldiers, commissioned both to guard His people, and execute judgment on His enemies. They are designated "the host of heaven" (1 Ki 22:19; Lk 2:13) — the Greek word meaning "soldiers" or, as we would term them, "men of war," the militia of heaven. In full accord with that concept we find the Saviour reminding His disciples that "more than twelve legions of angels" (Mt 26:53) were at His disposal, should He but ask the Father for protection against the armed rabble that had come to arrest Him. It was a host of them, in the form of fiery horses and chariots (cf. Ps 68:17) which here encamped around Elisha, ready to fight for him. How mighty the angels are we know. One, called "the destroyer" (Ex 12:23 and cf. 2 Sa 24:16) slew all the firstborn of the Egyptians, while another slew 185,000 Assyrians in a night (2 Ki 19:35). That their operations continue in this Christian era is plain from such passages as Acts 12:7-10; Hebrews 1:14; Revelation 7:1, 15:1; Matthew 24:31.

"And when they came down to him, Elisha prayed unto the LORD, and said, Smite this people, I pray thee, with blindness" (2 Ki 6:18). The "they" looks back to the armed host mentioned in verse 14. Formidable as was the force sent to slay him, or at least take him captive, the prophet stood his ground and calmly waited their approach. And well he might. Could he not say, "I will not be afraid of ten thousands of people, that have set themselves against me round about" (Ps 3:6); and again, "Though an host should encamp against me, my heart shall not fear" (Ps 27:3)! And should not the same confidence and courage be the Christian's? "The clearer sight we have of the sovereignty and power of heaven, the less shall we fear the calamities of this earth" (Henry). Perhaps the reader says, If I were favored with an actual view of protecting angels round about me, I would not fear physical danger or human enemies. Ah my friend, is that not tantamount to a confession that you are walking by sight? And may we not apply to you those words, "Blessed are they that have not seen, and yet have believed" (Jn 20:29)?

Why, think you my reader, has God chronicled here that which assured the heart of His servant of old? Is this nothing more than a registering of a remarkable incident in ancient history? Is that how you read and understand the sacred Scriptures? May we not adopt the language used by the apostle in connection with a yet earlier incident and say, "Now it was not written for his sake alone . . . But for us also" (Ro 4:23-24)? Most certainly we may, for later on in that very epistle we are expressly informed, "For whatsoever things were written aforetime were written for our learning, that we through patience and comfort of the scriptures might have hope" (15:4). God has recorded that sight of those protecting angels for our faith to lay hold of. But remember that if faith is to stand us in good stead in the hour of emergency, it must be regularly nourished by the Word; if it is not, then the terrors of earth will be real to us and the comforts of heaven unreal. Unless faith appropriates that grand truth, "If God be for us, who can be against us," we shall neither have peace ourselves nor be qualified to quiet the fears of others.

Second, the Means of the Miracle

"And when they came down to him, Elisha prayed unto the LORD" (2 Ki 6:18). That needs to be pondered and interpreted in the light of the previous verse, or we are likely to miss its beauty and draw a false inference. Very lovely was the prophet's conduct on this occasion. The presence of those horses and chariots of fire round about Elisha was virtually a sign that God had delivered these Syrians into his hands; he had only to speak the word and the angels would have destroyed them. But he bore his enemies no ill will. Had our present verse stood by itself, we might have concluded that the prophet was asking in self-defense, begging the Lord to protect him from his foes, but it opens with the word "And"; and in the light of the one preceding, we are obliged to revise our thought. It is quite clear that Elisha was in no personal danger, so it could not have been out of any concern for his own personal safety that he now sought God. Yet, though he calmly awaited their approach, he did not meet his enemies in his own strength, for prayer is an acknowledgment of insufficiency.

"Elisha prayed unto the LORD, and said, Smite this people, I pray thee, with blindness." At first glance it seems strange that he is referred to here by his personal name rather than as "the man of God," which the Holy Spirit generally uses when he was about to work a miracle; yet the variation in this place is neither fortuitous nor meaningless. It points to a blessed lesson for us, showing as it does the readiness of the Lord to hearken to the requests of His people. Though we do not possess the extraordinary powers of a prophet, yet it is our privilege to ask God to confuse and confound those of our natural enemies who seek our harm, and to subdue our spiritual ones. This incident has been recorded for our instruction and comfort, and one of the things we are to learn from it is that prayer avails to render our enemies impotent. Another preceding lesson, wherein we see another of Elisha's requests granted: success in prayer should encourage and embolden us to ask further favors from God.

Go back again for a moment to Elisha's situation. This petition of his was neither because he felt he was in any personal danger, nor did it proceed from any spirit of malice which he bore his enemies. Then what prompted it? Does not the miraculous healing of Naaman supply the answer to our question? When the king of Israel had rent his clothes in dismay, the man of God assured him that the king of Syria "shall know there is a prophet in Israel" (5:7-8), and when Naaman was recovered of his leprosy he sought unto the man of God and, before all his own retinue, testified, "Now I know that there is no God in all the earth, but in Israel" (v. 15). And now this heathen monarch had sent his forces to take the prophet prisoner! Very well, then, if he were not yet convinced that it was the true and living God whom Elisha served, he would receive further proof. It was Jehovah's glory which prompted Elisha's request. Weigh that well my reader. Everything depends upon the motive which inspires our petitions, determining whether or not we shall receive an answer. True and acceptable prayer rises above a sense of personal need, having in view the honor of God's name. Keep before you 1 Corinthians 10:31.

"And he smote them with blindness according to the word of Elisha" (2 Ki 6:18). That was an exact reversal of what took place under the foregoing miracle: there the prophet's servant was enabled to see what was invisible to others (v. 17), but here the Syrian soldiers were rendered incapable of seeing what was visible to others. But let us behold in this miracle the willingness of our God to respond to the cries of His own, that He is a prayer-hearing and prayer-answering God. If we self-distrustfully refuse to encounter foes in our own strength, if we confidently ask God to render their efforts impotent, and if we do so with His glory in view, we may be assured of His gracious intervention. No matter what may be our need, how drastic the situation, how urgent our case, how formidable our adversary, while simple faith is exercised and the honor of God is our aim, we may count upon His showing Himself strong on our behalf. "For I am the LORD, I change not" (Mal 3:6). He is the same now as He was in Elisha's day.

Third, the Mercy of the Miracle

"And Elisha said unto them, This is not the way, neither is this the city: follow me, and I will bring you to the man whom ye seek. But he led them to Samaria" (2 Ki 6:19). He did not abandon them in their blindness and leave them to themselves. Contrast Genesis 19:11, where God was dealing in wrath. Had they not been blinded, probably they would have identified the prophet by his attire; but being strangers to him, they would be unable to recognize him by his voice. Spiritually that illustrates a fundamental difference between the goats and the sheep: the former are incapable of distinguishing between teachers of truth and of error; not so the latter, for they "know not the voice of strangers" but "will flee from him" (Jn 10:5). But exactly what did Elisha signify by those statements? It is lamentable to find one commentator, in whose notes there is generally that which is sound and good, saying, "The prophet intended to deceive the Syrians, and this might lawfully be done, even if he had meant to treat them as enemies, in order to his own preservation; but he designed them no harm by such deception."

Apart from such a view giving the worst possible interpretation to the prophet's language, such an observation as the above is most reprehensible. It is never right to do wrong, and, no matter what may be our circumstances, for us to deliberately lie is to sin both against God and our fellowmen. Such an explanation as the above is also absurd on the face of it. Elisha was in no personal danger at all; and now that these Syrians were blinded, he could have walked away unmolested by them, had he so pleased. "This is not the way." What way? He could not mean to Dothan, for they were already there and must have known it. "I will bring you to the man whom ye seek." And who was that? Why, ultimately and absolutely, the king of Israel, for whom their master had laid an ambush (see 2 Ki 6:11), Elisha being merely an obstacle, who had hindered him. One who had just obtained from God such an answer to prayer, and who was now showing mercy to his enemies, would scarcely lie to them!

Fourth, the Counterpart of the Miracle

"And it came to pass, when they were come into Samaria, that Elisha said, LORD, open the eyes of these men, that they may see. And the LORD opened their eyes, and they saw; and, behold, they were in the midst of Samaria" (v. 20). Here was still further proof that Elisha harbored no malice against these Syrians and that he intended them no harm. Though they had hostile designs against him, yet he now uses his interest with the Lord on their behalf. Most gracious was that. What an example for every servant of God: "In meekness instructing those that oppose themselves" (2 Ti 2:25). Instead of cherishing ill will against those who are unfriendly to us, we should seek their good and pray to the Lord on their behalf. How this incident reminds us of a yet more blessed example when the Lord of glory in the midst of His sufferings made intercession for His crucifiers (Is 53:12; Lk 23:34).

A further miracle was now wrought in answer to Elisha's intercession, showing us once more the mighty power of God and His willingness to employ it in answer to the petitions of His people. Note how Elisha made good his promise: he led them to the man they really sought, for the next person mentioned is "the king of Israel"!

Fifth, the Accompaniment of the Miracle

"And the king of Israel said unto Elisha, when he saw them, My father, shall I smite them? shall I smite them?" (2 Ki 6:21). Very solemn is this: and in full accord with the king's character: the Lord did not open *his* eyes; consequently he was blind to the working of His goodness and incapable of appreciating the magnanimous spirit which had been displayed by the prophet. Here we see what man is by nature: fierce, cruel, vindictive. Such are we and all of our fellowmen as the result of the fall: "living in malice and envy, hateful, and hating one another" (Titus 3:3). Only the restraining hand of God prevents our enemies from falling upon us. Were that hand completely withdrawn, we should be no safer in a "civilized" country than if we were surrounded by savages or cast into a den of wild beasts. We do not sufficiently realize that God's restraining power is upon those who hate us: "I am with thee, and no man shall set on thee to hurt thee" (Ac 18:10).

"And he answered, Thou shalt not smite them: wouldest thou smite those whom thou hast taken captive with thy sword and with thy bow? set bread and water before them, that they may eat and drink, and go to their master" (2 Ki 6:22). Observe how Elisha kept full control of the situation, even though he was now in the royal quarters — something which every servant of God needs to heed, exercising the authority which Christ has given him. Note too how this verse teaches that mercy is to be shown to prisoners of war; or taking it in its wider application, how kindness is to be extended to our enemies. And this, mark it well, occurred under the Old Testament economy! The divine law commanded its subjects, "If thine enemy be hungry, give him bread to eat; and if he be thirsty, give him water to drink" (Pr 25:21, and see also Ex 23:4-5); much more so under the dispensation of grace are we required to "overcome evil with good" (Ro 12:21).

Sixth, the Sequel of the Miracle

Elisha had his way, and the king "prepared great provision for them: and when they had eaten and drunk, he sent them away, and they went to their master" (2 Ki 6:23), that he might learn anew that our times, the success or failure of our plans, our health and our lives, are in the hand of the living God, and that He is not only infinite in power but plenteous in mercy. The sequel was, "So the bands of Syria came no more into the land of Israel" (v. 23). God honored the magnanimity of His prophet and rewarded the obedience of his royal master by exempting the land from any further depredations from these savage bands.

Seventh, the Meaning of the Miracle

May we not see in the above incident another lovely gospel picture, viewing the graciousness of Elisha to those who had gone to take him captive as a shadowing forth of God's mercy to elect sinners? First, we are shown that they are by nature — at enmity with His servant. Second, we behold them as the subjects of His servant's prayers, that they may be granted a sense of their wretched condition. Third, in answer thereto they are duly brought to realize their impotency; who are so consciously helpless as the blind? Fourth, they were moved to follow the instructions and guidance of God's servant. Fifth, in due course their eyes were opened. Sixth, they were feasted with "great provision" at the king's own table! Seventh, the picture is completed by our beholding them as changed creatures — coming no more on an evil errand into Israel's land.

But is there not also an important spiritual meaning and lesson here for Christians? How are we to deal with those who seek to injure us, should Providence deliver them into our hands? We are to ask the Lord to nullify their efforts and render them powerless to injure us. But more. We are also to pray that God will open their eyes, and treat them kindly and generously (see Mt 5:44).

Chapter 23

FIFTEENTH MIRACLE
A GREAT FAMINE

THE PASSAGE which is now to engage our attention is much longer than usual, beginning as it does at 2 Kings 6:24 and running to the end of chapter 7. The whole of it needs to be read at a sitting, so as to perceive its connections, its unity, and its wonders. In it there is a striking mingling of light and shade: the dark background of human depravity and the bright display of the prophet's faith; the exercise of God's justice in His sore judgments upon a rebellious and wayward people, and the manifestation of His amazing mercy and grace. In it we are shown how the wrath of man was made to praise the Lord, how the oath of a wicked king was made to recoil on his own head, how the skepticism of his courtier was given the lie and how the confidence of Elisha in his Master's word was vindicated. In it we behold how the wicked was taken in his own craftiness, or to use the language of Samson's parable, how the eater was made to yield meat, and how poor outcast lepers became the heralds of good news.

Truth is indeed stranger than fiction. Were one to invent a story after the order of the incident narrated in our present portion, critical readers would scorn it as being too farfetched. But those who believe in the living and omnipotent God that presides over the affairs of this world, far from finding anything here which taxes their faith, bow in adoration before Him who has only to speak and it is done, to will a thing and it is accomplished. In this case, Samaria was beseiged by a powerful enemy, so that its inhabitants were completely surrounded. The situation became drastic and desperate, for there was a famine so acute that cannibalism was resorted to. Yet under these extreme circumstances Elisha announced that within twenty-four hours there would be an abundance of food for every-one. His message was received with incredulity and scorn, yet it came to pass just as he had said, without a penny being spent, a gift being made, or a blow being struck. The surrounding Syrians fled in panic and left their vast stores of food to relieve the famished city. Let us now begin our examination of this miracle.

First, the Reality of the Miracle

After our remarks above it may strike the reader that it is quite an unnecessary waste of effort to labor a point which is obvious and offer proof that a miracle was wrought on this occasion. The writer would have thought so too had he not, after completing his own meditations, consulted several volumes on the Old Testament, only to find that this wonder is not listed among the miracles associated with Elisha. Even such a work as *The Companion Bible,* which supplies what is supposed to be a complete catalog of the miracles of Elijah and Elisha, omits this one. We offer no solution to this oversight, but since other writers have failed to see in 2 Kings 7 one of the marvels of our prophet we feel that we should present some of the evidence which in our judgment furnishes clear proof that a supernatural event was wrought on this occasion, and that we are fully warranted in connecting it with Elisha.

The first thing that we would take note of is that when the people were in such desperate straits and the king was so beside himself that he rent his clothes and swore that the prophet should be slain that very day, we are told "But [contrastively] Elisha sat in his house, and the elders sat with him" (2 Ki 6:32), which suggests to us that they had waited upon the Lord and had received assurance from Him of His intervention in mercy. Second, that the prophet was in communion with and in possession of the secret of the Lord is borne out by the remaining words of the verse, where he tells his companions of Jehoram's evil intention and announces the approach of his agent before he arrived. Next, we find the prophet plainly declaring that an abundant supply of food would be provided on the morrow (7:1), and he did so in his official character as "the man of God" (vv. 2, 17, 18, 19), which, as we have seen in previous chapters, is the title that is usually accorded him when God was about to work mightily through him or for him in answer to his prayers.

Consider too the circumstances. "There was a great famine in Samaria: and, behold, they [the Syrians] beseiged it, until an ass's head was sold for fourscore pieces of silver, and the fourth part of a cab of dove's dung for five pieces of silver" (6:25). Nevertheless the prophet declared that there should suddenly be provided sufficient food for all; and the sequel shows it came to pass such an abundant supply. The manner in which that food was furnished clearly evidenced the supernatural, as an impartial reading of 7:6-7 will make clear, for it was their enemies who were made to supply their tables! Finally, if we give due weight to the "according to the word of the LORD" and "as the man of God had said" in 7:16-17 and link with 4:43-44 where another of his miracles is in view and so referred to, the demonstration is complete.

Second, the Occurrence of the Miracle

This was the terrible shortage of food in the city of Samaria, due to its being surrounded by an enemy, so that none of its inhabitants could go forth and obtain fresh supplies. "And it came to pass after this, that Ben-hadad king of Syria gathered all his host, and went up, and besieged Samaria" (2 Ki 6:24). Strange as it may at first seem and sound to the reader, we see here one of the many internal evidences of the divine inspiration of the Scriptures. This will appear if we quote the last clause of the verse immediately preceding: "So the bands of Syria came no more into the land of Israel." Had an impostor written this chapter, attempting to palm off upon us a pious forgery he surely would not have been so careless as to place in immediate juxtaposition two statements which a casual reader can only regard as a flat contradiction. No, one who was inventing a story certainly would have made it read consistently and plausibly. Hence, we arrive at the conclusion that this is no fictitious narrative from the pen of a pretender to inspiration.

"So the bands of Syria came no more into the land of Israel [of which 'Samaria' was a part, as v. 20 shows]. And it came to pass after this, that Ben-hadad king of Syria gathered all his host, and went up, and besieged Samaria" (vv. 23-24). Now the placing of those two statements side by side is a clear intimation to us that the Scriptures need to be read closely and carefully, that their terms must be properly weighed, and that failure to do so will inevitably lead to serious misunderstanding of their purport. It is because infidels only skim passages here and there and are so poorly acquainted with the Word, that they charge it with being "full of contradictions." But there is no contradiction here, and if it presents any so-called difficulty to us, it is entirely of our own making. The first statement has reference to the plundering and irregular "bands" which had from time to time preyed on the Samaritans (compare the "companies" of 5:2), what we would term today "commando raids"; whereas 6: 24 speaks of organized war, a mass invasion, Ben-hadad gathering together "all his host."

"And it came to pass after this, that Ben-hadad king of Syria gathered all his host, and went up, and besieged Samaria" (v. 24). The opening clause is far more than a historical mark of time; properly understood, it serves to bring out the character of this man. The introductory "And" bids us link his action here with what is recorded in the context. In the remote context (chap. 5), we saw how God graciously healed Naaman of his leprosy. Naaman was the commander-in-chief of Ben-hadad's army and had been sent by him into Samaria to be cured of his dread disease. But little did the Syrian monarch appreciate that signal favor; shortly after, he assembled an increased force of his bands and "warred against Israel" (6:8). His plan was to capture Jehoram, but being foiled by Elisha he sent his men to capture the prophet. In that too he failed, for in answer to Elisha's prayer, they were smitten with blindness; though instead of taking advantage of their helplessness, he later prayed for their eyes to be opened, and after having the king give them a feast, sent them home to their master, who had returned to Syria.

"And it came to pass after this"; not that Ben-hadad repented of his former actings, nor that he was grateful for the mercy and kindness which had been shown his soldiers; but that he "gathered all his host, and went up, and besieged Samaria." Not only was this base ingratitude against his human benefactors, but it was blatant defiance against Jehovah Himself. Twice the Lord had manifested His miracle-working power in grace on his behalf; and here was his response. Yet we must look further if we are to perceive the deeper meaning of "it came to pass after this," for we need to answer the question, Why did the Lord permit this heathen to invade Israel's territory?

The reply is also furnished by the context. Ben-hadad was not the only one who had profited by God's mercies in the immediate past; the king of Israel had also been divinely delivered from those who sought his life. And how did he express his appreciation? Did he promptly institute a religious reformation in his dominions and tear down the altars which his wicked parents had set up? No, so far as we are informed he was quite unmoved and continued in his idolatry.

It is written, "the curse causeless shall not come" (Pr 26:2). When God afflicts a people, be it a church or a nation, it is because He has a controversy with them. If they refuse to put right what is wrong, He chastises them. God, then, was acting in judgment on Samaria when He commissioned the Syrians to now enter their land in full force. "O Assyrian, the rod of mine anger, and the staff in their hand is mine indignation. I will send him against an hypocritical nation" (Is 10:5-6). So again, at a later date, the Lord said of Nebuchadnezzar "Thou art my battle axe and weapons of war: for with [or 'by'] thee will I break in pieces the nations, and with thee will I destroy kingdoms" (Jer 51:20). It is in the light of such passages as these we should view the activities of a Hitler or a Mussolini! Though God's time to completely cast off Israel had not come in the days of Jehoram, yet He employed Ben-hadad to grievously afflict his kingdom.

"And there was a great famine in Samaria: and, behold, they besieged it, until an ass's head was sold for fourscore pieces of silver, and the fourth part of a cab of dove's dung for five pieces of silver" (2 Ki 6:25). Troubles seldom come singly, for God means to leave us without excuse if we fail to recognize whose hand it is which is dealing with us. Ben-hadad chose his hour to attack when Israel was in sore tribulation, which serves also to illustrate Satan's favorite method of assaulting the saints. Like the fiend that he is, he strikes when they are at their lowest ebb, coming as the roaring lion when their nerves are already stretched to the utmost, seeking to render them both praiseless and prayerless while lying on a bed of sickness, or to instill into their minds doubts of God's goodness in the hour of bereavement, or to queston His promises when the meal has run low in their barrel. But since "we are not ignorant of his devices" (2 Co 2:11), we should be on our guard against such tactics.

"And there was a great famine in Samaria." It needs to be pointed out in these days of skepticism and practical atheism that the inhabitants of earth are under the government of something infinitely better than "fickle fortune," namely, a world which is ruled over by the living God. Goodly harvests or the absence of them are not the result of chance nor the effect of a blind fate. In Psalm 105:16 we read that God "called for a famine upon the land: he brake the whole staff of bread." And my reader, when He calls for a "famine," neither farmers nor scientists can prevent or avert it. We have read in the past of famines in China and in India, but how faintly can we conceive of the awful horrors of one in our day! As intimated above, the Lord called for this famine on Samaria because the king and his subjects had not taken to heart His previous chastisements of the land for their idolatry. When a people refuse to heed the rod, then He smites more heavily.

"And there was a great famine in Samaria: and, behold, they besieged it." Their design was not to storm but to starve the city, by throwing a powerful military cordon around it, so that none could either go out or come in. "And as the king of Israel was passing by upon the wall [probably taking stock of his defences and seeking to encourage the garrison], there cried a woman unto him, saying, Help, my lord, O king" (2 Ki 6:26). And well she might, for they were now deprived of the bare necessities of life, with a slow but painful death by starvation staring them in the face. Ah, my reader, how little we really value the common mercies of this life until they are taken from us! Poor woman, she turned to lean upon a broken reed, seeking relief from the apostate king, rather than making known her need to the Lord. There is no hint anywhere in the narrative that the people prayed to God.

"And he said, If the LORD do not help thee, whence shall I help thee? out of the barnfloor or out of the winepress?" (v. 27). That was not the language of submission and piety, but, as the sequel shows, of derision and blasphemy. His language was that of anger and despair: the Lord *will* not help; I *cannot,* so we must perish. Out of the abundance of his evil heart his mouth spoke. Calming down a little, "the king said unto her, What aileth thee? And she answered, This woman [pointing to a companion] said unto me, Give thy son, that we may eat him to day, and we will eat my son to morrow. So we boiled my son, and did eat him: and I said unto her on the next day, Give thy son, that we may eat him: and she hath hid her son" (vv. 28-29). This shows the desperate conditions which then prevailed and the awful pass to which things had come. Natural affection yielded to the pangs of hunger. This too must also be regarded as a most solemn example of the divine justice, and vengeance on idolatrous Israel.

It must be steadily borne in mind that the people of Samaria had cast off their allegiance to Jehovah and were worshiping false gods, and therefore according to His threatenings, the Lord visited them with severe judgments. They were so blockaded by the enemy that all ordinary food supplies failed them, so that in their desperation they were driven to devour the most abominable offals and even human flesh. Of old the Lord had announced unto Israel, "If ye will not for all this hearken unto me, but walk contrary unto me; Then I will walk contrary unto you also in fury; and I, even I, will chastise you seven times for your sins, and ye shall eat the flesh of your sons" (Lev 26:27-29). And again, "The LORD shall bring a nation against thee . . . And he shall besiege thee . . . And thou shalt eat the fruit of thine own body, the flesh of thy sons and of thy daughters, which the LORD thy God hath given thee, in the siege, and in the straitness" (Deu 28:49, 52-53). This was even more completely fulfilled at the destruction of Jerusalem in A.D. 70. No words of God's shall fall to the ground; His threatenings, equally with His promises, are infallibly certain of fulfillment!

"And it came to pass, when the king heard the words of the woman, that he rent his clothes; and he passed by upon the wall, and the people looked, and, behold, he had sackcloth within upon his flesh" (2 Ki 6:30). According to the customs of those days and the ways of Oriental people, this was the external garb of a penitent; but what was it worth while he renounced not his idols? Not a particle in the eyes of Him who cannot be imposed upon by any outward shows. It was a pose which the king adopted for the benefit of his subjects, to signify that he felt deeply for their miseries; yet he lamented not for his own iniquities, which were the underlying cause of the calamity. Instead of so doing, the very next verse tells us that he took an awful oath that Elisha should be promptly slain. "Rend your heart, and not your garments" (Joel 2:13) is ever the divine call to those under chastisement, for God desires truth (reality) in "the inward parts" (Ps 51:6).

As it is useless to wear sackcloth when we mourn not for our sins, so it is in vain to flock to church on a "day of prayer" and then return at once to our vanities and idols. Israel later complained, "Wherefore have we fasted, . . . and thou seest not? wherefore have we afflicted our soul, and thou takest no knowledge?" And God answered them by saying, "Behold, in the day of your fast ye find pleasure, and exact all your labours. . . . Ye shall not fast as ye do this day, to make your voice to be heard on high" (Is 58:3-4). Thus there is such a thing as not only praying but fasting which God pays no attention to. At a later date He said to them, "When ye fasted and mourned . . . did ye at all fast unto me, even to me? Should ye not hear the words which the LORD hath cried by the former prophets!" (Zec 7:5, 7). While a nation tramples upon the divine commandments, neither prayer and fasting nor any other religious performances are of any avail with Him who says, "Behold, to obey is better than sacrifice" (1 Sam 15:22). There must be a turning away from sin before there can be any real turning unto God.

Chapter 24

FIFTEENTH MIRACLE
THE WRATH OF MAN

"Then he said, God do so and more also to me, if the head of Elisha the son of Shaphat stand on him this day" (2 Ki 6:31). This was the language of hatred and fury. Refusing to admit that it was his own impenitence and stubbornness which was the procuring cause of the terrible straits to which his kingdom was now reduced, Jehoram turned an evil eye on the prophet and determined to make a scapegoat of him. As though the man of God was responsible for the famine, Israel's apostate king took a horrible oath that he should be promptly slain. He was well acquainted with what had happened in the reign of his parents, when in answer to the words of Elijah there had been no rain on Samaria (1 Ki 17:1), and he probably considered that his own desperate situation was due to Elisha's prayers. Though just as Ahab declined to recognize that the protracted drought was a divine judgment upon his own idolatry, so his son now ignored the fact that it was his personal sins that had called down the present expression of divine wrath.

This solemn and awful incident should be viewed in the light of that divine indictment, "The carnal mind is enmity against God" (Ro 8:7), and that my reader, is true of your mind and of my mind by nature. You may not believe it, but He before whose omniscient eye your heart is open, declares it to be so. You may be quite unconscious of your awful condition, but that does not alter the fact. If you were better acquainted with the true God, were aware of His ineffable holiness and inexorable justice, and realized that it is His hand that smites you when your body suffers acute pain or when your circumstances are most distressing, you might find it easier to discover how your heart really beats toward Him and the ill will you

198

bear Him. True, that fearful "enmity" does not always manifest itself in the same way or to the same degree, for in His mercy God often places His restraining hand upon the wicked and prevents the full
outbursts of their hostility and madness. But when that restraining
hand is removed, their case is like that described in Revelation 16:
10-11: "They gnawed their tongues for pain, And blasphemed the
God of heaven because of their pains and their sores, and repented
not of their deeds."

And why do we say that Jehoram's conduct on this occasion made
manifest the enmity of the carnal mind against God? Because, while
he was unable to do Jehovah any injury directly, he determined to
visit his spite upon Him indirectly, by maltreating His servant. Ah
my reader, there is important if solemn instruction for us in that.
Few people realize the source from which proceeds the bitterness,
the opposition made against, the cruel treatment meted out to many
of the ministers of the gospel. As the representatives of the holy One,
they are a thorn in the side of the ungodly. Though they do them
no harm, but instead desire and seek their highest good, yet are
they detested by those who want to be left alone in their sins. Nothing recorded in human history more plainly and fearfully displays
the depravity of fallen man and his alienation from God than his
behavior toward the most faithful of His servants — supremely manifested when the Lord of glory took upon Him the form of a servant
and tabernacled among men. It was just because He made known
and revealed the character of God as none else ever did, that man's
hatred of and enmity against Him was so inveterately and fiercely
exhibited.

"But Elisha sat in his house, and the elders sat with him" (2 Ki
6:32). This verse also needs to be pondered in the light of other
Scriptures. For example: "Whoso hearkeneth unto me shall dwell
safely, and shall be quiet from fear of evil" (Pr 1:33). The one
who truly fears the Lord, fears not man; and his heart is preserved
from those trepidations which so much disturb the rest and so often
torment the wicked. No, "he shall not be afraid of evil tidings"; he
shall neither have alarming anticipations of such, nor be dismayed
when they actually arrive. And why not? Because "his heart is fixed,
trusting in the LORD" (Ps 112:7). Rumors do not shake him, nor
does he quake when they are authenticated, for he is assured that his
"times" are in the hand of the Lord (Ps 31:15). And therefore is
he kept in peace. In the light of all that is recorded of him, who can

doubt that Elisha and his companions had been on their knees before the throne of grace, and now calmly awaited events. That is the holy privilege of the saints in times of acutest stress and distress: to "rest in the Lord, and wait patiently for him" (Ps 37:7).

"And the king sent a man from before him." This man was dispatched quickly ahead of Jehoram, either to announce his awful decision or to put it into actual execution. Had the king paused to reflect, he should have realized that it was one thing to form such a determination, but quite another to carry it out. Had not Ben-hadad, only a short time previously, sent a "great host" not only of footmen, but of "horses and chariots" against this servant of the Lord (2 Ki 6:14) only for them to discover their impotence against him! But when a soul (or a people) has abandoned the Lord, he is given up to a spirit of madness, so that not only does God have no place in his thoughts, but he is no longer capable of acting rationally — rationality and spirituality are closely connected. "But ere the messenger came to him, he [Elisha] said to the elders, See ye how this son of a murderer hath sent to take away mine head? look, when the messenger cometh, shut the door, and hold him fast at the door: is not the sound of his master's feet behind him?" (v. 32).

"And while he yet talked with them, behold, the messenger came down unto him: and he said, Behold, this evil is of the LORD: what should I wait for the LORD any longer?" (v. 33). We confess we do not find it easy to ascertain the precise force of this verse, not even its grammatical meaning. The first sentence is clear, for the "while he yet talked" evidently refers to what Elisha was saying to the elders. The difficulty is to discover the antecedent of the "And he said." The nearest is the "him" or Elisha, yet certainly he would not say his proposed murder ("this evil") was "of the Lord," ordered by Him. The next is "the messenger," but the prophet had given definite orders that he was not to be admitted, nor would this agree with what follows in 7:1-2. We therefore regard the second sentence as recording the words of the king himself, who had followed immediately on the heels of his messenger, thus the more remote but principal antecedent of verses 30-31; just as we understood "the man whom ye seek" as meaning Jehoram rather than Elisha (v. 19).

But what did the king signify by "this evil is of the LORD?" We certainly do not concur with Henry and Scott that he referred to the siege and famine, for not only is the grammar of the passage against such a view, but it is in direct opposition to everything else which is recorded of this son of Jezebel. He did not believe in Jehovah at all, and therefore his language must be regarded as that of derision and blasphemy. The context shows he was in a towering rage, that he regarded Elisha as being in some way responsible for the present calamity, and that he was determined to put a sudden end to his life. Fully intending to execute his murderous design, he now burst in on the prophet and said, "This evil is of the LORD." Those were the words of contemptuous mockery: you profess to be a servant of an all-powerful Jehovah; let's see what He can do for you now — behold me as His executioner if you please. "What should I wait for the LORD any longer?" Jehovah has no place in my thoughts or plan; the situation is hopeless, so I shall waste no more time, but slay you and surrender to Ben-hadad and take my chance.

"Then Elisha said —" The "Then" looks back to all that has been before us in the last ten verses of 2 Kings 6. "Then" when "all the hosts of Syria" were besieging Samaria; "then" when there was a great famine and things had come to such an extreme pass that the people were paying immense prices for the vilest of offals, and mothers were consuming their own infants. "Then" when the king of Israel had sworn that the prophet should be beheaded this very day; "then" when the king in a white heat of passion entered Elisha's abode to carry out his murderous intention. "Then" — what? Did the prophet give way to abject despair and break forth into bitter lamentations of murmuring rebellion? No indeed. Then what? Did Elisha fling himself at the king's feet and plead with him to spare his life? Very far from it; such is not the way the ambassadors of the King of kings conduct themselves in a crisis. Instead, "then Elisha said [calmly and quietly], Hear ye the word of the Lord." To what import? That His patience is exhausted, that He will now pour out His wrath and utterly consume you? No, the very reverse; the last thing they could have expected him to say.

"Then Elisha said, Hear ye the word of the Lord; Thus saith the LORD, To morrow about this time shall a measure of fine flour be sold for [as little as] a shekel, and two measures of barley for a shekel, in the gate of Samaria" (7:1). This brings us to the third area of consideration.

Third, the Announcement of the Miracle

In view of the next verse, it is quite clear that the prophet addressed himself to the king and those who had accompanied him. It was as though he said, I have listened to the derisive and insulting words which you have spoken of my Master; now hear what He has to say! And what was His message on this occasion? This: He is about to have mercy upon your kingdom. He is on the point of working a miracle within the next twenty-four hours which will entirely reverse the present situation, so that not only will the Syrians depart, but there shall be provided an abundant supply of food, which will fully meet the needs of your people, and that, without a blow being struck or your royal coffers being any the poorer.

Admire here the remarkable faith of Elisha. "Then." When things were at their lowest possible ebb, when the situation was desperate beyond words, when the outlook appeared to be utterly hopeless. Mark the implicit confidence of the prophet in that dark hour. He had received a message of good tidings from his Master, and he hesitated not to announce it. Ah, but put yourself in his place, my reader, and remember that he was "a man of like passions" with us, and therefore liable to be cast down by an evil heart of unbelief. It is a great mistake for us to look upon the prophets as superhuman characters. In this case, as in all parallel ones, God was pleased to place His treasure in an "earthen vessel," that the glory might be His. Elisha was just as liable to the attacks of Satan as we are. For all we know to the contrary and reasoning from the law of analogy, it is quite likely that the enemy of souls came to him at that time with his evil suggestions and said, May you not be mistaken in concluding that you have received such a word as this from the Lord? Nay, you are mistaken — your own wish is father to the thought. You are deluded into imagining that such a thing can be.

Those who are experimentally acquainted with the conflict between faith and unbelief, who are frequently made to cry out, "Lord, I believe, help thou mine unbelief," will have little difficulty in following what has just been said. They who know something from firsthand acquaintance of the tactics of the devil and the methods of his assaults, will not consider our remarks farfetched. Rather will they concur that it is more than likely Elisha was hotly assailed by the adversary at this very time. Would he not pose too as an angel of light, and preach a little sermon to the prophet, saying, A holy God is now acting in judgment, righteously scourging the idolatrous Jehoram, and therefore you must certainly be mistaken in supposing He is about to act in a way of mercy. At any rate, exercise prudence, wait a while longer lest you make a fool of yourself; it would be cruel to raise false hopes in the starving people! But if so, Elisha heeded him not, but being strong in faith, he gave glory to God. It was just such cases as this that the apostle had in mind when he mentioned the faith of "the prophets" in Hebrews 11:32.

Ah, my reader, Elisha was assured that what he had received was "the Word" of Him "that cannot lie," and no matter how much opposed it was to common sense and to all outward appearances, he firmly took his stand upon it. The "faith of God's elect" (Titus 1:1) is no fiction but a glorious reality. It is something more than a beautiful ideal to talk about and sing of. It is a divine gift, a supernatural principle, which not only overcomes the world but survives the "fiery trial," yes, issues therefrom refined. Elisha was not put to confusion. That divine "word," though perhaps quite unexpected and contrary to his own anticipations, was faithfully and literally fulfilled; and remember that this is recorded for our learning and consolation. We too have in our hands the Word of truth, but do we have it in our hearts? Are we really relying upon its promises, no matter how unlikely their accomplishment may seem to carnal reason? If so, we are resting upon a sure foundation, and we too shall have our faith vindicated, and God will be glorified through and by us.

But let us look higher now than Elisha's faith in that divine word to the One who gave it to him. It was the Lord manifesting Himself as the God of all grace to those who were utterly unworthy. In their dire extremity the Lord had mercy upon them and remembered they were the seed of Abraham, and therefore He would not entirely destroy them. He turned an eye of pity on the starving city and promised them speedy relief from the awful famine. How truly wonderful is His mercy! He was saying, "How shall I give thee up, Ephraim? how shall I deliver thee, Israel? how shall I make thee as Admah? how shall I set thee as Zeboim? mine heart is turned within me, my repentings are kindled together" (Ho 11:8). But that mercy rested on a righteous basis; there was a "handful of salt" in Samaria which preserved it from destruction — the prophet and the elders. Rightly was Elisha styled by a later king "the chariot of Israel and the horsemen thereof" (2 Ki 13:14), for his presence in their midst was a better defense than a multitude of infantry and cavalry; a British queen feared the prayers of Knox far more than any arm of flesh.

And may not what has just been pointed out provide a ray of hope for us in this, spiritually speaking, dark night? Of old Israel was reminded, "For what nation is there so great, who hath God so nigh unto them, as the LORD our God is in all things that we call upon him for?" (Deu 4:7).

Has not that been true of Britain the past four centuries as of no other people? God has shown us favors, granted us privileges, such as no other nation in the world has enjoyed. And we, like Israel of old, have evilly requitted Him and abused His great benefits. For years past His judgments have been upon us, and like Israel again, we have sadly failed to bow to His rod and turn from our sins. If God was so reluctant to abandon Israel, may He not continue to show us mercy, and for the sake of the little "salt" still left in our midst, spare us from destruction? Time will tell, but we are not left without hope.

"Then a lord on whose hand the king leaned answered the man of God, and said, Behold, if the LORD would make windows in heaven, might this thing be?" (2 Ki 7:2). There was the response that was made to Jehovah's word through His prophet. Instead of being received with thanksgiving and tears of gratitude, it met with a contemptuous sneer. The courtier's language expressed the skepticism of carnal reason. Unbelief dared to question the divine promise — illustrative of the unregenerate's rejection of the gospel. This man argued from what he could see: as no possible relief was visible, he scorned its probability, or rather certainty. "And he [Elisha] said, Behold, thou shalt see it with thine eyes, but shalt not eat thereof" (v. 2). Let it be noted that the prophet wasted no breath in reasoning with this skeptic. It is not only useless, but most unbecoming for a servant of the Lord to descend to the level of such objectors. Instead, he simply affirmed that this man would witness the miracle but be unable to share in its benefits. God Himself will yet answer the skeptics of this age, as He did that one, with appropriate judgment. Such will be the doom of unbelievers: they shall see the redeemed feasting at the marriage of the Lamb, yet not partake thereof (Mt 8:11-12).

Chapter 25

FIFTEENTH MIRACLE
FOUR LEPROUS MEN

Let us briefly review our last two chapters upon this miracle. First, we emphasized its reality, seeking to show it was indeed a miracle which took place and that it might justly be regarded as connected with Elisha. Second, we dwelt upon its occasion, which was the fearful shortage of food in the city of Samaria, resulting from its being so closely surrounded by the Syrians that none of its inhabitants could go forth and obtain fresh supplies (2 Ki 6:24-25). So acute did conditions become that the vilest of offals were sold at exhorbitant prices, and mothers had begun to consume their own babies. So far from humbling himself beneath the hand of divine judgment and acknowledging that it was his own idolatry and impenitence which was the procuring cause of reducing his kingdom to such sore straits, Israel's king turned an evil eye upon Elisha and determined to make a scapegoat of him, taking a horrible oath that he should be slain forthwith (6:31) — evidencing that he was a true son of Jezebel (1 Ki 18:4).

"But Elisha sat in his house, and the elders sat with him" (2 Ki 6:32); he calmly awaited events. Announcing that "this son of a murderer hath sent to take away mine head," he gave orders that the door should be shut and the royal messenger not be admitted. Jehoram himself hastened on just behind. The prophet and the king then came face to face, and the former announced the impending miracle. "Then Elisha said, Hear ye the word of the Lord; Thus saith the Lord, To morrow, about this time shall a measure of fine flour be sold for a shekel, and two measures of barley for a shekel, in the gate of Samaria" (2 Ki 7:1). That was tantamount to saying, God in His high sovereignty is going to show mercy on your wretched kingdom, and within a day will work a miracle that shall entirely reverse the present situation. Not only will the Syrians depart, but there shall be provided an abundant supply of food which will fully meet the needs of your people, without a blow being struck or your royal coffers being any the poorer.

"Then a lord on whose hand the king leaned answered the man of God, and said, Behold, if the LORD would make windows in heaven, might this thing be?" (7:2). Such a message of good news as the prophet had just proclaimed, of deliverance from the enemy and food for the starving, seemed utterly incredible to carnal reason, and therefore instead of being received with fervent thanksgiving, it was met with a contemptuous sneer. Unbelief presumed to call into question the divine promise. Arguing from what he could see, no possible relief being visible, this wicked lord scorned the likelihood of its fulfillment. That which Elisha had announced was indeed impossible to anyone but the living God, for only by a miracle could it be made good; yet it was the express word of Him that cannot lie and who is endowed with omnipotence. Despite the effort of his unbelieving courtier to prevent any weakening of his resolution, the king of Israel decided to wait another day before carrying out his murderous design, and during that interval the prediction was accomplished. We now continue this study.

Fourth, the Heralds of the Miracle

Heralds are the ones made use of by the Lord to proclaim the wonder of mercy which He had wrought. Strange indeed do the divine methods often appear to our dim vision, yet in the light of Scripture their significance is not lost upon those favored with anointed eyes. It was not "the elders of Israel" who had sat with Elisha in his house, nor was it "the sons of the prophets" whom the Lord honored on this occasion. God is sovereign and employs whom He pleases. Often He acts as He does in order to stain the pride of man, for He is jealous of His own honor and will suffer no flesh to glory in His presence. It is true that He has called certain men to the special work of the ministry and set them apart, and that He frequently works through them in the converting of His people; yet He is by no means tied to that particular agency, and often manifests His independence by making use of the most unlikely ones to be His agents — as appears in the more extreme cases of Balaam and Judas. So it was here.

"And there were four leprous men at the entering in of the gate: and they said one to another, Why sit we here until we die?" (2 Ki 7:3). More unlikely instruments could scarcely be imagined. They were pariahs, outcasts, men debarred from mingling with their ordinary fellow citizens. They were lepers, and as such excluded by the divine law (Lev 13:46). Yet these were the ones whom God was pleased to employ. How different are His thoughts and ways from man's! But let us observe the position which they occupied and the strange anomaly which that reveals. They were sitting "at the entering in of the gate," that is, of Samaria (7:1, 3), namely, on the outside of the city's walls — as the next verse shows. There we have a striking sidelight on the inconsistency of perverse human nature, especially in connection with religious matters. Though idolaters devoid of any respect for Jehovah, yet Jehoram and his officers were punctilious in carrying out the requirement of the ceremonial law as it respected the exclusion of lepers! They were diligent in tithing mint and anise while omitting the weightier matters of the moral law (Mt 23:23).

That to which we have called attention is frequently exemplified on the pages of Holy Writ. Instead of utterly destroying Amalek and all his possessions, as commanded when God delivered them into his hands, Saul permitted the people to spare the best of the sheep and oxen that they might offer them in "sacrifice unto the LORD." To these Samuel declared, "Behold, to obey is better than sacrifice, and to hearken than the fat of rams" (1 Sa 15:22). Because it was the eve of the Passover the Jews besought Pilate that the bodies of Christ and the two thieves who had been crucified with Him "might be taken away" (Jn 19:31), that their solemn feast might not be defiled. What a strange mixture human nature is! Those ceremonially unclean lepers must be shut out of Samaria, even though Jehovah Himself was treated with the utmost contempt! And do we not see the same principle illustrated in Christendom? Let a Christian attend morning services, and he may spend the remainder of Sunday as he pleases. Being a stickler for a particular form of baptism, breaking bread each Lord's day morning, or spending five days at a "communion," is a mockery if we love not our neighbor as ourselves.

"And there were four leprous men at the entering in of the gate: and they said one to another, Why sit we here until we die?" It will probably surprise many to know that some have been taught

that this is the proper attitude to assume when one has been convicted of his lost condition. Appeal for this is made to such passages as "Blessed is the man that heareth me, watching daily at my
gates, waiting at the posts of my doors" (Pr 8:34), "In these lay a
great multitude of impotent folk, of blind, halt, withered, waiting
for the moving of the water" (Jn 5:3). The awakened sinner is
told that he is utterly helpless to do anything for himself, entirely
dependent on God's sovereign pleasure, and then since there is a set
time to favor Zion (Ps 102:13), he must meekly wait for God's appointed hour of deliverance, should He deign to deliver him. But
such counsel is an utter misuse of both the truth of God's sovereignty
and of man's spiritual inability. Proof of its error is found in the
fact that it both clashes with the call of the gospel and is a repudiation of human responsibility.

The truth is that the spiritual inability of the natural man is both a
voluntary and a criminal one. He does not love and serve God because he hates Him; he believes not the gospel because he prefers to
cherish a lie; he will not come to the Light because he loves darkness. So far from his "I cannot repent, I cannot believe" expressing
an honest desire to do so, it is but an avowal of the heart's enmity
against God. If the doctrine of the cross and the glorious message
of the gospel contain nothing to overcome such enmity and attract
the soul to Christ, it is not for us to invent another gospel and bend
the Scriptures to the inclination of man's depravity. It is we who
must bend *to* the Scriptures; and if we do not, it will be to our eternal
undoing. The one who wrings his hands over his inability to believe
and asks, What can I do? is not to be soothed by something other
than the gospel of Christ, or encouraged to suppose that he is willing
to be saved in God's way. Yet that is the very delusion such souls
cherish, imagining they are as willing to be saved from their sins as
the impotent man by the pool was desirous of being made whole.

Neither Christ nor any of His apostles ever told a convicted soul
to passively wait for God's appointed hour of deliverance. Instead,
He bade the heavy laden "Come unto me." And instead of informing those who followed Him across the sea, "It lies not in your
power to do anything to secure the bread of life," He exhorted them
to, "Labour . . . for that meat which endureth unto everlasting life"
(Jn 6:27). Rather than tell men they must sit quietly before it,
Christ commanded, "Strive to enter in at the strait gate" (Lk 13:24).
When his hearers were pricked in their hearts and asked, "What

shall we do?", instead of saying, "You can do nothing, except wait until God speaks peace unto you," Peter bade them "repent" (Ac 2:37-38). Those who think they have been given a sense of their helplessness are quite content if some physician of no value will inspire them with a hope in the way they are now in, and encourage them to expect that if they remain passive, God will release them by a "moving of the waters." We do but miserably deceive souls if we give them any comfort or hold out any hope for them while they remain impenitent and away from Christ.

It is recorded that the passengers of a ship off South America went ashore on a brief expedition, ascending one of the mountains. But before they were aware, night and a very cold fog came on. They felt a strong inclination to sleep, but a medical man in the party remonstrated against any such indulgence, warning them that there would be the utmost danger of their never waking. As the one who chronicled this incident asks, "What had been thought of his conduct if, instead of urging his companions to escape from the mount, he had indulged them in their wishes? The Scriptures declare 'he that believeth not the Son shall not see life, but the wrath of God abideth on him,' and surely we ought not to contradict that, either by directing to the use of means short of 'believing' or by encouraging those who use them to hope for a happy issue." Paul did not offer the jailor comfort on the ground of his being in great distress, but bade him "believe on the Lord Jesus Christ." The word to troubled souls is not, "Sit still," but, "Seek and ye shall find; knock, and it shall be opened unto you."

But to return to the narrative. "They said one to another, Why sit we here until we die? If we say, We will enter into the city, then the famine is in the city, and we shall die there: and if we sit still here, we die also. Now therefore come, and let us fall into the host of the Syrians: if they save us alive, we shall live; and if they kill us, we shall but die" (2 Ki 7:3-4). How those poor lepers put to shame the "do nothing" fatalists! Those men rightly recognized the hopelessness of their case, perceiving that continued passivity would profit them nothing, and hence they decided to act. And if you, my reader, are already convicted of your perishing condition, do not rest content with that conviction and persuade yourself that in due time God will save you. Embrace the gospel offer and receive Christ as your Lord and Saviour, for He has declared, "Him that cometh to me I will in no wise cast out."

We ask the indulgence of others who have not been infected with such paralyzing teaching while we add a further word. We would ask them to beg God to use these paragraphs to deliver some souls from this subtle snare of the devil. If one who reads these lines has been made to feel his lost condition, then consider, we pray you, the far happier situation facing you from that in which those lepers were. They decided to come unto an enemy and cast themselves upon his mercy, while you are invited to betake yourself unto the Friend of publicans and sinners! They had no invitation from the Syrians, but you have from the Lord: "If any man thirst, let him come unto me and drink." They had nothing better than an "if they save us alive" to venture upon, whereas you have, "Believe on the Lord Jesus Christ, and thou shalt be saved." They were confronted with the possible alternative of being killed; not so you; "He that believeth on the Son hath everlasting life." Then why hesitate?

"And they rose up in the twilight, to go unto the camp of the Syrians: and when they were come to the uttermost part of the camp of Syria, behold, there was no man there" (v. 5). What was before us in verses 3-4 did not end in idle talk. The situation for those lepers was a desperate one; and prompted by a sense of urgency, they acted. Their sitting still had gotten them nowhere, so they "rose up" and proceeded at once to their proposed objective. They did not puzzle their heads about God's secret decree and whether or not His ordained hour had arrived, for that was none of their business. Instead, they responded to the instinct of self-preservation. Again we say, how far superior is the sinner's case: he need not wait a moment for the prompting of any instinct, but is invited, "Come; for all things are now ready" (Lk 14:17). Come just as you are with all your sinfulness and unworthiness; and if you cannot come to Christ with a melted heart and faith, then come to Him as a patient desperate for them.

Fifth, the Means of the Miracle

The divine narrative breaks in upon the account of the heralds of this miracle to show us its means. For before we see those lepers going forth to publish their good news, we are first informed how it was that they came to find the camp empty. "For the Lord had made the host of the Syrians to hear a noise of chariots, and the noise of horses, even the noise of a great host: and they said one to another, Lo, the king of Israel hath hired against us the kings of the Hittites, and the kings of the Egyptians, to come upon us" (2 Ki 7:6). This is to be regarded as the sequel to 6:24: Ben-hadad's purpose was to starve out Samaria. But man proposes and God opposes and disposes. "The LORD bringeth the counsel of the heathen to nought: he maketh the devices of the people of none effect" (Ps 33:10).

The Lord accomplishes His purpose by a great variety of measures and methods, sometimes employing the supernatural, more often using the natural. What were the means He used here? In the light of what is not said in verse 6, it seems strange that Thomas Scott should write, "The infatuation which seized the minds of the whole Syrian army was equal to the illusion put upon their senses, and both were from the Lord, but how produced we know not." Little better is Matthew Henry's "these had their hearing imposed upon." There was neither illusion nor imposition. It does not say, "The Lord made them to hear a noise *like as* of chariots and horses," but the actual thing itself. That is to say, He so attuned their auditory nerves that they registered the sound of what previously was inaudible to them. This is but another instance of how we create our own difficulties when reading the Word through failing to attend closely to exactly what is said.

If we allow scripture to interpret scripture, we should have no difficulty in ascertaining the precise means used on this occasion. On a previous one God had employed "horses and chariots of fire round about Elisha" (6:17), and as we showed, the reference there was to angelic beings. Then why not the same here! In the former case, God "opened the eyes of the young man" in order to see them; here, He opened the ears of the Syrians to hear them. It may well be that in their original condition our first parents were capacitated to both see and hear celestial beings, but the fall impaired those as well as all their faculties. The "clairvoyance" and "clairaudience" of spiritist mediums could be the devil's imitation of man's original powers. That the Syrians, unregenerate idolaters, misinterpreted what they heard is only to be expected. Those who heard the Father speaking to His Son thought "it thundered" (Jn 12:29), and those who accompanied Saul heard the voice which spoke to him (Ac 9:7) but "heard not the voice" (Ac 22:9) — distinguished not the words.

"Wherefore they arose and fled in the twilight, and left their tents, and their horses, and their asses, even the camp as it was, and fled for their life" (2 Ki 7:7). How true it is that "the wicked flee when no man pursueth." Supposing that a more formidable force had come to the relief of the besieged Samaritans, the Syrians were filled with consternation and at once abandoned their well-provisioned camp. So thoroughly panic-stricken were they that they left their "horses" which would have helped their flight. How easily can the Lord make the heart of the stoutest to quake, and how vain and mad a thing it is for anyone to defy Him! "Can thine heart endure, or can thine hands be strong, in the days that I shall deal with thee? I the LORD have spoken it, and will do it" (Eze 22:14). Then throw down the weapons of your warfare against Him and make your peace with Him now.

Chapter 26

FIFTEENTH MIRACLE
GLAD TIDINGS

IN CONTINUING our contemplation of this miracle, let us now pause and admire the marvel of it. Ben-hadad had become dissatisfied with the results achieved by his marauding bands, and, gathering together the whole of his armed forces, determined to reduce Samaria to utter helplessness. Throwing a powerful force around their capital he sought to bring its inhabitants to complete starvation by means of a protracted siege. In order to carry out his scheme, he had brought with his army large supplies of food and clothing, so that they might be in comfort while they waited for the stores of his victim to give out. How nearly his plan succeeded we have seen: the Samaritans were reduced to the most desperate straits in an effort to keep life in their bodies. Yet as Scott pointed out, "In extreme distress unexpected relief is often preparing, and whatever unbelievers may imagine, it is not in vain to wait for the Lord, how long soever He seems to delay His coming."

But in the instance now before us, there is not a word to indicate that the Samaritans had been crying unto the Lord and looking to Him for relief. They had openly turned away from Him and were worshiping idols. This it is which renders the more noteworthy the act of Jehovah on this occasion: He was found of them that sought Him not (Is 65:1). He showed Himself strong on the behalf of a people who had grievously despised and insulted Him. But where sin abounded, grace did much more abound. It was the Most High acting in His absolute sovereignty, having mercy on whom He pleased to have mercy and showing favor unto those who not only had no claim thereto but who deserved only unsparing judgment at His hands. The means which the Lord used on this occasion was as

213

remarkable as the exercise of His distinguishing mercy. He was pleased to use the stores of the Syrians, their deadly enemies, to feed the famished Samaritans. Thus were the wise taken in their own craftiness.

Four lepers outside Samaria's gates said, "Why sit we here until we die? If we say, We will enter into the city, then the famine is in the city, and we shall die there: and if we sit still here, we die also. Now therefore come, and let us fall unto the host of the Syrians: if they save us alive, we shall live; and if they kill us, we shall but die" (2 Ki 7:3-4). Observe how God wrought: it was not by an audible voice that He bade these lepers act — not such are the mysterious but perfect workings of Providence. It is by means of a secret and imperceptible impulse from Him, through the process of natural laws, that God usually works in men both to will and to do of His good pleasure. Those lepers acted quite freely of their own volition, in response to simple but obvious thoughts on their situation, and followed the dictates of common sense and the impulse of self-preservation. Mark, we are not here attempting to philosophize or explain the conjunction between the natural and the supernatural, but we are merely calling attention to what lies on the surface of our narrative, and which is recorded for our instruction.

When the four lepers arrived at the enemy's camp they found it to be deserted, "For the Lord had made the host of the Syrians to hear a noise of chariots, and a noise of horses, even the noise of a great host: and they said one to another, Lo, the king of Israel hath hired against us the kings of the Hittites, and the kings of the Egyptians, to come upon us. Wherefore they arose and fled in the twilight, and left their tents, and their horses, and their asses, even the camp as it was, and fled for their life" (vv. 6-7). That was indeed the employment of the supernatural — something over and above the ordinary workings of Providence, for though the Syrians misinterpreted the sound, we believe (as stated in our last chapter) that what they heard was the movement of angelic horses and chariots (cf. 6:17). The Lord allowed their ears to register what normally would have been inaudible to them. Yet even here there was a blending of the supernatural with the natural: those celestial beings did not slay the Syrians but only terrified them by the noise which they made.

It may not so strike the reader, but what most impresses the writer in connection with this incident is the remarkable blending together of the supernatural and the natural, the operations of God and the actions of men, and the light this casts on the workings of divine providence. Perhaps that would be made plainer by first reading verses 6-7, where we have recorded the miracle itself and the startling effect which it had upon the Syrians, and then verse 5 where we are told of the action of these four men which led to their discovery of a miracle having been wrought, thereby preparing the way for all that follows. Here we have another illustration of what we have frequently pointed out in these pages, namely, that when God works He does so at both ends of the line: here openly at one end and secretly at the other. Had not the lepers actually journeyed to the Syrians' camp, those in Samaria would have remained in ignorance that food was to be had. God therefore moved those lepers to go there, yet how naturally He wrought! They were not conscious that He had given them a secret inclination to move, nor had they any inkling of the miracle, as their words in verse 4 make clear.

"And when these lepers came to the uttermost part of the camp, they went into one tent, and did eat and drink, and carried thence silver, and gold, and raiment, and went and hid it; and came again, and entered into another tent, and carried thence also, and went and hid it" (v. 8). Solemn indeed is this, first, from the negative side. There was no recognition of the divine hand, no awesome explanation, "What hath God wrought!" no bowing before Him in thanksgiving for such a remarkable favor. They conducted themselves like infidels, accepting the mercies of heaven as a mere matter of course. And remember, they were lepers; but even such an affliction had not turned their hearts to the Lord. Be not surprised then that those whose homes are destroyed and whose bodies are injured by bombs are not brought to repentance thereby. After satisfying their hunger, they plundered the Syrian tents. Verily, "There is no new thing under the sun" (Ec 1:9). There was looting then as there is now, though theirs was not nearly so despicable and dastardly as what is now so common.

And why is it that "there is no new thing under the sun"? Because "as in water face answereth to face, so the heart of man to man" (Pr 27:19). Whether he be a man living in centuries B.C. or A.D., whether he be civilized or uncivilized, his heart is depraved. Civilization effects no change within any person, for civilization (not to be confused with morality and common decency) is but a veneer from without. But to return to our passage. The lepers, enriching themselves from the spoil of the Syrians, did not contribute to the relief of the starving Samaritans, and that was what Jehovah had promised. Mark then the sequel: "Then they said one to another, We do not well: this day is a day of good tidings, and we hold our peace: if we tarry till the morning light, some mischief will come upon us: now therefore come, that we may go and tell the king's household" (2 Ki 7:9). The divine design of mercy to the starving city was not to be thwarted by the greed of these lepers, for His counsel must stand. Yet note how it was now effected.

As God had wrought secretly in those lepers in verses 3-4, He again did so now. First it was by an impulse upon their instinct of self-preservation; here it is upon their conscience. Yet observe how conscience acts in the unregenerate, producing not horror and anguish at having offended a gracious God, but causing fear of the consequences. This is made clearer by the rendering: "If we tarry till the morning light, we shall find punishment." But unless God had wrought secretly upon them, they too would have been like our own generation, from whom His restraining hand is removed and who are "given up to their own hearts' lusts" — utterly reckless and regardless of consequences. In this instance, in order to carry out His benevolent purpose, God put a measure of fear upon these lepers and caused them to realize that not only were they playing an ignoble part, but were likely to swiftly be smitten by His wrath if they failed to announce the good news to their famished fellows.

"Now therefore come, that we may go and tell the king's household" (v. 9). Here, as everywhere, we need to be much on our guard against making a misapplication of Scripture. It is so easy to read our own thought into the Word and thus find what we are looking for. Those who are so enthusiastic in urging young believers to become evangelists by preaching the gospel to all and sundry, would likely find in this verse what they would consider a striking passage on which to base an address on the necessity of personal work; yet it would be an altogether unwarranted use to make of it. This verse is very far from teaching, by typical implication, that it is the duty of every Christian to announce the "good tidings" to all they contact. Holy Writ does not contradict itself, and none other than the Lord Jesus has expressly bidden us, "Give not that which is holy unto the dogs, neither cast ye your pearls before swine, lest they trample them under their feet, and turn again and rend you"

(Mt 7:6). That command is designed to bridle the restless energy of the flesh.

It was unto those who had been prepared for those "good tidings" who would welcome them, these lepers went forth, namely, to those who were fully conscious of their starving condition! There is a radical difference between those who are "lovers of pleasure" and satisfied with what they find therein, and the ones who have discovered the emptiness of such things and are deeply concerned about their eternal welfare; and there should be an equally radical difference in the way we deal with and speak to each of them. The gospel would not be "good tidings" to the former, but would be trodden beneath their feet if offered to them; yet it is likely to be welcomed by the latter. And if we unmistakably meet with the latter, it would be sinful for us to remain selfishly silent. "So they came and called unto the porter of the city: and they told them, saying, We came to the camp of the Syrians, and, behold, there was no man there, neither voice of man, but horses tied, and asses tied, and the tents as they were" (2 Ki 7:10).

Not being permitted to enter the city, the four lepers called out to those who were keeping watch at its gate. They announced the good news in plain and simple language, and then left the issue with them. The chief porter did not receive the strange tidings with incredulity, but "he called the [subordinate] porters;" and, while he remained at his post of duty, "they told it to the king's house within" (v. 11), middle of the night though it was. Here too we may perceive the continued, though secret, workings of the Lord. He it was who caused the porter to give heed to the message he had just heard. Altogether unexpected as it must have been, too good to be true as it would have sounded, yet he was divinely inclined to believe the glad tidings and promptly acquaint his royal master with them. Yet the porter acted quite freely and discharged his personal responsibility. How wondrous are the ways of Him with whom we have to do!

"And the king arose in the night, and said unto his servants, I will now shew you what the Syrians have done to us. They know that we be hungry; therefore are they gone out of the camp to hide themselves in the field, saying, When they come out of the city, we shall catch them alive, and get into the city" (v. 12). The king's reaction to the good news was thoroughly characteristic of him, being consistent with everything else recorded of him. Instead of expressing gratitude at the glad tidings, he voiced his skepticism; instead of perceiving the gracious hand of God, he suspected his enemies of laying a subtle snare. Perhaps some may be inclined to say, It was very natural for Jehoram to argue thus: the king was acting in prudence and wise caution. Natural it certainly was, but not spiritual! There was no thought that the Lord had now made good His word through the prophet, but simply the reasoning of a carnal mind at enmity against Him. One of the ways in which the carnal mind expresses itself is by a reasoned attempt to explain away the wondrous works and acts of God.

When God has spoken, plainly and expressly, it is not for us to reason, but to set to our seal that He is true and receive with unquestioning faith what He has said. If it is a promise, expect Him to make it good. The skepticism of the king only serves to show how the tidings borne by the lepers would have been lost on the porters and the entire royal household had not God wrought secretly but effectually in the one and the other. Accordingly we are next told, "And one of his servants answered and said, Let some take, I pray thee, five of the horses that remain, which are left in the city, (behold, they are as all the multitude of Israel that are left in it: behold, I say, they are even as all the multitude of the Israelites that are consumed:) and let us send and see" (v. 13). That too was "of the Lord." He it was who gave this servant both courage and wisdom to remonstrate with his master. He knew the man he had to deal with, as his "send and see" showed, reminding us at once of 6:10, when the king "sent" to see if Elisha's warning were a true one.

Nothing could be lost (unless it were the horses) by pursuing the policy proposed by the servant, and much might be gained. As the divine purpose could not be thwarted by the greed of the lepers, so it should not be by the skepticism of the king. It was God who gave the servant's counsel favor in his master's sight, and therefore we are told, "They took therefore two chariot horses; and the king sent after the host of the Syrians, saying, Go and see" (v. 14). God's ways and works are as perfect in their execution as they are in their devising. But be it noted that though Jehoram yielded to the solicitation of his servant, it was with some unbelief he did so, as his sending them "after the host of the Syrians" rather than "unto their camp" indicates. Nor was their errand in vain: "They went after them unto Jordan: and, lo, all the way was full of garments and vessels, which the Syrians had cast away in their haste" (v. 15). It was no temporary spasm of fear that possessed them but a thorough and lasting one. When God works, He works effectually.

"And the messengers returned, and told the king. And the people went out, and spoiled the tents of the Syrians. So a measure of fine flour was sold for a shekel, and two measures of barley for a shekel, according to the word of the LORD" (vv. 15-16). Of course it was, for no word of God's can possibly fall to the ground, since it is the Word of Him "that cannot lie" (Titus 1:2). Men may scoff at it, kings may not believe it, even when its definite fulfillment is declared to them; but that affects not its truth. "Blessed be the LORD, that hath given rest unto his people Israel, according to all that he promised: there hath not failed one word of all his good promise" (1 Ki 8:56). It is to be noted that the prediction made through Elisha was fulfilled in no vague and mere general way, but specifically and to the letter. That too is recorded both for our instruction and our consolation.

Sixth, the Meaning of the Miracle

After all we have sought to bring out upon this miracle, its spiritual significance should, in its broad outline at least, be plain to every Christian reader. We say "its broad outline," for every detail in it is not to be regarded as a line in the picture. First, the starving Samaritans may surely be viewed as portraying perishing sinners. They were not seeking God nor looking to Him for relief. So far from it, they had turned their backs upon Him and had given themselves up to idolatry. They were reduced to the most desperate straits, being quite unable to deliver themselves. As such they accurately represented the condition and position of the fallen and depraved descendants of Adam.

Second, in Ben-hadad and his hosts who sought the destruction of the Samaritans, we have a figure of Satan and his legions who are relentlessly attempting to destroy the souls of men, "seeking whom he may devour" (1 Pe 5:8).

Third, in the divine deliverance of the famished Israelites, by a miracle of sovereign mercy, we have a striking foreshadowment of the saving of God's elect. The particular aspect of the gospel here pictured appears in the strange means which God employed to bring about deliverance, namely, His causing the Syrians themselves to supply the food for those they had designed to be their victims. Does not this remind us forcibly of that verse; "that through death he might destroy him that had [as the executioner] the power of death, that is, the devil" (Heb 2:14)! As the Saviour Himself declared, "This is your hour, and the power of darkness" (Lk 22: 53); yet by allowing the serpent to bruise His heel, He set free his captives. Incredible as it seems to the proud philosopher, it is by Christ's humiliation His people are exalted, by His poverty they are made rich, by His death they have life, by His being made a "curse" all blessing comes to them!

Seventh, the Sequel of the Miracle

"And the king [God working secretly in him to do so] appointed the lord on whose hand he leaned to have the charge of the gate: and the people trode upon him in the gate, and he died, as the man of God [not simply 'Elisha'!] had said, who spake when the king came down to him. And so it fell out unto him" (2 Ki 7:17, 20). Thus in due course, the divine threat was executed, fulfilled to the very letter. Solemn indeed was this, being the awful sequel to what was before us in verses 1-2. In like manner God will yet answer the skepticism and blasphemous scoffing of this degenerate age. The great of this world may laugh at the Lord's servants now, but in eternity they shall gnash their teeth in anguish. This sequel completes the symbolic picture, showing as it does the doom of the reprobate. The gospel is a savor of death unto death as well as of life unto life. Unbelievers will "see" the elect feasting with Christ, as the rich man saw Lazarus in Abraham's bosom; but they shall not partake thereof.

Chapter 27

SIXTEENTH MIRACLE
THE SHUNAMMITE RETURNS

First, the Reality of the Miracle

THE FIRST SIX VERSES of 2 Kings 8 chronicle an incident which is rather difficult to classify in connection with the ministry of Elisha. By this we mean it is perhaps an open question whether we are to regard it as properly belonging to the miracles which were wrought through his instrumentality. Undoubtedly the majority of Christian writers would look upon this episode as an example of the gracious and wondrous operations of divine providence, rather than a supernatural happening. With them we shall have no quarrel, for it is mainly a matter of terms — some define a "miracle" in one way and some in another. No question of either doctrinal or practical importance is involved: it is simply a matter of personal opinion whether this series of events is to be viewed as among the ordinary ways of the divine government as God orders the lives of each of His creatures, and in a more particular manner undertakes and provides for each of His dear children, or whether we are to contemplate what is here narrated as something over and above the workings of providence.

The signal deliverances which the Lord's people experience under the workings of His special providence are just as truly manifestations of the wisdom and power of God as are what many theologians would technically term His "miracles," and are so to be regarded by us. While strongly deprecating the modern tendency to deny and decry the supernatural, we shall not now enter into a discussion as to whether or not "the day of miracles is past;" but this we do emphatically insist upon, that the day of divine intervention is most certainly not past. God is as ready to hear the cry of the righteous now as He was in the time of Moses and the prophets, and to so graciously and definitely answer the prayer of faith as cannot be explained by so called "natural laws," as this writer, and no doubt many of our readers, can bear witness. Whether you term His interpositions "miracles" or not, this is sure; the Lord still shows Himself strong on behalf of those whose heart is perfect (upright, sincere) toward Him.

Second, the Connection of the Miracle

This is intimated by the opening word of our narrative. That "then," which occurs so frequently in the Scriptures, should never be hurried over carelessly. There is nothing meaningless nor superfluous in God's Word, and every syllable in it should be given its due force and weight. "Then" is a sign of time, emphasizing the season or occasion when some particular event happened. To ascertain its significance we should always pause and ask, When? and in order to find the answer, refer back to the immediate context — often obliging us to ignore a chapter division. By so doing we are better enabled to perceive the connection between two things or incidents, and often the moral relation the one sustains to the other, not only of cause and effect, but of antecedent and consequent.

In passing, we may point out that "Then" is one of the key words of Matthew's gospel, with which should be linked "when" and "from that time" (see Mt 4:1, 17; 15:1, 21; 25:1; 26:14). The deeper significance of many an incident is discovered by observing this simple rule: Ask the "then" — when?

In our present instance the miracle we are about to contemplate is immediately linked to the one preceding it by this introductory "Then." There is therefore a close connection between them; the one is the sequel to the other. When considering 2 Kings 7, we saw how wondrously Jehovah wrought in coming to the relief of the famished Samaritans, furnishing them with an abundant supply of food at no trouble or cost to themselves, causing their enemies to supply their needs by leaving their own huge stores behind them. But, as we pointed out, there was no recognition of the hand that had so kindly ministered to them, no acknowledgment of His goodness, no praising Him for such mercies. He had no place in their thoughts, for they had grievously departed from Him and given themselves up to idolatry. Consequently, here as everywhere, we find inseparably linked together "unthankful, unholy" (2 Ti 3:2). Where there is no true piety, there is no genuine gratitude; and where there is no thankfulness, it is a sure sign of the absence of holiness. This is a criterion by which we may test our hearts: are we truly appreciative of the divine favors, or do we accept them as a matter of course?

It may seem a small matter to men whether they are thankful or unthankful for the bounties of their Maker and Provider, but He takes note of their response, and sooner or later regulates His governmental dealings with them accordingly. He will not be slighted with impunity. Whether He acts in judgment or in mercy, God requires us to acknowledge His hand, either by bowing in penitence beneath His rod, or offering to Him the praise of our hearts. When Moses demanded of Pharaoh that he should let the Hebrews go a three days' journey into the wilderness to hold a feast unto the Lord, he haughtily answered, "Who is the LORD, that I should obey his voice to let Israel go? I know not the LORD, neither will I let Israel go" (Ex 5:2). But before God's plagues were finished, the magicians owned, "This is the finger of God" (Ex 8:19), and the king himself confessed, "I have sinned against the LORD your God" (10:16). We are expressly bidden "O give thanks unto the Lord; for he is good" (Ps 136:1); and if men break that commandment, God will visit His displeasure upon them. One of the reasons why He gave up the heathen to uncleanness was because they were "unthankful" (Ro 1:21, 24).

Third, the Nature of the Miracle

God employs various methods and means in chastening an ungrateful people. Chief among His scourges are His "four sore judgments," namely, "the sword, and the famine, and the noisesome beast, and the pestilence to cut off from it man and beast" (Eze 14:21). In the present instance it was the second of these judgments. "Then spake Elisha unto the woman, whose son he had restored to life, saying, Arise, and go thou and thine household, and sojourn wheresoever thou canst sojourn: for the LORD hath called for a famine; and it shall also come upon the land seven years" (2 Ki 8:1). This we regard as a miracle, and as connected with Elisha. First, because this pronouncement was a prophecy, a supernatural revelation which he had received from God and then communicated to the woman. Second, because his announcement here is expressly said to be "the saying of the man of God" (v. 2), indicating he was acting in his official character. Third, because both in verse 1 and verse 5, this incident was definitely linked with an earlier miracle — the restoring of her dead son to life.

But our present miracle is by no means confined to the famine which the Lord here sent upon Samaria, nor to the prophet's knowledge and announcement of the same. We should also contemplate the gracious provision which the Lord made in exempting the woman from the horrors of it. A famine is usually the outcome of a prolonged drought with the resultant failure of the crops and the drying up of all vegetation, though in some cases it follows incessant rains which prevent the farmers from harvesting their grain. Now, had the Lord so pleased, He could have supplied this woman's land with rain, though it was withheld from her adjoining neighbors (see Amos 4:7), or He could have prevented her fields from being flooded, so that her crops might be garnered; or in some mysterious way He could have maintained her meal and oil that it failed not (1 Ki 17: 16). Yet, though the Lord did none of those extraordinary things, nevertheless He undertook for her just as effectually by His providences.

Fourth, the Duration of the Miracle

This particular famine lasted no less than seven years, which was double the length of time of the one God sent on Samaria in the days of Elijah (Ja 5:17). When men refuse to humble themselves beneath the mighty hand of God, He lays His rod more heavily upon them, as the successive plagues which He sent upon Egypt increased in their severity, and as the judgments mentioned in the Revelation are more and more distressing in nature. Of old God called upon Israel, "Consider your ways" and complained that His house was neglected, while they were occupied only with rebuilding and attending to their own. But they heeded Him not, and accordingly He told them, "Therefore the heaven over you is stayed from dew, and the earth is stayed from her fruit. And I called for a drought upon the land, and upon the mountains, and upon the corn, and upon the new wine, and upon the oil, and upon that which the ground bringeth forth, and upon men, and upon cattle, and upon all the labour of the hands" (Hag 1:10-11). Thus it was now upon the rebellious and idolatrous Samaritans.

Fifth, the Beneficiary of the Miracle

This was "the woman whose son Elisha restored to life." She was before us in 2 Kings 4. There we saw that she was one who had a heart for the servant of God, not only inviting him into her house for a meal whenever he passed by her place, but building and furnishing for him a chamber (vv. 8-10). Then we beheld her remarkable faith; for instead of wringing her hands in despair upon the sudden death of her child, she promptly rode to Mount Carmel where Elisha then was, with the evident expectation that God would undertake for her in that extremity through His servant. Nor was her hope disappointed; a miracle was wrought and her dead son quickened. But now that the seven years' famine was imminent, Elisha did not keep to himself the knowledge he had received from the Lord, but put it to a good use, thinking of the family which had shown him kindness in his earlier days, warning the woman of the sore judgment that was about to fall upon the land of Samaria.

The prophet's action contains important instruction for us, especially for those who are the ministers of God. First, we are shown that we are not to selfishly keep to ourselves the spiritual light God gives us, but pass it on to those ready to receive it. Second, the servant of God is not to lose interest in those to whom God made him a blessing in the past, but seek opportunities to further help them in spiritual things, particularly endeavoring to express his gratitude to those who befriended him in earlier days. Often this can be most effectively accomplished by prayer for them or by sending them a special word of greeting (see Ro 16:6; 2 Ti 1:16). Elisha did not consider he had already discharged his indebtedness to this woman by restoring her son to life, but as a fresh emergency had arisen, he gave timely counsel. Third, here too we see God honoring those who honored Him. In the past she had ministered to the temporal needs of His servant, and He had not forgotten this. Having received a prophet in the name of a prophet, she now received the prophet's reward — light on her path.

"Then spake Elisha unto the woman, whose son he had restored to life, saying, Arise, and go thou and thine household, and sojourn wheresoever thou canst sojourn" (2 Ki 8:1). As there is no mention of her husband throughout the whole of this narrative it is likely he had died in the interval between chapters 4 and 8 and that she was now a widow. If so, it illustrates the special care the

Lord has for widows and orphans. But let us observe the exercise of His sovereignty on this occasion, for He does not always act uniformly. In an earlier famine He had miraculously sustained the widow of Zarephath by maintaining her meal and oil. He could have done the same in this instance, but was pleased to use other means, yet ones just as real and effective in supplying her every need. We must never prescribe to the Lord, nor limit Him in our thoughts to any particular form or avenue of deliverance, but trustfully leave ourselves in His hands and meekly submit to His imperial but all-wise ordering of our lot.

"Arise, and go thou and thine household, and sojourn wheresoever thou canst sojourn." How frequently are we reminded that here have we no continuing city, which should cause us to hold all earthly things with a very light hand. This incident also reminds us that the righteous are occasioned many inconveniences because of the conduct of the wicked; nevertheless the Lord evidences His particular care of His own when His judgments fall upon a nation. Observe to what a severe test this woman's faith was now submitted. It was no small matter to leave her home and property and journey with her household into another land, the inhabitants of which had for so long time been hostile to the Israelites. It called for implicit confidence in the veracity of God's servant. Ah, my reader, nothing but a genuine faith in God and His Word is sufficient for the human heart in such an emergency; but the mind of one who trusts Him will be kept in perfect peace.

"And the woman arose, and did after the saying of the man of God" (v. 2). Note well how that is phrased: she regarded Elisha's instruction as something more than the kindly advice of a personal friend, viewing him as the messenger of God to her. In other words, she looked above the prophet to his Master, and accepted the counsel as from Him. Thus she acted in faith, which was in entire accord with what was previously recorded of her. There is no hint that she murmured at her lot or complained at the severity of her trial. No, when faith is in exercise, the spirit of murmuring is quelled. Contrariwise, when we grumble at our lot, it is sure proof that unbelief is dominant within us. Nor did she yield to a fatalistic inertia and say, If God has called for a famine, I must bow to it; and if I perish, I perish. Instead she acted as a rational creature, discharged her responsibility, forsook the place of danger, and took refuge in a temporary haven of shelter.

"And she went with her household, and sojourned in the land of the Philistines seven years" (v. 2). Not in the adjoining territory of Judah, be it noted, for probably even at that date the Jews had "no dealings with the Samaritans" (Jn 4:9). It is sad, yet true, that a Christian will often receive kinder treatment at the hands of strangers than from those who profess to be the people of God. This Israelite woman had not been warranted when she took refuge among the Philistines without divine permission, for God had said unto Israel, "ye shall be holy unto me: for I the LORD am holy, and have severed you from other people, that ye should be mine" (Lev 20:26); and therefore did He declare, "the people shall dwell alone, and shall not be reckoned among the nations" (Num 23:9). But note well that it is not said that she and her household "settled down" in the land of the Philistines but only that she "sojourned" therein, which means that she did not make herself one with them, but lived as a stranger in their midst (cf. Gen 23:4; Lev 25:23).

"And sojourned in the land of the Philistines seven years." That is surely remarkable, and very blessed. The Philistines had long been the enemies of Israel, and had recently made war against it. Yet here was this Israelite woman, and her household, was permitted to live peacefully in their midst with her temporal needs supplied by them! In that we must see the secret power of God working on her behalf and giving her favor in their eyes. The Lord never confounds those who truly trust Him, and as this woman had honored His word through His prophet, so now He honored her faith. Her ways pleased the Lord, and therefore He made her enemies to be at peace with her. "And it came to pass at the seven years' end, that the woman returned out of the land of the Philistines" (2 Ki 8:3). This too is equally blessed. She had not found the society of the Philistines so congenial that she wished to spend the remainder of her days with them. But observe how it is worded: not "when the famine was over" she returned to Samaria, but "at the seven year's end" mentioned by the prophet — the word of God through His servant was what directed her!

"And she went forth to cry unto the king for her house and for her land" (v. 3). It is not clear whether her property had reverted to the crown upon her emigration, or whether someone had unlawfully seized it and now refused to relinquish it; but whichever it was, she did not shirk her duty, but actively discharged her responsibility. She was neither a believer in passive resistance nor in looking to

God to undertake for her while she shelved her duty — which would have been highly presumptuous. Scott has pointed out how this verse illustrates "the benefit of magistracy," and rightly added in connection therewith, "Believers may, on important occasions, avail themselves of their privileges as members of the community: provided they are not actuated by covetousness or resentment, do not manifest a contentious spirit and make no appeal in a doubtful or suspicious cause; and rulers should award justice without respect of persons, and compel the injurious to restitution." Had not this woman now appealed to the king for the restoration of her own property, she would have condoned a wrong and refused to uphold the principles of righteousness.

Sixth, the Sequel of the Miracle

This is equally striking, for the anointed eye will clearly perceive the power of the Lord working on behalf of His handmaid. "And the king talked with Gehazi the servant of the man of God, saying, Tell me, I pray thee, all the great things that Elisha hath done. And it came to pass, as he was telling the king how he had restored a dead body to life, that, behold the woman, whose son he had restored to life, cried to the king for her house and for her land. And Gehazi said, My lord, O king, this is the woman, and this is her son, whom Elisha restored to life. And when the king asked the woman, she told him. So the king appointed unto her a certain officer, saying, Restore all that was hers, and all the fruits of the field since the day that she left the land, even until now" (vv. 4-6). Who can fail to see the superintending hand of God in the king's desire to hear of Elisha's miracles, the presence of one well qualified to inform him, the timing of such an occurrence, the interest in this woman which would be awakened in the King, and his willingness to grant her full restitution!

Seventh, the Lesson of the Miracle

In the course of our remarks, we have called attention to many details of this incident which we may profitably take to heart, but there is one outstanding thing in it which especially claims our notice, namely, the wonder-working providences of God in behalf of the woman — through Elisha, the Philistines, Gehazi, and the king of Israel. And thus it is that He still acts on behalf of His own, making gracious provision for them in an evil day. Whatever be the means or the instruments He makes use of in providing a refuge for us in a time of trouble, it is as truly "the Lord's doing" and should be just as "marvelous in our eyes," especially when God constrains the wicked to deal kindly with us, as if He openly worked for us what are technically called "miracles." At the close of Psalm 107, after recounting the various deliverances the Lord wrought for those who cried unto Him, this comment is made: "Whoso is wise, and will observe these things, even they shall understand the lovingkindness of the LORD." The greater pains we take to observe God's hand undertaking for us by His providences, the better shall we understand His "lovingkindness" and the more confidence we shall have in Him.

Chapter 28

SEVENTEENTH MIRACLE
DEATH OF A KING

THE OPENING VERSE of 2 Kings 8 informs us that the Lord had called for a seven years' famine on Samaria, and we considered one of the things which transpired during that "sore judgment" from heaven. That which is now to claim our attention is not to be regarded as something which occurred after the expiration of the famine, but rather as what took place at its beginning. After tracing the experiences of the woman from Shunem, the Holy Spirit picks up the thread of verse 1 and informs us of the movements of the prophet himself. "And Elisha came to Damascus" (v. 7). He too left Samaria, for it was no place for him now that the indignation of the Lord was upon it. When God deals in judgment with a people, His temporal plagues are usually accompanied by spiritual deprivations, often by removing His servants "into a corner" (Is 30: 20), and then the people of God are left "as sheep without a shepherd" — one of the acutest afflictions they can experience. It was thus with Israel in the earlier famine days of Ahab. There is no intimation that Elijah did any preaching during these three and a half years, for the Lord sent him to Cherith and then to Zarephath.

Sad indeed is the plight of any people when they are not only scourged temporally but have their spiritual blessings taken from them too. During the times of the judges, when "every man did that which was right in his own eyes" (Judg 21:25), we are told, " . . . in those days; there was no open vision" (1 Sa 3:1). This signifies there was no accredited servant of God to whom the people could go for a knowledge of the divine mind and will. So again in the days of Ezekiel it was announced, "Mischief shall come upon mischief, and rumour shall be upon rumour;" and as the climactic calamity: "Then shall they seek a vision of the prophet; but the law shall perish from the priest" (Eze 7:26). Little as it is realized by the present generation, the most solemn, fearful, and portentous of all the marks of God's anger is the withholding of a Spirit-filled, faithful, and edifying ministry. For then there is "a famine in the land, not a famine of bread, nor a thirst of water, but of hearing the words of the Lord" (Amos 8:11). There is much more than appears on the surface in that short statement, "And Elisha came down to Damascus."

Solemn indeed is that brief and simple sentence, denoting as it does that the prophet had left Samaria, left it because his ministry there was unwelcome, wasted. How often we find a parallel to this in the gospels. At the very beginning of His public ministry, we read that Christ "came down to Capernaum" (Lk 4:31). Why? Because at Nazareth they were filled with wrath at His teaching (vv. 28-29). "He entered into a ship, and passed over." Why? Because at Capernaum the whole city "besought him that he would depart out of their coasts" (Mt 8:34; 9:1). He "withdrew himself from thence" because the Pharisees had "held a council against him" (Mt 12:14-15). "He could there do no mighty work . . . because of their unbelief". What follows? "And He went round about their villages teaching" (Mk 6:5-6). "It was necessary that the word of God should first have been spoken to you, but seeing ye put it from you . . . lo, we turn to the Gentiles" (Ac 13:46). When God calls a pastor to another charge, the church he has left has reason to search itself before the Lord as to the cause.

First, the Connection of the Miracle

"And Elisha came to Damascus" (2 Ki 8:7). The opening "And" links the incident which follows with the first verse of our chapter. But more, as was the case in several previous instances, it points a series of striking contrasts between this and the events recorded in the context. There, the central character was a godly woman; here it is a wicked man. In the former the prophet took the initiative, communicating with the woman; now, a king sends to inquire of the man of God. There his prophetic announcement was promptly credited; here it is scornfully ridiculed (v. 13). In the first, the king's servant told him the truth (v. 5); in this, another king's servant tells him a lie (v. 13). There God put forth His power and graciously provided for one of His own; here He removes His restraining hand and lets one of the reprobate meet with a violent end. The previous miracle closed with the restoration of the woman's property to her; this ends with a callous murder and the usurper occupying the throne.

Though there is nothing in the narrative to intimate specifically when it was that Elisha "came to Damascus," yet the introductory "And" seems to make it clear that the prophet took this journey during "the seven years' famine," and probably at an early stage. As the Lord was not pleased on this occasion to work in a mysterious and extraordinary way for the temporal preservation of the woman of Shunem (as He had for the widow at Zarephath) but provided for her needs by the more regular yet not less wonderful ordering of providence on her behalf, so it would seem that He did for His servant. And as she sojourned in the land of the Philistines, so he now sought refuge in the capital of Syria, even though that was the very country which had for so long been hostile to Samaria. Nor did he go into hiding there, but counted upon his Master's protecting him even in the midst of a people who had so often preyed upon Israel. That Elisha's presence in Damascus was no secret is clear from what follows.

Second, the Occasion of the Miracle

"And Elisha came to Damascus" — the most ancient city in the world, with the possible exception of Jerusalem. Josephus says that "it was founded by Uz, the son of Aram, and grandson of Shem." It is mentioned as early as Genesis 14:15, in the days of Abraham, 2000 B.C. It was captured and occupied in turn by the Persians, the Greeks, and the Romans. Paul commenced his ministry there (Ac 9:19-22). It remains to this day. In the time of Ahab, Benhadad, after his defeat by the Samaritans and the sparing of his life, said to the king of Israel, "Thou shalt make streets for thee in Damascus, as my father made in Samaria." Upon which Ahab said, "I will send thee away with this covenant. So he made a covenant with him, and sent him away" (1 Ki 20:34). Whether Ben-hadad ever made good his promise Scripture does not inform us, but his "covenant" with Ahab certainly gave Elisha the right of asylum in Damascus.

That Elisha had not fled to Damascus in the energy of the flesh in order to escape the hardships and horrors of the famine, but had gone there in the will of the Lord is evident from the sequel. In what follows we are shown how that while he was here he received communications from God and was used by Him. That is one of the ways in which the child of God may ascertain whether or not he is in the place he should be, or whether in self-will he has forsaken the path of duty. "He that hath my commandments, and keepeth them, he it is that loveth me: . . . and I will love him, and will manifest myself to him" (Jn 14:21), make Myself a living reality to his soul, make discoveries of My glory to him through the written Word. But when we take matters into our own hands and our ways displease the Lord, communion is severed, and He hides His face from us. When we choose our own way and the Spirit is grieved, He no longer takes the things of Christ and shows them to us, but disquiets our hearts because of our sins.

Yes, God made use of Elisha while he sojourned in Damascus. But how varied, how solemnly varied, are the several ways in which He is pleased to employ His servants. Not now was he commissioned to heal a leper, nor to restore a dead child to life, but rather to announce the death of a king. Herein we have shadowed forth the more painful and exacting side of the minister's duty. He is required to set before men the way of life and the way of death. He is under bond to faithfully make known the doom awaiting the wicked, as well as the bliss reserved for the righteous. He is to preach the law as well as the gospel; to describe the everlasting torments of hell, as well as the unending glory of heaven. He is bidden to preach the gospel to every creature, and announce in no uncertain tones, "He that believeth and is baptized shall be saved; but he that believeth not shall be damned" (Mk 16:16). Only by so doing will he be warranted in saying, "I am pure from the blood of all men. For I have not shunned to declare unto you all the counsel of God" (Ac 20:26-27).

"And Ben-hadad the king of Syria was sick; and it was told him, saying, The man of God is come hither" (2 Ki 8:7). The wearing of a crown does not exempt its possessor from the common troubles to which man is born; rather does it afford additional opportunities for gratifying the lust of the flesh, which will only increase his troubles. It is only by being temperate in all things that many sicknesses can be avoided, for walking according to the rules of Scripture promotes health of body as well as health of soul. When sickness overtakes a saint his first concern should not be its removal, but a definite seeking unto the Lord to ascertain why He has afflicted him (Job 10:2). His next concern should be to have his sickness sanctified to the good of his soul, that he may learn the lessons that chastisement is designed to teach him, that he may be able to say, "It is good for me that I have been afflicted; that I might learn thy statutes" (Ps 119:71). But it is the privilege of faith to become better acquainted with *Jehovah-Rophi,* "the Lord that healeth thee" (Ex 15:26).

In the case before us it was not a child of God who had fallen sick, but a heathen monarch. "And the king said unto Hazael, Take a present in thine hand, and go, meet the man of God, and enquire of the LORD by him, saying, Shall I recover of this disease?" (2 Ki 7:8). What a startling antithesis this presents from what was before us in 6:31! Only a short time previously, the king of Israel had sworn a horrible oath that Elisha should be slain; here a foreign king owns him as "the man of God" and makes inquiry concerning his own life or death. Striking too is the contrast between Ben-hadad's action here and the last thing recorded of him when he sent his forces to take Elisha captive (6:14)! How fickle is human nature: Man is one day ready to pluck out his eyes and give them to a servant of God, and the next regards him as an enemy because he told the truth (Gal 4:15-16). But now the Syrian king was concerned about his condition and anxious to know the outcome of his illness.

It appears to have been the practice in those days for a king who was seriously ill to make a formal inquiry from one whom he regarded as endowed with supernatural knowledge. Thus we read that when Jeroboam's son fell sick, he sent his wife to ascertain of Ahijah the prophet "what shall become of the child" (1 Ki 14:1-3); and again we are told that Ahaziah sent messengers "to enquire of Baal-zebub the god of Ekron whether I shall recover of this disease." (2 Ki 1:2). From what is recorded in 1 Kings 20:23 and the sequel, we may conclude that Ben-hadad had lost confidence in his own "gods" and placed more reliance upon the word of Elisha; yet it is to be noted that he neither asked for his prayers nor expressed any desire for a visit from him; seriously sick as he felt himself to be, he was not concerned about his soul but only his body. Throughout the whole of his career there is nothing to indicate he had the slightest regard for the Lord, but much to the contrary.

"So Hazael went to meet him, and took a present with him, even of every good thing of Damascus, forty camels' burden, and came and stood before him, and said, Thy son Ben-hadad king of Syria hath sent me to thee, saying, Shall I recover of this desease?" (2 Ki 8:9). The "present" was to intimate that he came on a peaceful and friendly mission and with no design of doing the prophet an injury or carrying him away as a prisoner. This too was in accord with the custom of those days and the ways of Orientals. Thus when Saul wished to consult Samuel about the lost asses of his father, he lamented the fact that he had "not a present to bring to the man of God" (1 Sa 9:7), and when the wife of Jeroboam went to inquire of the prophet Ahijah she took a present for him (1 Ki 14:3). But looking higher, we may see in the lavish nature of Ben-hadad's present the guiding hand of God and an "earnest" for His servant that He would spread a table for him in the presence of his enemies! We are not told that Elisha refused this present, nor was there any reason why he should; perhaps he sent a goodly portion thereof to relieve the distress of the schools of the prophets still in Samaria.

"And Elisha said unto him, Go, say unto him, Thou mayest certainly recover: howbeit the LORD hath shewed me that he shall surely die" (2 Ki 8:10). Observe first a significant omission. Elisha did not offer to go and visit Ben-hadad! That was not because he was callous, for the very next verse shows he was a man of compassion. Rather was he restrained by the Lord, who had no design of mercy unto the Syrian king. Very solemn was that. But what are we to make of the prophet's enigmatical language? The disease from which your master is suffering will not produce a fatal end; nevertheless, the Lord has showed me that his death is imminent — by violence: another proof that the Lord God "revealeth his secret unto his servants the prophets" (Amos 3:7). It is on this same principle we discover the harmony between there being "an appointed time to man upon earth" (Job 7:1) and "why shouldest thou die before thy time?" (Ec 7:17) — before the normal course of nature; and the fifteen years "added to" the course of Hezekiah's life — God intervening to stay the ordinary working of his disease.

Third, the Accompaniment of the Miracle

"And he settled his countenance steadfastly, until he was ashamed:

and the man of God wept" (2 Ki 8:11). The first clause must be interpreted in the light of all that follows. Had it stood by itself, we should have understood it to signify that Hazael was deeply grieved by the prophet's announcement and sought to control his emotions — though that would not account for the prophet bursting into tears. But the sequel obliges us to conclude that, far from being horrified at the news he had just received, Hazael was highly gratified, and the settling of his countenance was an endeavor to conceal his elation. Accordingly, we regard the "until he was ashamed" (the Hebrew word is often rendered, "confounded," and once, "put to confusion") as denoting that, under the piercing gaze of Elisha he realized he had not succeeded and was chagrined that his countenance revealed the wicked pleasure he found in the prophet's reply. God has wisely, justly, and mercifully ordered that to a considerable extent, the countenance is made to betray the workings of our minds and the state of our hearts.

The servant of God was not deceived by Hazael's playacting, for he not only had the aid of his own eyes to perceive the attempted deception, but also had a direct revelation from heaven concerning the sequel. The weeping of the man of God was not occasioned by his knowledge of the violent end awaiting Ben-hadad, but rather from what the Lord had also shown him concerning the fearful horrors which should shortly be inflicted upon Israel. In his tears we behold Elisha foreshadowing his incarnate Lord, who wept over Jerusalem (Lk 19:41). Elisha was no heartless stoic: even though he knew that his nation fully deserved the still sorer judgments which God would shortly visit upon it through the agency of the man who now stood before him, yet Elisha could not be unmoved at his prophetic foreview of their terrible afflictions. The prophets were men of deep feelings, as the history of Jeremiah abundantly manifests. So too was Paul (Phil 3:18). So is every true servant of Christ.

Fourth, the Nature of the Miracle

"And Hazael said, Why weepeth my lord? And he answered, Because I know the evil that thou wilt do unto the children of Israel: their strong holds wilt thou set on fire, and their young men wilt thou slay with the sword, and wilt dash their children, and rip up their women with child" (2 Ki 8:12). Like the two preceeding

ones, this miracle consists of a supernatural disclosure, the announcing of a prophetic revelation which he had received directly from
God — in this case a double one: the death of Ben-hadad and the
judgments which should come upon Israel. Hazael was far from
being melted by Elisha's tears (he was probably nonplussed by
them), and in order to gain time for composure of mind, he asked
the question which he did. It is solemn to note that while Elisha
announced what he foresaw would happen, he made no effort to
dissuade or deter Hazael — as our Lord foretold the treachery of
Judas, but sought not to turn him from his evil purpose.

Fifth, the Challenge of the Miracle

"And Hazael said, But what, is thy servant a dog, that he should
do this great thing?" (v. 13). Hotly did he resent such a charge,
nor did he at that moment deem himself capable of such atrocities,
nor did he wish the prophet to regard him as such a wretch. How
little do the unregenerate realize or suspect the desperate wickedness
of their hearts! How anxious are they that others should not think
the worst of them! When not immediately exposed to temptations,
they do not believe they are capable of such enormities, and are
highly insulted when the contrary is affirmed. "And Elisha answered, The LORD hath shewed me that thou shalt be king over
Syria." Again we see the extraordinary powers with which the prophets were invested, though Elisha gives God the glory for his. When
Hazael ascended the throne, all human restraint would be removed
from him, and enlarged powers and opportunities would be his for
working evil.

Sixth, Fulfillment of the Miracle

"So he departed from Elisha, and came to his master; who said to
him, What said Elisha to thee? And he answered, He told me that
thou shouldest surely recover" (v. 14). Thus did Hazael seek to put
off his guard the one he intended to murder by deliberately lying to
him. "And it came to pass on the morrow, that he took a thick
cloth, and dipped it in water, and spread it on his face, so that he
died: and Hazael reigned in his stead" (v. 15). And this was the
man who a few hours before indignantly denied he had the character of a savage dog! In the fearful doom of Ben-hadad we see the
righteous retribution of God. Having been a man of violence, he

met with a violent end — as he had lived, so he died (see 1 Ki 20:1, 16, 21, 26, 29; 22:1; 2 Ki 6:8, 24). And for Hazael in the future: 2 Kings 10:32.

Seventh, the Meaning of the Miracle

This is so obvious that very few words are needed: it is the glaring contrast between the faithful and the unfaithful servant. Elisha had unflinchingly declared the counsel which he had received from the Lord, however unpalatable it was to his hearer. But Hazael gives us a picture of the hireling, the false prophet, the deceiver of souls. Ostensibly he went forth in obedience to his master's commission (2 Ki 8:9); in reality he was playing the part of a hypocrite (v. 11). When he delivered his message he falsified it by withholding the most pointed and solemn part of it (v. 14). How many there are like him, uttering "smooth things" and remaining guiltily silent on the doom awaiting the wicked. As surely as Hazael slew Ben-hadad, the unfaithful preachers of our day are murdering souls. As Hazael became king, so the most faithless now occupy seats of power in Christendom.

Chapter 29

ELISHA'S YOUNG DEPUTY

WE REGARD THE INCIDENT recorded in 2 Kings 9:1-10 as relating to the mission of Elisha. In order to better understand it, we refer the reader back to the first two chapters. There we pointed out that the missions of Elijah and Elisha formed two parts of one whole, much the same as did those entrusted to Moses and Joshua. While there was indeed a striking difference between what was accomplished through and by Moses and the one who succeeded him, and while their respective missions may be considered separately, yet in the wider view the latter should be regarded primarily as the complement of the former. Such was also the case with Elijah and Elisha. The analogy between Moses and Joshua and Elijah and Elisha is not perfect in every detail, yet there is sufficient agreement in the broad outline as to enable us to perceive more clearly the relation which the second sustained to the first in each of those two pairs. By such perception, light is cast upon the ministries of those we are now more especially concerned with.

The very similarity of their names intimates a more than ordinary connection between them. According to that important rule of interpretation, the very first mention of Elisha in the Scriptures clearly defines his relation to his predecessor. Unto Elijah the Lord said, "Elisha the son of Shaphat of Abel-meholah, shalt thou anoint to be prophet in thy room" (1 Ki 19:16). Those words signify something more than that he was to be his successor in the prophetic office; Elisha was to take Elijah's place as his accredited representative. This is confirmed by the fact that when he found Elisha, Elijah "cast his mantle upon him" (v. 19), which denotes the closest possible identification between them. In perfect accord with that is the reply Elisha made when, later, he was asked by the one whose place he was to take, "Ask what I shall do for thee, before I be taken away [not from 'Israel,' but] from thee. And Elisha said, "I pray thee, let a double portion of thy spirit be upon me" (2 Ki 2:9), which request was granted. Elisha, then, was far more than the historical successor of Elijah; he was appointed and anointed to be his representative, we might almost say his "ambassador."

Elisha was the man called by God to take Elijah's place before Israel. Though Elijah had left this scene and gone on high, yet his ministry was not to cease. True, he was no longer here in person, yet he was so in spirit. The starting point of Elisha's ministry was the supernatural rapture of his master, and that the one was to carry on the work of the other was symbolically intimated by his initial act, for his first miracle was an exact duplication of the last one wrought by his predecessor, namely, the smiting and opening up of the waters of Jordan so that he crossed over dry-shod — the instrument used being Elijah's own mantle (2 Ki 2:14)! The immediate sequel supplies further evidence for what we have just pointed out: "And when the sons of the prophets which were to view at Jericho saw him, they said, The spirit of Elijah doth rest on Elisha. And they came to meet him, and bowed themselves to the ground before him" (v. 15).

In 2 Kings 2 we read of "the sons of the prophets that were at Beth-el" (v. 3), and in verse 5 we are also told of "the sons of the prophets that were at Jericho," the latter numbering more than fifty (v. 17). By that expression (a Hebrewism) we understand that these young men had been converted under the ministries of Elijah and Elisha, for the latter had accompanied the former for some years previous to his rapture — and who were organized into schools. As we saw in an earlier chapter, there was yet another school of them at Gilgal (4:38), and from their "sitting before him" (cf. Deu 33: 3; Lk 2:46 and 10:39) it is evident that Elisha devoted much of his time to their instruction and edification. Their owning him as "thou man of God" (2 Ki 4:40) and "master" (6:5) reveals plainly enough the relation which he sustained to them, as does also their appeal to him for the enlarging of their living quarters (6:1). He acted then as their rector or superintendent, and gained both their respect and their affection.

In the course of our studies we have seen how Elisha wrought more than one miracle for the benefit of these students. Thus, through his intervention on her behalf, he enabled the widow of one of the children of the prophets, who had appealed to him in her dire extremity, to pay off her debt and save her two sons from being made bondmen to her debtor (4:1-7). Next he delivered a whole company of them from being poisoned when there was "death in the pot" which they were about to partake of (4:38-41). Then he rescued the head of the ax borrowed by another of them (6:4-7). Not only were the schools of the "sons of the prophets" which were established by the Tishbite continued throughout the life of his successor, but in the above instances we see how Elisha acted toward them as Elijah would have done had he remained among them — using his extraordinary powers on their behalf as need arose and occasion required.

Let us now point out the relevancy of this somewhat lengthy preface to the incident we are now to contemplate. Our narrative opens by saying: "And Elisha the prophet called one of the children of the prophets, and said unto him, Gird up thy loins, and take this box of oil in thine hand, and go to Ramoth-Gilead. And when thou comest thither, look out there Jehu the son of Jehoshaphat the son of Nimshi, and go in, and make him arise up from among his brethren, and carry him to an inner chamber. Then take the box of oil, and pour it on his head, and say, Thus saith the LORD, I have anointed thee king over Israel. Then open the door, and flee, and tarry not" (2 Ki 9:1-3). That can only be rightly apprehended in the light of what has just been pointed out.

If we turn back to 1 Kings 19:15-16 it will be found that Elijah received the following commission: "And the LORD said unto him, Go, return on thy way to the wilderness of Damascus: and when thou comest, anoint Hazael to be king over Syria: And Jehu the son of Nimshi shalt thou anoint to be king over Israel: and Elisha the son of Shaphat of Abel-meholah shalt thou anoint to be prophet in thy room." Concerning the anointing of Hazael, Scripture is silent; that of Elisha was accomplished when Elijah "cast his mantle upon him" (v. 19). At first sight the long delay in the anointing of Jehu seems to present a problem, but compare an earlier passage, and the difficulty is at once removed. Jehu was to be the Lord's instrument of executing His vengeance on the wicked house of Ahab — a solemn announcement of which was made to that apostate monarch by Elijah in 1 Kings 21:21-24, and Jehu's agency in connection therewith was intimated in 1 Kings 19:17.

Upon hearing that dreadful announcement from the lips of the Lord's messenger, we are told that Ahab "rent his clothes, and put sackcloth upon his flesh, and fasted, and lay in sackcloth, and went softly" (1 Ki 21:27). Because of that external humbling of himself before Jehovah, He declared unto the prophet, "I will not bring the evil in his days: but in his son's days will I bring the evil upon his house" (v. 29). Since that divine decision was communicated to Elijah personally, we infer that it was tantamount to bidding him defer the anointing of Jehu: a respite having been granted unto Ahab, the commissioning of the one who was to execute the judgment was also postponed. For the same reason we conclude that since the time for the anointing of Jehu had not arrived before Elijah left this earth, that he transferred this particular duty to his successor, to the one who became "prophet in his room," as the Lord Jesus is said to have baptized those who were immersed by His disciples acting under His authority (Jn 4:1-2).

But now the question arises, Why did not Elisha personally perform the task assigned him by the one whose representative he was? Why entrust it to a deputy? The principal reason given by Matthew Henry (and adopted by Thomas Scott) is that it was too dangerous a task for Elisha to undertake, and therefore it was not fit that he should expose himself; that being so well known, he would have been promptly recognized, and therefore he selected one who was more likely to escape observation. But such an explanation by no means commends itself to us, for it is entirely out of accord with everything else recorded of Elisha. The one who had spoken so boldly to king Jehoram (2 Ki 3:13-14), who was not afraid to give offence unto the mighty Naaman (5:9-11), who had calmly sat in the house when the king had sworn he should be slain that day (6:31-32), and who possessed such power from God as to be able to smite with blindness those who sought to take him captive (6:18), was hardly the one to shrink from an unpleasant task and invite another to face peril in his stead.

Since the Scriptures do not implicitly reveal to us the grounds on which Elisha here acted, none may attempt to dogmatically define them. The most any writer can do is to form his own judgment from what is revealed, state his opinion, and submit it to the readers. Personally we prefer to interpret Elisha's action on this occasion in the light of the particular stage which had now been reached in his career. Nothing more is recorded about him after this incident, save what immediately preceded his death. It appears then that, for some reason unknown to us (for he lived many years afterward), that he was about to retire from the stage of public action, and therefore that he would prepare the "sons of the prophets" and perhaps this one more particularly to take a more prominent part in the public life of Israel, and consequently was placing more responsibility upon them. It is not to be lost sight of that it was also an important and distinguished mission this young man was now entrusted with, and that a high honor was conferred upon him.

"And Elisha the prophet called one of the children of the prophets and said unto him, Gird up thy loins and take this box of oil in thy hand, and go to Ramoth-Gilead" (2 Ki 9:1). Elisha is not here designated "the man of God" because no miracle was involved in what follows. Only here is he termed "Elisha the prophet" and only in 1 Kings 8:36 was his predecessor called "Elijah the prophet": it intimated the identification of the one with the other. Elisha's calling one of the children of the prophets to him manifests the relation which he sustained unto them, namely, as one having authority over them — compare the section on 6:1-7. In the light of what was pointed out in the preceding paragraph we may see in Elisha's action an example which elderly ministers of the gospel may well emulate: Endeavoring to promote the training of their younger brethren, seeking to equip them for more important duties after they will have left this scene. This is a principle which Paul acted upon: "The things that thou hast heard of me . . . the same commit thou to faithful men, who shall be able to teach others also" (2 Ti 2:2).

"And when thou comest thither, look out there Jehu the son of Jehoshaphat the son of Nimshi, and go in, and make him arise up from among his brethren, and carry him to an inner chamber" (2 Ki 9:2). Here we behold another example of the extraordinary powers possessed by Elisha. He knew where Jehu was to be found, that he would not be alone, the precise company he would be in, that he would be seated, and yet not in the inner chamber! But it was a trying ordeal to which he now subjected his deputy and a solemn errand on which he sent him. The wicked Jehoram (also called "Joram") was still on the throne and at that time sojourning in Ramoth-gilead, where he was recovering from the wounds which the Syrians had given him in the recent battle at Ramah (8:29). With him was the son of the king of Judah, who was visiting him in his sickness, and with him too were other members of the reigning house. The mission entrusted to the young prophet involved his entry into the royal quarters, his peremptory ordering one of the princes to accompany him to a private chamber, and then discharging the purpose for which he had come.

That purpose was not only to anoint and make him king, but to deliver an announcement which would to most temperaments be very unpleasant. But the minister of God, be he young or old, is not free to pick and choose either his sphere of labor or the message he is to deliver. No, being but a "servant" he is subject only to the will of his Master, and therefore any self-seeking or self-pleasing is nothing else than a species of insubordination. Implicit obedience to the Lord, no matter what it may involve or cost him in this life, is what is required of him, and only by rendering such obedience will he be rewarded in the next life, by hearing from the lips of Christ himself, "Well done, thou good and faithful servant . . . enter thou into the joy of the Lord." Oh that each young minister of Christ who reads these lines may be constrained to earnestly seek enabling grace that he may live and act now with the day to come before him.

"Then take the box of oil, and pour it on his head, and say, Thus saith the LORD, I have anointed thee king over Israel. Then open the door, and flee, and tarry not" (2 Ki 8:3). The young prophet was to make it unmistakeably clear that he was acting in no private capacity, not even as an agent of Elisha, but under the immediate authority of Jehovah Himself. It is most important that the minister of Christ should similarly conduct himself. He is to make it evident that he is commissioned by heaven, not delivering a message of his own devising nor acting as the agent of his denomination. Only thus is God honored and only thus will His servant preserve his true dignity and speak with divine authority. When he has fulfilled his charge, then let him "tarry not"; that is, not stay around in order to listen to the compliments of his hearers. Note that kingship is of divine appointment and institution (cf. Pr 8:15), and therefore are God's people bidden to "honor the king" (1 Pe 2:17). It is one of the marks of an apostate and degenerate age when "dominion" is despised and "dignities" are evil spoken of (Jude 8).

"So the young man, even the young man the prophet, went to Ramoth-gilead" (2 Ki 9:4). Observe how the Holy Spirit has emphasized his youth! Often the babe in Christ is more pliable and responsive than an older Christian. Note there is nothing to show he asked for an easier task, objected to this one on the score of his youth, nor that he felt unworthy for such a mission — which is more often the language of pride than of humility, for *none* is "worthy" to be commissioned by the Almighty. It is entirely a matter of sovereign grace, and in nowise one of personal merit, that anyone is called to the ministry. Said the apostle Paul, "I was made a minister, according to the gift of the *grace* of God given unto me by the effectual working of His power." He at once added, "Unto me, who am less than the least of all saints, is this grace given, that I should preach among the Gentiles the unsearchable riches of Christ" (Eph 3:7-8). He referred to a two-fold "grace": in calling and equipping him. When God calls one to His service, He also *furnishes* him. This is illustrated in this incident by "the box of oil" put into the young prophet's hand.

"And when he came, behold, the captains of the host were sitting; and he said, I have an errand to thee, O captain. And Jehu said, Unto which of all us? And he said, To thee, O captain. And he arose, and went into the house" (2 Ki 9:5-6). We regard the "behold" as having a threefold force. First, as calling attention to the accuracy of Elisha's indirect but obvious prediction in verse 2. Second, as emphasizing the severity of the ordeal which then confronted the young prophet: Jehu being surrounded by companions of note, and the likelihood that he would resent such an intrusion. Third, in view of what follows, as intimating the gracious hand of God so ordering things that Jehu promptly and unmurmuringly complied with the prophet's order, thus making it much easier for him. In that we see how God ever delights to honor those who honor Him and show Himself strong in the behalf of those whose heart is perfect toward Him.

That which is recorded in verses 7-10 was evidently included in the commission which the young man had received from the Lord through Elisha, and which he now faithfully discharged. The fact that the prophet here made such an announcement appears to supply strong confirmation of what was pointed out in our opening paragraphs, namely, that this deputy of Elisha was acting in the stead of Elijah or as his representative. For if it is compared with 1 Kings 21:21-24 it will be found that it is practically an echo of the Tishbite's own words to Ahab. In the charge here given to Jehu we are shown how he was to be God's battle-ax (Jer 51:20) or sword of justice. Man might see in Jehu's conduct (see remainder of 2 Ki 9) nothing more than the ferocity of a human fiend, but in these verses we are taken behind the scenes as it were and shown how he was appointed to be the executioner of God's judgments. "For the vision is yet for an appointed time, but at the end, it shall speak and not lie: though it tarry wait for it; because it will surely come" (Hab 2: 3). This is equally true whether the "vision" of prophecy foretells divine mercy or wrath, as the wicked house of Ahab was to discover.

"And he opened the door and fled" (2 Ki 9:10). This was most praiseworthy, and should be duly taken to heart by us. The servant of God is not free to please himself at any point but must carry out the orders he has received to the last letter. In all probability, if this young man had lingered, Jehu, after receiving such a high favor at his hands, would have evidenced his appreciation by bestowing some reward upon him, or at least feasting him at his royal table. But Elisha had bidden him, "Open the door [as soon as he had performed his errand] and flee, and tarry not" (v. 3); and here we see his implicit obedience to his master. Oh that we may in all things render unqualified compliance with our Master's will. It is not without signifiance that in the very next verse the young prophet is scornfully referred to as "this mad fellow" (v. 11) by one of the servants of the king. For the unregenerate are quite incapable of assessing at their true value the motives which prompt the faithful minister of Christ, and judging him by their own standards, regard him as crazy. But what is the contempt and ridicule of the world if we have the approbation of the Lord? Nothing, and less than nothing, especially if we expect it, as we should do.

Chapter 30

ELISHA'S DEATH

WE HAVE NO MEANS of ascertaining the exact age of Elisha when he was overtaken by his fatal sickness, for we know not how old he was when called to the prophetic office (though from the analogy of Scripture, he would probably be at least thirty at that time). Nor does there appear any way of discovering how long a period he accompanied and ministered to Elijah before his rapture (some writers think it was upwards of ten years); but if we total up the years which the various kings reigned over Israel, who were all outlived by our prophet (beginning with Ahab), it will be seen that he was a very old man. One commentator supposes him to have been "at this time fully one hundred and twenty years of age." Good it is to be assured that, whether our appointed span be long or short, our "times" are in the hands of the One who gave us being (Ps 31:15). God recovers His people from many sicknesses, but sooner or later comes one from which there is no deliverance. It is well for us if, when that time arrives, we conduct ourselves as Elisha did and use our remaining strength to the glory of the Lord.

Elisha's Last Times

The final incidents in connection with Elisha are in striking keeping with the whole record of his remarkable mission. No commonplace career was his and most extraordinary are the things which mark its closing scenes. First, we learn that the reigning monarch called upon him during his fatal illness! Kings are not accustomed to visit dying people, least of all the servants of God at such times; it might be good for them if they did. Still more unusual and remarkable was it for the king to weep over the prophet because he was on the eve of leaving the scene. Even more noteworthy was the language used by the king on this occasion. Second, so far was Elisha from considering

247

himself flattered by the presence of such a visitor that he took complete charge of the situation, gave orders to the king, and honored him by giving a message from Jehovah, which was as striking as any he had delivered on earlier occasions. Third, after his death God honored the remains of the prophet by raising to life one who had been cast into his sepulchre.

That which is recorded in the second half of 2 Kings 13 speaks of what was really another miracle in Elisha's memorable life. This is intimated by the Spirit referring to him there as "the man of God" (v. 19), which, as we have so frequently pointed out, was used only when he was acting in his official character and discharging his extraordinary office, a fact which seems to have escaped the notice of other writers. Like several others which have been before us, this miracle consisted of a divine revelation being communicated through him, his uttering a supernatural prophecy. Previous to this incident nothing is recorded about his activities or how he was employed, yet it must not be concluded that he was under a cloud and rusting out. No, that lengthy silence is broken in such a way as to preclude any thought that he had been set aside by his Master, for the Lord here makes signal use of him as He had done formerly. Elisha, like other (though not all) of God's servants, brought forth "fruit" in his old age (Ps 92:14).

"Now Elisha was fallen sick of his sickness whereof he died" (2 Ki 13:14). "The Spirit of Elijah rested on Elisha and yet he is not sent for to heaven in a fiery chariot, as Elijah was, but goes the common road out of the world. If God honors some above others, who yet are not inferior in gifts and graces, who should find fault? May He not do what He wills with His own?" (Henry). God does as He pleases and gives no account of His matters. He asks counsel of none and explains His actions to none. Every page of Holy Writ registers some illustration and exemplification of the exercise of His high sovereignty. "Moses was an hundred and twenty years old when he died: his eye was not dim, nor his natural force abated" (Deu 34:7). Whereas of Joshua, who lived ten years less (Jos 24:29), we read that he "waxed old" and was "stricken in age" (23:1); yet certainly he was not inferior in spirituality, nor did he occupy a less eminent position in the Lord's service than did his predecessor. So it is still; God preserves the faculties of some unto old age, yet not so with others.

"And Joash the king (also called 'Jehoash' in 2 Ki 11:21, the grandson of Jehu; he is to be distinguished from 'Joash the king of Judah' in 2 Ki 13:10-13), came down unto him" (v. 14). This indicates that the prophet had not spent his closing years in isolated seclusion, for the king of Israel, not long come to the throne, knew the place of his abode. But this mention of the king's visit also informs us that the man of God was held in high esteem, and though the royal house had sadly failed to respond to his teachings, yet they recognized his value to the nation. Israel's fortunes had fallen to a very low point, for a little earlier than this we are told, "In those days the LORD began to cut Israel short: and Hazael smote them in all the coasts of Israel; From Jordan eastward, all the land of Gilead, the Gadites, and the Reubenites, and the Manassites, from Aroer, which is by the river Arnon, even Gilead and Bashan" (10:32-33). What would the end be if Elisha were now removed!

"And Joash the king of Israel came down unto him, and wept over his face, and said, O my father, my father, the chariot of Israel, and the horsemen thereof" (2 Ki 13:14). While this visit of the king probably indicated his respect for Elisha, yet his tears are not to be regarded as proof of his affection for him; the second half of the verse really interprets the first. The king was worried over the assults of Hazael, and greatly feared that upon the death of this man whose counsels and miracles had more than once been of service to the royal house and saved the nation from disaster (3:16-25, 6:9, 7:1), it would henceforth be left completely at the mercy of their enemies. Joash regarded the prophet as the chief bulwark of the nation, and the prospect of his speedy removal filled him with consternation and sorrow. Thus there was a strange mingling of esteem and selfishness behind those tears; and is not that generally the case even in connection with the departure of a loved one?

The practical lesson for us here is plain. In the words of another,

> Let us seek so to live that even ungodly men may miss us when we are gone. It is possible for us in a quiet, unobtrusive manner, so to adorn the doctrine of God our Saviour in all things, that when we die many shall say "Let me die the death of the righteous, and let my last end be like his," and men shall drop a tear, and close the shutter, and be silent and solemn for an hour or two when they hear that the servant of God is dead. They laughed at him while he lived, but they weep for him when he dies: they could despise him while he was here, but now that he is gone they say: — "We could have better missed a less-known man, for he and such as he

are the pillars of the commonweal: they bring down showers of blessing upon us all." I would covet this earnestly, not for the honor and esteem of men, but for the honor and glory of God, that even the despisers of Christ may be compelled to see there is a dignity, a respect, about the walk of an upright man.

"And said, O my father, my father, the chariot of Israel, and the horsemen thereof" (2 Ki 13:14). This was an acknowledgment that Joash regarded Elisha as the chief security of his kingdom, his best defense against aggressors, as the piety and prayers of God's people are today the nation's best protection in a time of evil, being far more potent than any material weapons. But we must note the striking language used by the king on this occasion as he gave expression to that truth. In the opening paragraphs of our last chapter we dwelt at some length upon the connection which the ministry of Elisha has to that of his predecessor: how he was raised up to act in his stead and carry forward the work which he began. The final confirmation of the identity of the latter with the former is found in these words of the king, for they unmistakably make clear the unusually intimate relation he sustained to the Tishbite. As he had gazed on the departing form of his master, Elisha had cried "My father, my father, the chariot of Israel, and the horsemen thereof" (2:12), and now that he was on the eve of taking his departure from this world, another utters the same words over him!

Elisha's Last Prophecy

We turn now to consider Elisha's response to the king's visit, his tears, and his acknowledgment. The prophet was very far from acting as a flatterer before Joash on this occasion, but maintained and manifested his official dignity to the end of his course. He was an ambassador of the King of kings, and conducted himself accordingly. Instead of any indication that he felt himself to be honored by this visit or flattered by the monarch's tears, the man of God at once took charge of the situation and gave orders to his earthly sovereign. Let not young ministers today conclude from this incident that they are thereby justified in acting haughtily and high-handedly in the presence of their seniors and superiors. Not so. Such an inference would be entirely unwarranted, for they do not occupy the extraordinary office which Elisha did, nor are they endowed with his exceptional gifts and powers. Nevertheless, they are to maintain their dignity as the ministers of Christ: "Let no man despise thy youth: but be thou an example of the believers, in word, in [behavior], in [love], in spirit, in faith, in purity" (1 Ti 4:12).

"And Elisha said unto him, Take bow and arrows. And he took unto him bow and arrows" (2 Ki 13:15). What follows is virtually a parable in action. It should be remembered that in Eastern lands, instruction by means of symbolic actions is much more common than it is with us; and thus we find the prophets frequently using this method. When Samuel would intimate unto the self-willed Saul that "the Lord hath rent the kingdom of Israel from thee this day," he "laid hold upon the skirt of his mantle, and it rent" (1 Sa 15:28, 27). When the prophet Ahijah announced that the Lord would "rend the kingdom out of the hand of Solomon and give ten tribes to another," he caught hold of the new garment upon Jeroboam and "rent it in twelve pieces" and bade him "take thee ten pieces" (1 Ki 11:29-31). Even the false prophets employed such means (see 1 Ki 22:10-11). Significant emblems were presented to the eye to stir up the minds of those who beheld them and evoke a spirit of inquiry (see Jer 27:2 and cf. 28:10-11 and see Eze 24: 17-19). To this custom God referred when He said, "I have also spoken by the prophets, and I have multiplied visions, and used similitudes, by the ministry of the prophets" (Hos 12:10). For a New Testament example see Acts 21:10-11.

When Elisha bade Joash "Take bow and arrows," he was making use of a visual "similitude." The articles selected at once explain it. In response to the king's lamentation the prophet said, in effect, Weeping over my departure will avail the nation nothing: stand fast in the faith, quit you like a man, be strong (1 Co 16:13). Take not the line of least resistance, but assemble your forces, lead your army in person against the enemy. Though I be taken away from the earth, Jehovah still lives and will not fail those who put their confidence in Him. Nevertheless, you must discharge your responsibility by making good use of the means at hand.

Thus Joash was informed that he was to be the instrument of Israel's deliverance by means of his own military efforts, and that if he trusted in the Lord and followed out His servant's instructions, He would grant him full success. There was no need then for the king to be so distressed. If he acted like a man, God would undertake for him!

"And he said to the king of Israel, Put thine hand upon the bow.

And he put his hand upon it: and Elisha put his hands upon the king's hands" (2 Ki 13:16). Here again we see the commanding authority and influence which the prophet had, under God, for Joash made no demur but meekly did as he was ordered. By placing his hands upon the king's, Elisha signified his identification with what he should yet do, thereby intimating that he owed it to the prophet's mission and ministry that Israel was to be spared and that God would again intervene on their behalf. By symbolic action, Elisha was saying to him, "The battle is not your's, but God's" (2 Ch 20:15). How little is that recognized today! "He teacheth my hands to war" (Ps 18:34) was what Elisha now sought to impress upon his royal master.

"And he said, Open the window eastward. And he opened it. Then Elisha said, Shoot. And he shot. And he said, The arrow of the LORD's deliverance, and the arrow of deliverance from Syria: for thou shalt smite the Syrians in Aphek, till thou hast consumed them" (2 Ki 13:17). In those words the prophet explained to the king the meaning of his symbolic actions, and what should be the outcome of them. It evidenced that Elisha's mind was still occupied with the welfare of Israel. It demonstrated that he still acted as the servant of Jehovah; it was the final use of his prophetic gift and proof of his prophetic office. "Eastward" was the portion of the land which Hazael had already conquered (10:33), and in bidding the king shoot in that direction Elisha indicated where the fighting would have to be done. Notice the striking conjunction of the divine and human elements here, and the order in which they were made. It should be "the arrow of the LORD's deliverance," yet "thou (Joash) shalt smite the Syrians." God would work, yet by and through him!

"And he said, Take the arrows. And he took them. And he said unto the king of Israel, Smite upon the ground. And he smote thrice, and stayed" (v. 18). In the light of what follows it is clear that the king's faith was here being put to the test; the prophet would have him indicate his reaction to the reassuring message he had just heard. "Smite upon the ground" and intimate thereby how far you believe the words which I have spoken and really expect a fulfillment of them. Did the Lord's promise sound too good to be true, or would Joash rest upon it with full confidence? Would he lift up his heart and eyes to God and say with David, "Thou hast also given me the necks of mine enemies; that I might destroy them that hate me"

(Ps 18:40), or would he follow the temporizing course which Ahab had pursued, when instead of following up his victory by slaying Ben-hadad whom the Lord had delivered into his hand, spared his life, made a covenant with him, and then sent him away (1 Ki 20: 29-31)?

"And the man of God was wroth with him, and said, Thou shouldest have smitten five or six times" (2 Ki 13:19). There are some who teach that a saint should never lose his temper, that all anger is sinful, which shows how little their thoughts are formed by Scripture. In Ephesians 4:26-27 Christians are thus exhorted: "Be ye angry, and sin not," though it is at once added, "let not the sun go down upon your wrath: Neither give place to the devil." There is a holy and spiritual anger — a righteous indignation — as well as a carnal and sinful one. Anger is one of the divine perfections, and when the Son became incarnate we read that on one occasion He "looked round about on them with anger, being grieved for the hardness of their hearts" (Mk 3:5). Elisha was disgusted at the half-hearted response made by the king to his message, and from love for Israel, he was indignant that Joash should stand in their way and deprive them of full deliverance from their foes. And if we had more zeal for God and love for souls we would be angry at those who deprive them of their privileges.

"Thou shouldest have smitten five or six times; then hadst thou smitten Syria till thou hadst consumed it: whereas now thou shalt smite Syria but thrice" (2 Ki 13:19). What possible difference to the issue could be made by the number of times the king smote upon the ground? If God had foreordained that the Syrians should be "consumed" (v. 19), then could any failure on the part of Joash prevent or even modify it? But do not Elisha's words plainly signify that the extent to which the Syrians would be vanquished turned upon the response made by him to the divine promise? We shall not here give a solution to this problem.

Instead of wasting time on metaphysical subtleties let us learn the practical lesson which is here pointed, namely, "According to your faith be it unto you" (Mt 9:29). For it was at that point Joash failed; he did not thoroughly believe the prophet's words. The majority of God's people today need to realize that the exercise of faith does make a real difference in what they obtain or fail to obtain from God, as real and as great a difference as between Joash "consuming" the Syrians (the Hebrew word is rendered "destroy utterly" in Lev 26:44 and "make an utter end of" in Nah 1:8-9) and the "three times" he beat Hazael (2 Ki 13:25). Most Christians expect little from God, ask little, and therefore receive little, and are content with little. They are content with little faith, little knowledge of the deep things of God, little growth and fruitfulness in the spiritual life, little joy, peace, and assurance. And the zealous servant of God is justified in being wroth at their lack of spiritual ambition.

"And Elisha died, and they buried him" (2 Ki 13:20). It is to be noted that nothing is said here of any burial service. Nor is there anywhere in the Scriptures, either in the Old Testament or the New Testament. Elaborate, mournful ceremonies are of pagan origin and are neither authorized nor warranted by the Word of God. If the body of Christ was tenderly and reverently interred without the mummery of any "service" over His corpse, shall the disciple be above his Master! What slaves many are to "the way of the heathen" (Jer 10:2), and in what bondage do they let themselves be held through fear of public opinion, afraid of what their friends and neighbors would think and say if they should be regulated only by Holy Writ.

"And the bands of the Moabites invaded the land at the coming in of the year. And it came to pass, as they were burying a man, that, behold, they spied a band of men; and they cast the man into the sepulchre of Elisha: and when the man was let down, and touched the bones of Elisha, he revived, and stood up on his feet" (2 Ki 13:20-21). Behold here once more the sovereignty of God; He honored Elijah at his departure from this world, but Elisha, in a different way afterward. It was the Lord's seal upon His servant's mission. It indicated that the Lord was his God after death as well as before, and thus furnished evidence both of the immortality of the soul and the final resurrection of the body. It was an intimation that other miracles would yet be wrought for Israel in response to his prayers and as the result of his labors. Thus to the end, miracles are connected with the mission of Elisha.

Moody Press, a ministry of the Moody Bible Institute, is designed for education, evangelization, and edification. If we may assist you in knowing more about Christ and the Christian life, please write us without obligation: Moody Press, c/o MLM, Chicago, Illinois 60610.